CW01510133

Is Medical Ethics in Armed Conflict Identical to Medical Ethics in Times of Peace?

Is Medical Ethics in Armed Conflict Identical to Medical Ethics in Times of Peace?

By

Janet Kelly

CAMBRIDGE SCHOLARS

PUBLISHING

Is Medical Ethics in Armed Conflict Identical to Medical Ethics in Times of Peace?,
by Janet Kelly

This book first published 2013

Cambridge Scholars Publishing

12 Back Chapman Street, Newcastle upon Tyne, NE6 2XX, UK

British Library Cataloguing in Publication Data
A catalogue record for this book is available from the British Library

ISBN (10): 1-4438-4414-4, ISBN (13): 978-1-4438-4414-7

To
Mum and Dad

CONTENTS

ACKNOWLEDGEMENTS

It is my pleasure to thank those who made this book, as without their help and support, I would not have been able to complete this work. I am indebted to Professor Julie Jomeen and the Reverend Doctor Peter Draper for their constructive feedback and constant encouragement throughout.

I wold also like to thank my colleagues and friends in the Territorial Army and in particular Major Rozalind Peel, QARANC and Major Caroline Whittle RAVC for their encouragement and constructive comments on the authenticity of the vignettes. I am also most grateful to Rebecca Wilkinson, Specialist Nurse from the Humber Traumatic Stress Service, Humber NHS Foundation Trust for her guidance in updating me in military healthcare and her enthusiasm in reading the vignette chapters to ensure that they remained realistic. Her input and constructive comments were particularly useful.

I would also like to thank my family and in particular Ruth Lawford and Jean Zimmerman. To Ruth in particular, for sharing my passion and exuberance in striving to reach this achievement, and for her constructive comments on each chapter in their early stages, and to Jean for her final proof reading of the work.

Above all, I owe my loving thanks to my Mum and Dad for their endless love and support throughout, and their continuing encouragement to complete this book

ABSTRACT

This book challenges The World Medical Association's (WMA) International Code of Ethics statement in 2004, which declared that **'medical ethics in armed conflict is identical to medical ethics in times of peace'.** This is achieved by examining the professional, ethical, and legal conflicts in British Military healthcare practice that occur in three distinct military environments. These are (i) the battlefield, (ii) the operational environment and (iii) the non-operational environment. As this conflict is exacerbated by, the need to achieve Operational Effectiveness, this book also explores the dual loyalty conflict that Military Health Care Professionals (MHCPs) encounter between following military orders and professional codes of practice.

The method used to challenge the WMAs statement and explore these conflicts is by real-life problem-solving vignettes, which mirror actual ethical and professional conflicts and dilemmas that may occur in the three environments. The areas of law analysed similarly reflect the difficulties that MHCPs face when caring for the sick and wounded in violent locations when under attack. In particular, the book questions whether it is right for a MHCP to owe their patients a duty of care in hostile environments. This leads onto to questioning if any MHCP could be protected by combat immunity where no duty of care is owed to fellow soldiers in the battlefield.

The book also questions whether the standard of care should be variable in hostile environments. It also explores the dual loyalty conflict of a wounded senior officer refusing treatment from a junior officer. In addition, it examines the difficulties of a doctor maintaining patient confidentiality when a soldier refuses treatment for a psychological injury but wishes to redeploy to the battlefield.

The book successfully challenges the WMAs statement. It also concludes by suggesting that neither a military-focused approach nor a professional healthcare-focused approach towards military healthcare is the best way to solve the dual loyalty conflict.

CHAPTER ONE

PREAMBLE

This first chapter briefly outlines the aim of the book and outlines the contents of each chapter. In 2004, The World Medical Association's International Code of Ethics (WMA 2004; Hallgarth, 2007) claimed that **'medical ethics in armed conflict is identical to medical ethics in times of peace'**, thus suggesting that the patients' clinical needs in war remain sacrosanct, above all other considerations (Annas, 2008). This book aims to challenge the WMA's statement and assert that medical ethics in British Military Healthcare Practice, as encountered by Military Healthcare Professionals (MHCPs) on the battlefield and in the operational environment, is *not* identical. This is underpinned by arguments, which demonstrate that medical ethics are constrained and questionable under existing ethical, professional, and legal parameters. Therefore, new professional regulatory solutions to solve these ethical conflicts are required.

Summary of Chapters

Chapters 2, 3, 4 and 5 details the main themes of the book in order to set the context. This is to aid an understanding of the concept of military healthcare in the battlefield, operational environment and non-operational environment in which MHCPs serve. Chapters 3 and 4 further explain the historical background and importance of international, humanitarian and military law and discipline to the present day and its relationship with civil law and healthcare professional regulations.

Chapter 5 continues by highlighting the complexities of solving ethical and professional dilemmas in diverse military environments (Tschudin, 2002). It highlights the paucity of existing research on the ethical and professional complexities of MHCPs caring for the sick and wounded in war (Vetter, 2007; Robinson 2007 and Fleischmann, 2006). The chapter does, however, critically analyse one specific quantitative study by Verweij, Hofhuis and Soeters (2007), which was conducted to emphasise how the Dutch Military view the ethical and moral training of its military personnel. This paper arose in an attempt to avoid a repetition of events that involved Dutch troops when Serbian soldiers allegedly murdered Bosnian Muslims during the Balkan Wars in the 1990's. The significance of this study is that it highlights the complexities of ethical decision making in challenging military environments. In addition, chapter 5 illustrates a study by Boyd, Himmelstie, Lasser, McCormick, Bor, Cutrona and Woolhandler (2007) conducted at selected universities across the United States, that examined how much knowledge and understanding medical students had about military medical ethics and the Geneva Conventions'. As a result of these two studies, this chapter indicates that both a *military-focused* approach and a *professional healthcare-focused* approach could, perhaps, be used to solve the difficulties that a MHCP might face when having to follow both military orders and professional codes of conduct in diverse military environments.

Chapter 6 explains the rationale for using vignettes to Address Military Clinical Ethical Issues. It explains that real-life vignettes based on the experiences of military nurses with problem-solving questions to give 'recognisable snapshots' of events that require legal analysis to solve their outcomes (Schofield, 2009 at pg. 1109) were uniquely used in three distinct military environments: the **battlefield,** the **operational environment,** and the **non-operational environment.** These were then critically analysed by legal methodology. Legal methodology involved **(i)** Identification of the legal area and relevant legal issues. This was medical law and included issues such as refusal of treatment, confidentiality and mental capacity, **(ii)** the use of relevant legal authority by case law and statutory authority and then, **(iii)** giving the legal advice. Legal methodology was enhanced by using Howe's (2003) three role-specific military ethical model. These consisted of a **military role-specific ethic** where MHCPs would follow military orders above everything else. This ethic follows a *military-focused* approach. A **medical role-specific ethic,** which follows a *professional-healthcare focused* approach and where MHCPs would follow professional codes of practice and put their patients first (Howe, 2003 at pp. 333-334). Finally, the third role is **a discretionary role-specific ethic** where the MHCPs use some discretion in deciding when and whether the needs of the military are absolute (Howe, 2003 at p.335).

Using legal sources from the common law and statutes, **chapter 7** introduces the first vignette that concerns the law concerning a MHCP owing a duty of care to a patient. Similarly, chapters 7 and 8 present a legal literature review of the law concerning Crown Immunity and the doctrine of combat immunity. By the use of problem-solving vignettes which, according to Hughes and Huby (2000) are useful tools to simulate real life situations and examine difficult complex concepts in context, **chapters 6 to 12** highlight realistic ethical, professional and legal difficulties which can occur in hostile and non-hostile military environments. In view of the author's first hand experiences, **chapter 7** explains that military healthcare in the battlefield environment is distinctly different to civilian healthcare, even in an emergency and thus a question emerges: 'Should a duty of care apply to Military Healthcare Professionals in this environment?' The chapter explains that although MHCPs have a legal and professional obligation to care for the wounded on the battlefield, this obligation can contradict the following of military orders, causing a dual loyalty conflict. As further discussed in this chapter, soldiers are part of a 'fighting force' so that they are fit to fight the enemy and win the battle. They are thus seen as being more of a commodity rather than individuals with distinct healthcare needs. Such distinct differences in wartime can override normal peacetime professional ethics to the extent that the duty of care owed by MHCPs to their patients on the battlefield can be constrained and questionable under existing ethical and legal parameters.

Following a legal literature review of combat immunity, **chapter 9** extends the discussion of a duty of care owed by MHCPs to their patients on the battlefield being problematic under existing ethical and legal parameters. It does this by explaining that the combatant soldier on the battlefield remains protected from any claim in negligence by the doctrine of *combat immunity* for any negligent act or omission they may make when fighting. In other words, the combatant soldier *does not* owe a fellow soldier a duty of care on the battlefield, as the duty of care is non-justiciable. However, the non-combatant MHCP, although sometimes operating in the same hostile circumstances as the fighting soldier, is currently unlikely to benefit from combat immunity for any negligent act or omission that they make on the battlefield, as they continue to owe their patient a duty of care. The chapter, therefore, considers if the MHCP could ever be protected by combat immunity. It then further considers if a unique and a modified form of immunity, namely *Military Healthcare Battlefield Immunity,* could be a viable and exclusive doctrine to protect MHCPs against a claim by a patient for an alleged negligent act or omission. The chapter demonstrates that it is unlikely that a MHCP could enjoy combat immunity due to their non-combatant status. Instead, the chapter proposes that this unique form of immunity may be viable, but *only* in rare circumstances and to a much lesser degree than combat immunity.

Chapter 10 explains that the battlefield is a hostile environment for MHCPs. The chapter considers whether the current standard of care on the battlefield is sufficiently viable to protect the Ministry of Defence (MoD) against a claim of a breach of a duty of care for any negligent act or omission by a MHCP. In addition, as MHCPs have both legal and professional obligations to care for the wounded on the battlefield, as well as an obligation to follow military orders, the chapter considers the effect that dual loyalty conflict has when giving emergency care and treatment in this environment. The chapter concludes that the law is sufficiently viable to protect the MoD and that dual loyalty conflict does not unduly influence healthcare professionals, as decisions are made quickly, thus giving the MHCP little time to consider this dual role conflict issue.

In contrast to chapters 7, 9 and 10, which consider ethical, professional, and legal conflicts on the *battlefield,* **chapter 11** considers ethical, professional, and legal conflicts in an *operational* environment. It explores the law concerning consent and refusal of medical treatment where the capacity of a patient soldier is questionable. This is discussed in the context of dual loyalty conflict, where the patient soldier, who is a senior military officer, refuses life-saving treatment and gives a military order to a healthcare professional not to give him treatment. This chapter concludes by suggesting that, ordinarily, it is unlawful and unethical to exert any undue influence over a patient in persuading them to accept medical treatment. However, in an operational environment, where the MHCP and the patient's safety may be at risk from enemy attack, it is understandable that some undue influence may be exerted by the MHCP on their patient.

Chapter 12 considers ethical, professional, and legal conflicts in a *non-operational* environment. It explains that military doctors have a legal and professional obligation to maintain patient soldier confidentiality and allow a competent patient soldier to refuse consent to medical treatment. However, this obligation can be inconsistent with following military orders, causing a dual loyalty conflict. This can become more problematic when the military doctor believes he has a professional duty to disclose confidential medical information to a senior military officer in the public interest, so that an unfit soldier can be prevented from deploying on an operational tour. The chapter concludes by suggesting that dual loyalty conflict in the context of a *non-operational* vignette is best managed via a discretionary ethic-role. This then allows independent clinical judgment, whilst at the same time minimising harm and conflict to a Commanding Officer as an interested third party.

Chapters 13 and **14** suggests that professional codes of practice by the General Medical Council and the Nursing Midwifery Council are not a sufficient solution to the existing and emerging ethical and professional conflicts that occur in the battlefield and operational environments. It further suggests that 'medical ethics in armed conflict is *not* identical to medical ethics in times of peace'. In doing so, chapters 13 and 14 critically analyse each vignette from a *military-focused* approach and a *professional healthcare-focused* approach and concludes that neither of these approaches to military medical ethics is appropriate. This is due to the difficulty in determining whether the military duty to follow military orders or the medical duty to follow professional codes of practice should override one another. Chapters 13 and 14 further suggest that both of these approaches contradict with the principles of healthcare ethics, thus potentially compromising patient care. In addition, as explained in chapter 5, they also contradict with achieving Operational Effectiveness and thus could potentially compromise a set military mission. **Chapter 15** concludes the book by recommending that new professional regulatory solutions by the General Medical Council and the Nursing Midwifery Council may be required to help solve ethical conflicts in the diverse and harsh military environments in which MHCP serve. This final chapter highlights some limitations and boundaries of the book, but also its uniqueness and originality.

In conclusion, this book, therefore, successfully highlights that medical ethics in armed conflict is *not identical* to medical ethics in times of peace. This is primarily due to MHCPs providing healthcare in more controlling, distinct and hostile environments compared to civilian healthcare professionals. Furthermore, it is also due to MHCPs having a dual loyalty conflict between following military orders and professional codes of practice. It suggests that, although dual loyalty conflict can exist in other areas of healthcare apart from the military, the conflict is less problematic than it is in a military environment. This is because the duty to follow military orders can be incompatible with the duty to follow professional clinical codes of practice.

CHAPTER TWO

CONTEXTUAL BACKGROUND

Introduction

These next three chapters highlight the mains themes of the book to aid an understanding of the concept of military healthcare in the diverse environments in which Military Healthcare Professionals (MHCPs) operate and serve. This chapter draws attention to the organisational and cultural differences between civilian and military personnel and the military's relationship with civil law and healthcare professional regulations. The following chapter gives a review of international and humanitarian law followed by chapter 4, which gives an historical review of military law and the importance of military discipline, which is a core value for the British Armed Forces and is a fundamental requirement towards achieving Operational Effectiveness. Chapter 5 highlights two studies on the moral and ethical judgment of individuals in a military context.

Civil and Military Values

Regarding civil and military values, there are significant differences regarding **(i)** the physical environment and **(ii)** the context of where care is given. It is also clear that there is some distinction regarding the philosophy of care, which is discussed next from a *military philosophical perspective* and a *National Health Service philosophical perspective*.

Military philosophical perspective

From a military philosophical perspective, the British Army perceives that wherever a service person is serving, military law and discipline must underpin Operational Effectiveness (Soldier Management, 2004). In other words, Operational Effectiveness, which is examined in more detail in chapters 7, 10, 13 and 14, is the British Army's ultimate and primary objective. The implication of this for MHCPs within the environment they serve, means that to achieve Operational Effectiveness, they must be ready and prepared to give treatment and healthcare to military personnel who are about to deploy, or who are already deployed, in any military operation (Delivering Our Armed Forces' Healthcare Needs, 2007). Present examples of such deployments are those formerly in Iraq and now in Afghanistan. When not deployed on operations or military exercises, Operational Effectiveness is achieved in other ways. This is by regular military training at military bases, acquisition of new knowledge and maintenance of clinical skills within a primary care location, such as a General Practitioner's surgery, a medical centre or via a secondary care establishment such as at a Military Defence Hospital Unit (Queen's Regulation, 1975, section 5.181).

Nonetheless, it is reasonable to suggest that switching between a battlefield, an operational environment and a non-operational environment, and having to maintain Operational Effectiveness constantly is challenging both physically and psychologically (Gross, 2006). Smith and Arthur (1992) remark that there is an expectation by Commanding Officers that MHCPs can easily switch and adapt to delivering the unique healthcare requirements provided by service personnel from that of a peacetime environment to that of a war zone. Anything that compromises or challenges that ability undermines the successful functioning of the army in achieving its given mission (Soldier Management, 2004). To adapt efficiently and effectively to that change of environment, all military service personnel must, therefore, demonstrate individual fitness. This is currently achieved by successfully passing Military Annual Training Tests (Queen's Regulations, 1975), which is necessary and essential to ensure that Operational Effectiveness is sustained. However, as explained in the next section, outside a military environment, Operational Effectiveness is, perhaps, not a consideration or issue that front line civilian personnel in the NHS are preoccupied with, as it rather different in a NHS context.

National Health Service philosophical perspective

The Darzi Report in 2008 highlighted the need for the NHS to provide high quality patient care that prevents illness, as well as treating illness (High Quality Care For All, 2008). In addition, a strong emphasis was placed on the need to encourage people to live healthier lives, to raise standards of care by empowering patients and professionals and also by providing the most effective diagnostics and subsequent treatments to detect diseases earlier (High Quality Care For All, 2008). The legal mandate for this was originally via the National Health Service Acts of

1977 and 2006 and more recently, the Health and Social Care Act 2012. Clearly, despite the expected political changes ahead, the function and aim of the NHS is *not* to support the British Armed Forces in achieving Operational Effectiveness, although it may be sympathetic to that cause.

Clearly, the core ideology and beliefs of either a *military philosophical perspective* or a *National Health Service philosophical perspective* are significantly different from each other, yet it is apparent that the military personnel who work within this structure are subject to *both* military and civilian laws that govern this core NHS ideology.

In addition and as discussed in the next chapter, military personnel including MHCPs *must* also follow International Law, which main aim is to manage relations between states during war and peace as stipulated by the International Committee of the Red Cross (The Joint Service Manual of the Law of Armed Conflict, 2004 at para 1.1). As explained in the next chapter, the implications of International Committee of the Red Cross parameters for the MHCP therefore, is that it reinforces the need for the MHCP to have an understanding of how military healthcare practice and professional codes of practice, must be compatible with several facets of law i.e. international, domestic and military law (Lamp, 2011).

CHAPTER THREE

INTERNATIONAL LAW

Military personnel including Military Healthcare Professional (MHCPs) *must* also follow International Law, which main aim is to manage relations between states during war and peace (The Joint Service Manual of the Law of Armed Conflict, 2004 at para 1.1). Whilst international and humanitarian law is not explicitly addressed in the vignettes apart from in chapter 9, it is abundantly clear that, international law places obligations on states to act within defined humanitarian parameters as stipulated by the International Committee of the Red Cross (ICRC) within their own country, and to commence any legal action against personnel through their domestic courts when these parameters are breached (Orakhelashvili, 2006; Akander and Sangeete, 2010). Thus, it is clear that the ICRC is the 'guardian' of humanitarian law and is a major player in the protection of the sick and wounded in war (Ratner, 2011). This is clearly highlighted in the vignette in chapter 9 when the MHCP believes he is protecting his wounded patient by firing at the enemy. The implications of ICRC parameters for the MHCP therefore, is that it reinforces the need for the MHCP to have an understanding of how military healthcare practice and professional codes of practice, must be compatible with several facets of law i.e. international, domestic and military law (Lamp, 2011).

Historical Background of Humanitarian Law

The earliest form of humanitarian law stems as far back as 3000 BC in Africa and Ancient Greece to protect victims of war and control how war was conducted in relation to the use of weapons and proportionality (Sassòli et al, 2011). There is also evidence of humanitarian law from the Saracens in the Middles Ages during the Crusades when they followed the principles laid down in the Koran and allowed the lives of the civilians living in Jerusalem at that time, to be saved from attack and certain death (Detter, 2000; Algasse, 1977). Following this, there was little intervention on the conduct of warfare against armed forces and civilians until the 19th century when during the American Civil War (1861-1865), President

Lincoln successfully codified the behaviour of Union forces via the Lieber Code (Rogers, 2004). Shortly afterwards, the St Petersburg Declaration of 1868 gave greater clarity on the prohibition of certain weapons in war (Schindler and Toman, 1988). In modern humanitarian law, however, the protection of the wounded, civilians and property (the law of property is not discussed in this book) arises principally from the 'Law of Geneva' through the Geneva Conventions and the 'Law of Hague' through the Hague Conventions of 1899 and 1907.

Humanitarian law has two distinct branches, these are, the **'Law of Geneva'** and the **'Law of Hague'** (International Humanitarian Law, 2002). The Law of Hague commonly known as the Hague Conventions are two international agreements (referred to as Treaties) that were negotiated and agreed between States at international peace conferences at The Hague in the Netherlands. The First Hague Conference was in 1899 and the Second Hague Conference in 1907. The Law of Hague refers to the 'rights and obligations of belligerents in the conduct of military operations' or as Bugnion (1995) remarks more succinctly, how nation's conduct war on each other. For example, following the atomic bomb attacks on the Japanese cities on Hiroshima and Nagasaki that ended the Second World War, an ICRC delegate, Fritz Bilfinger, sent a telegram stating the following:

> "Visited Hiroshima thirtieth, conditions appalling stop city wiped out, eighty percent all hospitals destroyed or seriously damaged; inspected..." (Bugnion, 1995).

Following this observation on Hiroshima, the ICRC strongly encouraged all states to ban the use of nuclear weapons and any type or weapons that caused the devastating destruction on the two Japanese cities and their peoples. As suggested by Reisman and Stevick (1998), whilst collateral damage during war is unavoidable, it is essential that lawful primary targets be clearly defined to establish boundaries of what can and cannot be attacked. These two authors further remarked that the use of weapons is neither lawful nor unlawful but must be used in the specific context that they were defined for, so that they can separate between combatants and non-combatants. Thus, when targeting a military establishment the principle of proportionality needs to be taken into account (Fenrick, 2001). Although the differentiation between combatants and non-combatants is explored in detail in chapter 9, the use of weapons by non-combatants clearly has implications for MHCPs as they are bound to respect international and humanitarian law as well as national and military law (Bianchi, 2007).

The 'Law of Geneva', was inspired by a Geneva businessman, Henry Dunant at the battle of Solferino, in northern Italy between French, Italian and Austrian forces in 1859. Dunnat was concerned about the lack of care for the wounded soldiers on the battlefield that were left to die without any treatment or care (Sassòli et al, 2011. As a consequence of his experiences, he published a book, *A Memory of Solferino* with recommendations on how to care for the sick and wounded in war that was quickly endorsed by other countries. This resulted in a small committee being created, which was the inauguration of the modern ICRC. Thus, the First Geneva Convention was written and implemented by countries in 1864. Presently, the Geneva Conventions comprise of four treaties, which are commonly known as the 'Geneva Conventions of 1947' or the 'Geneva Conventions'; they also include three Additional Protocols (Rogers, 2004), which have been updated throughout the years to meet the demands of modern warfare in protecting the wounded and sick in war. The Geneva Conventions and the Hague Conventions were merged together by the adoption of Protocols I and II in 1977.

The importance of the Geneva Conventions has recently been re-affirmed in two documents by the ICRC; *'Health Care in Danger'* (ICRC, 2011) and *'How Does Law Protect in War?'* (Sassòli et al, 2011) where it reiterated that protective emblems such as wearing the Red Cross, Red Crescent or Red Crystal must be respected by all sides and that all military personnel including MHCPs must follow the international and humanitarian law. As explored in chapter 9, both these documents have stated the importance of distinguishing between combatants and non-combatants and that health facilities and personnel will lose their protection if they engage in harmful acts against the enemy that are not, for their own, or their patients' protections. Thus, the ICRC is clear about what the role of all MHCPs involves, this is, they must have an understanding of the importance of humanitarian law and the Law of Armed Conflict.

International and humanitarian law within the context of the vignettes

Although this book explores *British* military healthcare practice, the essential features of humanitarian law are nonetheless, clearly acknowledged, and entrenched implicitly within the vignettes and in particular, more explicitly in chapter 9, which critically explores the legitimacy of a non-combatant MHCP firing at the enemy when under attack. In addition, the Geneva Conventions Act 1957 and more recently the Geneva Conventions

(Amendments) Act 1995 ratifies the Geneva Conventions into United Kingdom law. Section 1 of this 1957 Act also states that any violation of the Geneva Conventions will be punishable via either a civil court or a court martial for military personnel and may involve a custodial sentence pending the severity of the crime. The 1957 Act is now strengthened by the Armed Forces Act 2006, which allows Commanding Officers to deal more readily with offences committed whilst on operations. The 2006 Act also confirms British military law's compatibility with international and humanitarian law. For example, schedule 2, section 12 (t) of the Armed Forces Act 2006, directly refers to section 1 of the Geneva Conventions Act 1957 thereby reinforcing the United Kingdom's commitment to conforming to the Geneva Conventions and its Additional Protocols.

Regarding chapter 9 of this book, Chapter 3, Article 19 of the First Geneva Convention (the Amelioration of the Condition of the Wounded and Sick in Armed Forces in the Field) refers to 'Medical Units and Establishments' and states that 'mobile medical units' such as military medical vehicles or military personnel travelling in light armoured tactical vehicles where their Red Cross insignia is clearly visible, may not in any 'circumstances', be attacked. In addition, Chapter 5, Article 35 of the same convention also states that medical transport vehicles when escorting the sick and wounded to medical establishments must not be attacked. Further, Chapter 7, Article 40 of the First Geneva Convention also refers directly to the 'Distinctive Emblem' i.e. the Red Cross that all personnel must legally wear on their upper left arm. The position of the protective emblem is further enhanced in Protocol III, which is the Third Protocol additional to the Geneva Conventions of 1949 relating to the Adoption of an Additional Distinctive Emblem (Protocol III). Accordingly, in each vignette, all military personnel wear this distinctive insignia i.e. the Red Cross apart from chapter 12 as this vignette is not based in a theatre of war and therefore there is no legal requirement for any medical personnel to wear this emblem at this time.

In chapter 9 of the book, the battlefield vignette also explains that the MHCP is wearing an upper left armband with a Red Cross on it that denotes his protected medical status as stated above. In Chapter 3, Article 24 of the First Geneva Convention under 'protected persons' the phrase, 'medical personnel proper', further categories doctors and nurses as personal who give direct care to the wounded. Thus, all of the MHCPs in the vignettes are 'medical personnel proper'. As further explained in chapter 9, the wearing of a Red Cross armband denotes that the enemy *must not* fire at him. Equally, it also signifies that medical personnel must not fire at the enemy, *unless;* it is for the protection of their patient's or their own life. Nonetheless, as the vignette explains, the enemy are firing at him and consequently, the MHCP fires back. In the context of this vignette, because the wearing of a protective emblem directly relates to the First Geneva Convention and the use of the protective Red Cross emblem on a white background, it is therefore important to explicitly mention the key principles of international law via the Geneva Conventions. In addition, chapter 9 also mentions that British combatants are firing back at the enemy. By way of Protocol I (Protocol Additional to the Geneva Conventions of 1949 relating to the Protection of Victims of International Armed Conflicts), section 3 on 'Combatants and Prisoners of War', Article 43 (2) (Protocol I), combatants are defined as being personnel who are legitimately permitted to engage in hostilities against the enemy. In chapter 9 therefore, it is clear that the combatant soldiers are legally allowed to fire at the enemy when under attack. Accordingly, it is therefore essential and relevant to critically analyse the differences between combatants and non-combatants regarding the consequences of their actions when under fire and the contrasting actions that they are lawfully permitted to undertake when under the rules and regulations of international law.

Similarly, in chapter 10, as this battlefield vignette also involves a MHCP giving care and treatment to a wounded soldier when under enemy fire, the requirements of international law and the Geneva Conventions are clearly relevant in the same context as in chapter 9. This is, that the enemy *must not* fire at any medical personnel when they are treating a wounded soldier. For instance, Chapter 2, Article 12 of the First Geneva Convention (the Amelioration of the Condition of the Wounded and Sick in Armed Forces in the Field) refers to the wounded and sick and medical personnel treating them. In this section, it clearly states that the wounded and medical personnel treating them *must not* be fired upon by the enemy. However, unlike chapter 9, in chapter 10, the importance of international law and the Geneva Conventions is implicitly applied. This is to avoid repetition from the previous chapter, but also, in contrast to chapter 9, where the importance of international law and the Geneva Conventions cannot be overlooked and must be unequivocally addressed, it is to highlight that the main focus of chapter 10, is to examine the *standard of care* in the battlefield and whether there is a *dual loyalty conflict* between following military orders or professional codes of practice in the context of the vignette. Accordingly, although important, the aim of chapter 10 is *not* to explore the relevance of international law in this context.

In the same way, the aim and focus of the operational vignette in chapter 11 is to explore dual loyalty conflict when a senior military officer *refuses* life-saving medical treatment from a junior MHCP and when the senior officer's *capacity* to consent is questionable due to their injury. In this vignette, although international law will clearly apply because of the vignette indicating that the injury is sustained within enemy and hostile territory, the purpose of the vignette is *not* to discuss international law. Instead, the aim of the vignette in chapter 11, is to critically discuss professional requirements as required by professional bodies such as the General Medical Council (GMC) and the Nursing Midwifery Council (NMC) on *capacity to consent* and allowing a competent patient to *refuse life-saving treatment.* In the context of the vignette, this is when the patient is being given treatment in a hostile and dangerous environment and when the MHCPs life is at risk. However, if international law were the focus of the discussion, then Part II, Article 21 of Protocol I, would apply, as 'medical vehicles' such as the medical helicopter carrying the emergency surgical team in chapter 11, must not be attacked. Further, Part II, Article 11 (5) of Protocol I, similarly would be relevant as this concerns refusal of treatment and any act or omission that endangers the physical health of another person; however, clearly this discussion would be outside the scope of professional guidance and requirements from either the GMC or NMC.

In contrast, the non-operational vignette of chapter 12 is based in a United Kingdom environment and is therefore outside the theatre of war. This vignette involves *refusal of treatment* and *confidentiality* of a soldier suffering from a psychological injury. Accordingly, the implications of international law and the Geneva Conventions are less significant in this environment and context compared to the other vignettes in more hostile situations. However, as in chapter 11 if the psychological injury did occur in a battlefield or operational environment then Part 2, Article 11 (1) and (4) of Protocol I would apply as this concerns the care and treatment for the mental health of wounded personnel.

In not openly mentioning or having the main focus of analysis throughout each vignette on international and humanitarian law and the Geneva Conventions, this book *does not,* in any way whatsoever, diminish or dismiss the extreme importance and practical relevance of this area of law. On the contrary, because this area of law is so important, as already discussed, chapter 9 explores separately international law within the context of a realistic vignette. This is before the book discusses the next battlefield vignette and the operational and non-operational vignettes in the subsequent chapters. This allows the remaining vignettes to explore the areas of medical law discussed above, in the context of British military law and its compatibility with professional codes of practice and *not* international law or the specific criteria mentioned in the four Treaties of the Geneva Conventions and the 'Additional Protocols'. More specifically, the main focus of the book is *not* about international and humanitarian law. Instead, and as mentioned in chapter 1, its emphasis is to **(i)** challenge the World Medical Association's claim that medical ethics during armed conflict is *identical* to medical ethics in times of peace in the context of British Military Healthcare Practice, **(ii)** to discuss British Military law in conjunction with professional codes of practice from either the General Medical Council or Nursing Midwifery Council and **(iii)** to explore the dual loyalty conflict between either following military law of professional codes practice. Clearly, if the context of each vignette were more directed towards exploring international and humanitarian law and the Geneva Conventions, then the book would quite evidently not address or challenge the WMAs statement. However, as mentioned above, this does not mean that the book has relegated international law in favour of domestic, civil, and military law or dismissed its significance. On the contrary, international law clearly *does* merit attention and exploration within a military discourse. However, this should only be done where appropriate and in this book, a thorough examination of international law, would detract from the main aim and purpose of it and would be outside the scope of this work. Accordingly, this area of law is best dealt with in a separate book.

However, notwithstanding the above, in addition to the legal requirement of having to follow international and humanitarian law, as discussed in the next chapter, military law also makes it imperative to obey and follow military orders without question and acquire military discipline. Using real life vignettes, this book, therefore, considers how this can cause ethical and professional constraints between either following professional codes of practice or following military orders to achieve Operational Effectiveness, and whether the World Medical Association's statement that **'medical ethics in armed conflict is identical to medical ethics in times of peace'** can be successfully challenged (WMA 2004; Hallgarth, 2007).

CHAPTER FOUR

MILITARY LAW AND DISCIPLINE

Modern Military Law

Military law is entrenched via international obligations under military and humanitarian rules and regulations such as the Geneva Conventions of 1949 and Protocol 1 of 1977 (Rogers, 2004). Its aim is **(i)** to establish and maintain military discipline so that the underlying functional effectiveness of the military at all levels is not compromised and **(ii),** to ensure that the instructions and orders of the military commander can be achieved within any environment (Soldier Management, 2004). It is, as mentioned by Savitsky et al (2009), characterised by mobility and on 'mission readiness'.

Although it is a separate judicial system to civilian law, it is not exclusive from it; meaning that military personnel are equally subjected to the civilian law of any particular country wherever they are serving, including international law (Soldier Management, 2004). This means that, like any other employer, the military has a procedural system whereby it can discipline its employees if they fail to meet the required standards or fail to follow that which governs them. This also includes disciplining MHCPs for not obeying military orders. Therefore, as demonstrated in the real-life vignettes and unique to the military, is that they can discipline any soldier, irrespective of where they are serving, and whether the environment is hostile and violent from enemy attack. To aid this process, currently the British Army uses Army General and Administrative Instructions (AGAIs) (1998). The AGAIs, however, do not give any guidance on whether the standard for disciplining MHCPs changes in line with the context of the situation and the hostile, challenging environments that the MHCP can work in when caring for wounded personnel. The AGAIs do not also give any guidance over which order takes precedence if conflict arises between obeying and following military orders or following professional codes of practice. Although no rationale is given for this, it may be because the Army *does not* identify and/or appreciate that such conflict could ever arise, as it may have assumed that whatever rank a person is, he/she will unquestionably obey a military order from a senior officer. For example, as discussed in chapters 7 and 9 in a battlefield environment military orders could be for MHCPs to treat military personnel only and not civilians; contrasted with the non-operational environment to treat military and civilian casualties alike. This order may have adverse ethical, professional, and legal implications for a MHCP, which will be discussed further throughout the book. The complexity is self-evident when one has to consider that, to civilian healthcare professionals; not treating wounded civilians would be morally repugnant and contradict the entire underpinning principles of healthcare (Crowe, 1991). Moreover, feasibly and fundamentally, it contradicts the World Medical Association's philosophy, that 'medical ethics in armed conflict is *identical* to medical ethics in times of peace' (Hallgarth, 2007). Clearly, the military system appears to be more authoritarian than that to which civilian employees adhere and, as further discussed in the next paragraphs, this military system is re-enforced via military statutory authority.

Military Statutory Authority

When medical and nursing services were recognised in a military capacity and became officially attached within their respective military framework, they became governed by military law and hence subject to stringent military discipline. These single service discipline Acts were the Army Act 1955, the Naval Discipline Act 1957, and the Royal Air Force Act 1955 (Explanatory Notes to Armed Forces Discipline Act 2000). However, it was recognised following the Strategic Defence Review in 1997, that military personnel from the three services often worked and were commanded by military personnel from a different armed service (Queen's Regulations 1975). It, therefore, seemed appropriate to have one Act to command all service personnel, irrespective of their service. These three discipline Acts, therefore, led to the creation of the Armed Forces Discipline Act 2000, which now exerts command over all military personnel in the British Armed Forces. Unique to MHCPs, however, is that they are also governed by their respective professional regulations, irrespective of the environment within which they are serving.

The Armed Forces Discipline Act 2000, modernised and updated the previous three single service Acts in relation to military discipline. In addition, it also reinforced and highlighted the need for military discipline and 'mission readiness' and a need for a separate military justice system rather than a reliance of civilian law alone. However, of importance is that this Act did not highlight whether the military duty flowing from the need for military discipline and following military orders takes a legal precedence over professional codes of practice in the different environments in which a MHCP serves. In addition, this Act also did not take into consideration the effects of a dangerous environment and when a MHCP's life may be at risk when caring for an injured soldier.

More recently, the Army Act 1955, the Naval Discipline Act 1957 and the Royal Air Force Act 1955 were all repealed via the Armed Forces Act 2006, which received Royal Assent in November 2006. As recent conflicts in Iraq and Afghanistan have shown, the three services increasingly work closer together than ever before. The intention of this new Act is, therefore, to 'align discipline and command responsibilities' to create universal equity and fairness amongst the three services and create harmony with the Armed Forces Discipline Act 2000 (Armed Forces Act 2006). Like the Armed Forces Discipline Act 2000, however, it does not take into consideration the dual nature of the MHCP as subject to both professional codes of practice and military regulations in battlefield, operation, and non-operational environments. In the Armed Forces Act 2006, medical practitioners are only mentioned under the heading of Sentencing: Principles and Procedures (The Armed Forces Act 2006, part 9, chapter 1-2, and schedule 16). This involves assessing a soldier's fitness to stand trial or be imprisoned in a military correction centre and instructions what to do if a soldier is considered unfit to stand trial. Rubin (2002) asserts that even though the military law has undergone significant recent changes in becoming 'civilianised', the Armed Forces Act 2006 does not address the ethical dilemmas that MHCPs may face in battlefield, operation, and non-operational environments. Therefore, without clear military statutory authority or guidance from the GMC and the NMC for MHCPs when serving in these diverse environments, there may be tensions towards ensuring Operational Effectiveness and achieving military discipline.

Military Discipline

Napoleon Bonaparte stated, '*Il n'y a pas de victoire sans discipline*' meaning, victory cannot be achieved without discipline (Carney, 1996). Discipline is, therefore, the soul of any army, which only prevails and succeeds when soldiers are obedient to commands. Helvetius in Cramer (1921 at p. 774), in the eighteenth century, defined discipline as 'the art of inspiring soldiers with more fear for their own officers than they have for the enemy'. Other authors describe discipline as, '...the long-continued habit by which the very muscles of the soldier instinctively obey the command; even if his mind is too confused to attend, yet his muscles will obey'(Murray, 1921). More recently, General Sir Mike Jackson (the retired former head of the British Armed Forces), in his autobiography, indicated that army discipline is ensuring 'immediate obedience when necessary' to any soldier or officer, irrespective of their specific role or their location (Jackson, 2007). More comprehensively, the British Army defines discipline as follows:

'Discipline is teaching, which makes a man do something which he would not, unless he had learnt that if was the right, the proper, and the expedient thing to do. At its best, it is instilled and maintained by pride in oneself, in one's unit, in one's profession; only at its worst by fear of punishment' (Field Marshall Sir William Slim, 1956).

Discipline is, therefore, the 'backbone' that promotes efficiency in the Army' (Soldier Management, 2004). This efficiency incorporates the army in peacetime and during war; at home in the United Kingdom and overseas and relies on teamwork, trust, loyalty and a set of values and standards for all those who are employed within it. It, therefore, applies to every British service person in the world, no matter what their specific role is, or whether that person is a MHCP with a dual responsibility to a professional body such as the GMC or the NMC. However, as the following quotation illustrates, before these collective values can be achieved, self-discipline needs to be acquired, which was described by Field Marshal The Viscount Montgomery of Alamein as:

'All of us have in our make-up good and bad points. Training in self-discipline consists in analysing a man's character and then in developing the good points whilst teaching him to hold in subjection the bad points. This leads on, automatically, to collective discipline, in which the outstanding factor is the subordination of self for the benefit of the community.' (Field-Marshall the Viscount Montgomery of Alamein, 1958).

This quotation indicates that not only self-discipline must be enforced, but also it must be enforced whatever the situation, for the collective benefit of all (Warbuton, 2006). It clearly, however, does not permit deviance and hence it would not allow a MHCP to decide to follow professional codes of practice or military orders. Thus, prioritising professional codes of practice over following military orders can cause conflict and become problematic, if not impossible, since a lack of self-discipline in the military is viewed as misconduct, and an offence according to the Armed Forces Act 2006, chapter 25, sections 2, 11, 12, and 13.

Professional Regulation and its Conflict with Military Law

All healthcare professionals have a duty to follow regulations from their respective professional bodies. This duty is also a legal one, since professional codes of practice are created via secondary legislation and statutory instruments. In addition, the National Institute for Health and Clinical Excellence, formerly known as the National Institute for Clinical Excellence (NICE), which is an independent organisation, guides all healthcare professionals in delivering care within an evidence-based framework, promoting health and preventing ill-health, irrespective of whether they are civilian or military healthcare professionals. Although they are more generalised than NICE guidelines, National Service Frameworks (NSFs), also have some effect on the way that patient care is delivered.

In contrast, and unlike civilian healthcare professionals, MHCPs are also regulated by military law via the Armed Forces Act 2006. The ethical and professional implications of such are explained in more detail in the vignettes. The potential problem for MHCPs in adhering to all elements of relevant military law, professional codes of practice, NICE guidelines, and NSFs is if any of them conflict with Operational Effectiveness. A number of examples concerning the management and prevention of self-harm serve to illustrate this point. For instance, NICE recommends that once a patient has deliberately injured him or herself, they should be treated 'in an atmosphere of respect and understanding' (NICE, 2004). Whilst this may be possible in a non-operational environment, such as the United Kingdom or in any Military Defence Hospital Unit and although on occasion a MHCP may have empathy towards a self-harm patient, generally it is difficult to imagine in a battlefield or operational environment that such respect and understanding would or could be accorded to that individual soldier by the majority of his or her colleagues, or by their Commanding Officer if it compromised Operational Effectiveness. Likewise, if a soldier were to refuse medical treatment, then according to the Armed Forces Act 2006, Part 1 (Offences), section 16 - Malingering (1) c, 'A person subject to service law commits an offence if, to avoid service – by any act or omission he aggravates or prolongs any injury of his'. Refusing treatment is examined in detail in chapters 11 and 12. However, a soldier refusing treatment may be considered to deliberately and perhaps with premeditated intent, prevent himself from becoming fit to fight (Gross, 2006). It may, therefore, be considered as a military offence in accordance with the Armed Forces Act 2006.

The consideration of refusal of treatment raises several interesting issues. In spite of its statutory authority, the Armed Forces Act 2006 also appears to conflict with civilian rights and conflict with case law, thus causing MHCPs difficulties in the management of patient care. For example, in *Re T (Adult: Refusal of Medical Treatment, 1992)*, refusing treatment was held to be an absolute right. In addition, as cited by Wheatley (2001), the European Convention of Human Rights (1950), the Human Rights Act 1998 (HRA 1998) being the UKs implementation, provides minimum standards on civil rights. Thus, Article 3 provides that: 'No one shall be subject to torture or to inhuman or degrading treatment or punishment'. In *Ahmed v Austria* (1996), it was held that Article 3 'enshrines one of the fundamental values of democratic societies' and, therefore, absolutely prohibits any form of degrading treatment. Consequently, this judgment should allow a competent soldier, who is a patient, to make a choice over whether to accept or refuse medical treatment. However, as discussed in chapter 12, this is clearly not the case. Nonetheless, the HRA 1998 provides a model 'framework' that allows consideration of issues concerning choice, consent and refusal of medical treatment (Wicks, 2001). What the HRA 1998 emphasises is that, although soldiers relinquish many of their rights when they join the armed forces, such as the right to claim unfair dismissal (Employment Rights Act 1996, part xiii, s. 192); they do not relinquish their healthcare rights. Thus, if a military patient soldier refuses medical treatment, this can be problematic. As examined in more detail in chapters 11 and 12, the tension between either allowing the patient to refuse medical treatment or being obedient to military orders and ensuring that all soldiers are fit to fight can be problematic for the MCHP (Tricarico, 1998).

These examples, therefore, highlight the countless challenges that MHCPs face when caring for soldiers in difficult and dangerous environments. It also emphasises Lutzen's (2004) opinion in that there are no easy answers to solving dilemmas in war and conflict. Unfortunately, however, although the following two studies in the next chapter highlight the moral and ethical judgment of individuals in a military context, there is little research on the ethical and professional complexities of Military Healthcare Professionals caring for the sick and wounded in war (Moreno, 2008) and in a military context (Verweij et al, 2007), to determine what education and approach MHCPs should take when faced with ethical and legal dilemmas in hostile military environments. Tschudin and Schmitz (2003) suggest that caring for the sick and wounded in war is complex, and, therefore, for military doctors and nurses to fully comprehend and understand the issues around caring for the sick and wounded in these hostile environments, better education and knowledge within the military to learn about the effects of war is necessary.

CHAPTER FIVE

MORAL JUDGMENT IN THE MILITARY

Study of Military Ethical Dilemmas

Due to a paucity of information regarding military ethical dilemmas in the battlefield, operational and non-operational environments, the following study by Verweij et al (2007), which used a Moral Judgment Test developed from the work of Lind (1999) is discussed in depth. In this study, participants were asked *to listen to and evaluate moral arguments about a moral dilemma, especially arguments that opposed their standpoint of the dilemma* (Kohlberg, 1964 and 1984; Lind, 1999). Verweij and colleagues analysed the moral judgment skills of Dutch military officers, officer-candidates, and university students in relation to four different ethical dilemmas to determine how military personnel should act according to different ethical problems. The Moral Judgment Test asked the participants to judge whether they agreed or disagreed with the decisions made by the key players within the scenarios posed. For each dilemma, the respondents were asked the pros and cons of each decision, which were as follows:

1)   An 'employee dilemma', where employees suspected that their employers were conducting unauthorised surveillance of the workforce. Here the employee had to decide whether to disclose this information to the trade union, but consider that if they did so, then their decision may result in them being dismissed from the company.

2)   A 'medical dilemma', where a doctor accedes to a dying patient's wishes to help him/her end their life, in contravention of their professional codes of practice, which forbids a doctor from assisting a person die.

3)   The 'Gerard dilemma', where a French soldier witnessed friends on a tape shooting in the direction of innocent civilians. The soldier considered whether 'he should hand over the tape to the police'.

4)   The Special Air Service (SAS) dilemma where soldiers on a secret mission in Iraq were discovered by a boy. They let the boy go

free, but were consequently captured by Iraqi soldiers, as a direct result of not killing the boy. The soldiers then questioned whether they made the correct decision in compromising the mission by not following military orders and failing to kill the boy.

In addition to the Moral Judgment Test, the authors utilised their own Ethical Awareness Model (EAM) (Verweij et al, 2007). The aim of EAM was to provide a practical tool to enable multinational military personnel to deal appropriately with moral questions and dilemmas in the course of their duty and to guide them in dealing with difficult ethical situations in different military environments, similar to the environments defined in this book; namely, the battlefield, operational or non-operational environments. Gross (2006), explains that when soldiers are faced with a moral or ethical dilemma in war, they will generally make a decision that favours their comrades before the enemy and any civilian, even when that decision could be perceived as the wrong decision. Therefore, a practical tool can eradicate such subjectivity, as it will allow soldiers to act more benevolently and impartially (Rubenstein, 2004). In this study, the EAM itself was developed from a Code of Conduct, which emerged from moral judgments of Dutch military personnel following conflict in the Former Yugoslavia in the 1990's. In particular, this was the Srebrenica tragedy in 1995, where Dutch Armed Forces failed to create a safe haven and protect Bosnian Muslims from Bosnian Serbs, leading to the subsequent alleged murder of approximately 8,000 Bosnian Muslims.

The Code of Conduct comprised of **(i)** behavioural rules, which emerged from Dutch societal norms and **(ii)** level and phases of moral development, which were identified from the work of Kohlberg, (1981; 1984) a psychologist who studied cognitive development. Although Kohlberg's work is not singularly related to military personnel, he did, however, establish that every person progresses through three levels of moral development. **Firstly,** the *precondition level,* which is based on punishment and obedience, in that individuals learn that they will be punished if they do not obey. **Secondly,** the *conventional phase*, where individuals seek peer approval and become aware of the expectations of others within a group and **thirdly,** the *post-conventional and principal phases*. In this final phase, the individual is able to progress from obeying rules and being influenced by others to form their own moral values. By doing so, they then learn that rights, such as the 'right to live', the 'right to justice' and the 'right to be free from torture' is a universal right that should be respected in all societies. The use of this Code of Conduct was intended to assist Dutch military personnel in having common moral and ethical values to deal more appropriately with future ethical dilemmas than they had done at Srebrenica.

The importance of this study is that, although it did not indicate whether the participants would perform the same actions as the personnel in each dilemma, they were aware of the moral and ethical dilemmas of each scenario. The Code of Conduct could be considered to have limited value, however, due to its basis in Dutch societal norms and rules. It would, therefore, be difficult to predict how transferable it would be and what value it would have to, for example, British MHCPs. Despite this, it seems reasonable to concur with Verweij and colleagues that having some code of conduct is advantageous, as it could assist soldiers in their decision-making process, given any ethical dilemma.

A further criticism of the study is that the questions appear too restrictive to predict what decision a military person might make when faced with other ethical dilemmas. In particular, of relevance to this book, is a choice a British MHCP would make if similarly faced with ethical dilemmas as those described by Verweij and colleagues (2007). Thus, overall, the utility of the framework used is limited in cultural terms and limited in its transferability across professionals. Although the research attempted to assist military personnel in dealing with ethical dilemmas, clearly, Dutch military behavioural rules are not consistent with other countries' military behavioural rules. For example, in the British Military, junior soldiers are trained and instructed to follow orders without question (Jackson, 2007) whereas in the Dutch military, a huge cultural difference is evident insofar as questioning orders by a junior soldier is acceptable, so as to promote an analysis of the order they have been given (White, 2010). Therefore, the benefits within a multinational military operation governed by separate national commanders can be questionable. It may only be beneficial if the same national countries are serving in an operational tour that is either North Atlantic Treaty Organisation (NATO) or United Nations (UN) led, where one country is the dominant force and the lead country is able to ascribe the same values to other countries that they command, thus reducing any cultural differences and tensions.

Noteworthy, however, is that with the military scenario, there was a significant difference between whether the participants had served in a battlefield or in an operational environment. Those who had battlefield and operational experience were more able to recognise the complexities of making decisions in such intense and dangerous environments. However, a more significant criticism of the study was the use of a methodological approach that did not allow the researchers to focus on the soldiers' personal experiences in determining what the best response to an ethical dilemma could be in a hostile environment (Culet and Bluff 2006). Hence, this study was unable to take into account the ethical aspects of how a soldier may react in an environment that is stressful, dangerous, and unfamiliar. Nonetheless, the study appears to have three useful facets for this book. **Firstly,** the study highlighted the complexities of solving ethical and professional dilemmas in military environments. Verweij et al (2007) go as far as to suggest that when trying to solve an ethical dilemma in a military environment, there is 'no solution that does not cause any pain'. **Secondly,** to prevent any repeat of the Srebrenica massacre from occurring, the study also highlighted the necessity for the military to focus and have greater awareness of ethical issues and training (Richardson et al, 2004). As remarked by Badaracco (1997), if a person is able to analyse an ethical dilemma, they are then more likely to estimate the consequence of their actions. **Thirdly,** the study highlighted the complexities of having to follow both military orders and professional codes of practice in different and challenging environments. Thus, this puts emphasis on a dual loyalty conflict where the aim of the military is to defeat the enemy. Killing them is regarded as lawful and an unavoidable and accepted consequence, in contrast to the aim of military medicine, which is to save, lives (Powell, 2005). This appears to suggest that in the military, the conflict for a MHCP between being obedient to both military orders and professional codes of practice is unavoidable (Clarke, 2006). In addition, as will be discussed later in the vignettes and chapters 13 and 14, the study emphasised the complex situation of when an MHCP simultaneously **(i)** may be acting legally and ethically in one sense when following either military orders or professional codes of practice but **(ii)** may also compromise legality and act unethically in the other when they follow the same military orders or professional codes of practice. Moreover, the study raises the question of whether following either *military orders* or *professional codes of practice* is the best way to solve ethical medical dilemmas in diverse military environments that are distinct from normal civilian healthcare environments (Kelly, 2010); examples of which are highlighted in the vignettes. Further, it raises the importance of military personnel having knowledge and understanding of military medical ethics.

Study of Medical Students' Knowledge and Understanding of Military Medical Ethics, the United States Military, and the Geneva Conventions

Boyd, Himmelstie, Lasser, McCormick, Bor, Cutrona, and Woolhandler (2007) generated a computer based survey. They then sent it via the internet inviting approximately **5,000** medical students in different years of their programme from **8** universities to examine how many hours they had been taught and what their knowledge was of **(i)** military medical ethics, **(ii)** the Geneva Convention and **(iii)** their likely response to compulsory mobilisation of medical personnel. The impetus for the study was the proven mistreatment by United States guards and complicity of United States healthcare professionals in the interrogation of prisoners who were suspected of being members of Al-Qaida and the Taliban at Abu Ghraib prison in Iraq during the second Gulf War, and Guantanamo Bay in Cuba after the Trade Centre attacks in New York on the 11 September in 2001. What occurred at these locations, and the alleged involvement of US MHCPs, arguably damaged the reputation of the US Armed Forces and explicitly highlighted the need for the US military medical services to review the military training of its personnel (Miles, 2004).

The response rate varied from each university from 19.4% to 60.5% giving a disappointing average response rate of 35% or 1,756 students. Whilst 51% of the respondents were male, overall, there was no significant difference between male and female responses and the actual year of their programme. Regarding military medical ethics, the study revealed that 94.2% of the students had had less than *1 hour* of education on this topic and just 4.3% had received between *1 to 5 hours* regarding military healthcare professional responsibilities and obligations towards their patients whilst serving in the military. Only 5.7% of the students were 'very familiar' with the Geneva Conventions. 66.1% were 'somewhat familiar', which meant they answered correctly that a military healthcare professional should 'treat the sickest first, regardless of nationality'. However, 26.5% answered incorrectly when they said that they should 'treat their own soldiers first according to the level of severity and then attend to the wounded enemy'. When asked 'under what circumstance is a [medical] officer ethically required to disobey a direct order from a superior' they were offered three options:

Option 1 'when ordered to threaten a prisoner with an injection of a psychoactive drug that will not actually be administered'.
Option 2 'when ordered to inject a harmless bolus of saline into a prisoner who fears he is receiving a lethal injection'.
Option 3 'when ordered to inject a lethal drug into a prisoner'.

Although a small percentage, but nonetheless still rather alarming, **6%** would obey all three options as a direct order. This highlights the notion of unquestionable obedience to act in a way that under any other circumstance would be abhorrent. A bigger minority, at **27%**, believed that only option 3 was unacceptable, whereas the majority, **66%**, believed that all of the options were unacceptable. Although the study did not give any statistical evidence for the students with future military obligations, the authors commented that these students had 'scarcely more knowledge than the other [none military medical] students'. These figures are significant, since individuals only possess effective moral and ethical judgment skills when they can appreciate the interests at stake concerning a given situation (Verweij et al, 2007) and their own individual personal values (Lere and Gaumnitz, 2003). The figures suggest that **33%** of the respondents did not have the skills and knowledge to recognise the ethical and moral issues at stake concerning all of the options. This is important because, in addition, the figures suggest that, although the law deals with right and wrong acts, ethics deals with good and bad acts (Johnson, 1999). General Sir John Hackett remarked 'What the bad man cannot do is be a good sailor, or soldier, or airman' (Hackett, 1963). In other words, military personnel need to act both lawfully and ethically (Jackson, 2007). The results further indicate that military ethics appear to be strongly influenced by a sword approach, with the importance of following military duty and orders before anything else (Toner, 2006). Meaning that in ethical terms and as discussed in the vignettes, achieving Operational Effectiveness and unquestionably following military duty as discussed earlier, is a desirable characteristic that every military person must acquire and anything after that, such as autonomy or self-determination for the soldier-patient and MHCP is secondary and selfish (Gross, 2006).

In a duty-based approach, therefore, soldiers should perform their duties as soldiers and health professionals should perform their duties as health professionals (Warbuton, 2006). However, the difficulty with this approach is in determining which duty is the most important. It may mean that a MHCPs professional duty could yield to the military duty to following military orders if the goal is to achieve Operational Effectiveness. Koch (2006) describes this as 'weaponising medicine', a phrase created by Donald Rumsfeld, the Secretary of Defence (for the USA in 2006), where he contentiously indicated that when medical personnel are faced with non-medical matters i.e. following military orders, a patient-doctor relationship does not exist. Likewise, an unreported US Southern Command policy statement instructed MHCPs caring for prisoners at Guantanamo Bay that 'communication from "enemy persons under US control" are not confidential and are not subject to the assertion of privileges' and that MHCPs must "convey any information concerning... the accomplishment of military or national security mission" in the course of any treatment given' (Bloche and Marks, 2005). Although this concerns the US military only, this clearly indicates the conflict between following military orders and professional codes of practice.

Boyd et al (2007), assert that although the results were interesting, a criticism of the study was that by using *only* 8 medical schools and considering the poor response rate overall, it was unlikely that this was an accurate representation and reflection of all medical students in the US, regarding their knowledge and understanding of military medical ethics, their knowledge of the US military and the Geneva Conventions. In addition, the study indicated that only **5.4%** of the respondents had any past or present experience of military medical ethics. This indicates that further research is required to gain more knowledge of what participants understand of military medical ethics. Indeed, Verweij et al (2007) highlighted that 'military personnel who have had previous experiences' in dealing with dilemmas in hostile military environments 'differ from military personnel without such experiences in assessing the dilemmas that were presented' to them. This therefore questions if the responses they gave would **(a)** mirror their actions if they were *presently* in the military, **(b)** would mirror their actions if in the *future* they were to become part of the military or **(c)** whether training is the key to personnel understanding and being able to act both ethically and lawfully when faced with a military medical dilemma. Clearly, the study could have been strengthened in that regard to **firstly,** address these questions and **secondly,** if it had involved qualified doctors, to ascertain if they would give the same responses as the medical students.

Nonetheless, in contrast, there are three benefits of the study for this book. **Firstly,** it highlights the need for greater awareness and analysis of dilemmas in military medical ethics and the medical aspects of the Geneva Conventions if any medical student, doctor, or nurse later joins the military to become Military Healthcare Professionals or works for the military in a civilian capacity. **Secondly,** it highlights an overall general lack of knowledge and understanding of military medical ethics, thereby acknowledging the need for greater education for military healthcare professionals to become advocates for wounded soldiers and prisoners everywhere in war. **Thirdly,** it suggests that possibly a *military-focused* approach and or a *professional healthcare-focused* approach could perhaps be the solution to the dual loyalty conflict and solving medical ethical dilemmas in war.

Concluding Comments

According to Gross (2006), before attempting to resolve ethical, professional, and legal conflicts in a military healthcare environment, 'an understanding of the principles at stake' are required. This chapter has highlighted the lack of consideration of military medical ethics and the ethical and professional complexities of MHCPs caring for the sick and wounded in military environments. In addition, it has illustrated the conflict that MHCPs face in either following professional codes of practice or following military law. This chapter has also shown that solving ethical and professional conflicts in a military environment is as challenging as determining what the best course of action is to take is problematic (Tasioulas, 1998). This chapter has also illustrated that, currently, neither the GMC nor the NMC give any definitive guideline to assist MHCPs as to what the best solution is when faced with ethical and professional problems in battlefield, operational and non-operational military environments.

This chapter has also highlighted that, despite some professional cohesiveness between civilian and military healthcare, its limitations are manifested when ethical and legal dilemmas occur in intense and dangerous environments such as the battlefield and operational environment, to the extent that a 'patient's needs' may be subjugated to ensuring that Operational Effectiveness is achieved. In spite of the World Medical Association's International Code of Ethics in 2004 claiming that *'medical ethics in armed conflict is identical to medical ethics in times of peace'* (WMA 2004; Hallgarth, 2007), it is apparent that ethics in wartime situations is complex. For example, as remarked by Gross (2004) in his essay on 'Bioethics and Armed Conflict', in times of war, patient welfare may need to yield to the interests of a State's national security, thus suggesting that WMAs assertion is problematic.

CHAPTER SIX

USING VIGNETTES TO ADDRESS MILITARY CLINICAL ETHICAL ISSUES

Introduction

This chapter starts with explaining why the WMAs statement is problematic. It also explains why vignettes are not new to healthcare and are a useful way of interpreting, evaluating, and solving ethical problems (Vellinga et al, 2005). This chapter also describes what a vignette is, explains the content of each vignette utilised in this book and provides the rationale for why vignettes are used to address the WMAs statement that **'medical ethics in armed conflict is identical to medical ethics in times of peace'**. This chapter also describes and explains why the book uses legal methodology to analyse each vignette and emphasises the importance of legal precedent and statutory interpretation. In addition, it explains and describes why a military ethical model is also used to analyse the ethical dilemmas in each vignette.

Why is the World Medical Association's International Code of Ethics statement problematic?

Although explored in more detail throughout the book, **the World Medical Association's International Code of Ethics statement** in chapter 1 is problematic for several reasons. **Firstly,** although some of the difficulties of this have already been highlighted in chapter 1, meeting the expectation that *medical ethics in war* is the same as *medical ethics in peace* is both challenging and demanding. This is because healthcare decisions are influenced by the urgent demands of combat and a military Commander's need to achieve his/her military mission (Benatar and Upshur, 2008). As remarked by Michael Gross (2006 at page 232), 'War does not transform or affect ethics in any meaningful way. Rather, it sets ethics aside entirely'. **Secondly,** despite choice assuring that a person has the right to decide what they want or do not want to do, in a military setting, wherever there is an ethical dilemma and a choice has to be made, there is always a greater consequence, with more potential for an undesirable side effect to another person (Appiah, 2006). Therefore, a choice is often a 'defining moment', as it is based on the moral judgment of the person making that choice (Coleman, 2009). **Thirdly,** unique to a Military Healthcare Professional (MHCP) is that sometimes they are more defined by the rank they hold, as opposed to their healthcare professional qualification (Kelly, 2010). Thus, they have to make a defining choice between following military orders and or following their professional obligations. Making this choice becomes more problematic when they have to make a decision quickly and they are situated in an intense and frightening environment, such as the battleground or an operational area where their life could be at risk (Howe, 2003). This is further exacerbated when a MHCP generally has firsthand knowledge of the devastating effects of war on the wounded, both physically and emotionally, as the choice they may have to make may appear to involve determining an impossible value (Tschudin and Schmitz, 2003). **Fourthly,** clarifying military and professional responsibilities in differing and demanding environments can sometimes result in an adverse outcome for either MHCPs or their patient (Badaracco, 1997). With an ethical and moral dilemma, whatever choice is made, it may be perceived by another as the wrong choice (Ohlsson, 1993). For a MHCP, a superior officer or their patient will sometimes perceive the choice made as the incorrect one. Hence, in demanding and hostile environments, such as those currently in Iraq or Afghanistan, where wounded soldiers require urgent medical care, such ethical dilemmas may be exacerbated due to the speed at which decisions have to be made (Sandman and Nordmark, 2006).

According to Lantz (2005), although war creates an 'all-embracing threat to human and moral values', there is no specific direction from previous literature or professional guidance from either the General Medical Council (GMC) or the Nursing Midwifery Council (NMC) to advise MHCPs as to the best course of action when working in a hostile military environment and when faced with ethical conflicts and dilemmas. As explained in more detail in chapter 9, the only guidance in caring for the sick and wounded in such situations arises from the Geneva Conventions of 1864, 1949 and Additional Protocol 1 of 1977 (Rogers, 2004).

Via a legal methodological approach, using real life vignettes, this book substantiates four sub-requirements, which are as follows:

1) Although there are similarities between civilian and military healthcare practices, the hostile and diverse environments that MHCPs work in is significantly different to a civilian healthcare environment, even in an emergency (discussed in chapter 7).

2) Although, a dual loyalty conflict may exist in other areas of healthcare apart from the military, it is not problematic to the same extent as it is in diverse military environments (discussed in chapters 7 and 9 to 12).

3) Current professional codes of practice by the GMC and the NMC are not a sufficient solution to the existing and emerging ethical and professional conflicts in battlefield and operational environments.

4) Medical ethics in armed conflict are constrained and questionable under existing ethical, professional, and legal parameters. Therefore, new professional regulatory solutions to solve these ethical conflicts should be considered by the professional bodies i.e. the GMC and NMC.

Using a legal methodological approach of the Royal Prerogative, statutory interpretation, and judicial precedent that will be explained later in this chapter, the book addresses the following:

1) To establish if a duty of care should apply to MHCPs in the **battlefield** environment (discussed in chapters 7).

2) To examine if MHCPs can be protected by combat immunity or a modified and unique form of combat immunity named as *Military Healthcare Battlefield Immunity* on the **battlefield** (discussed in chapter 9).

3) To ascertain if the current standard of care on the **battlefield** is sufficiently viable to protect the Ministry of Defence against a claim of a breach of a duty of care for any negligent act or omission by a MHCP (discussed in chapter 10).

4) To clarify if the medical obligation to respect a competent patient soldier's wish to refuse medical treatment and confidentiality is compromised in an **operational** and **non-operational** military environment (discussed in chapters 11 and 12).

5) To ascertain if a MHCP should follow military duties before professional codes of practice (discussed in chapters 7 and 9 to 12).

6) To ascertain if a MHCP should follow professional codes of practice before military duties (discussed in chapters 7 and 9 to 14).

7)   To determine if the consequences of not following military duties should be more important than the consequences of not following professional codes of practice (discussed in chapters 7 and 9 to 14).

8)   To determine if a MHCP can exhibit ethical behaviour that is both compatible to the military and to their respective professional bodies such as the GMC and the NMC. If this is the case, to consider if it will then allow them to practice military healthcare in the battlefield, operational and non-operational environments without legal, professional, and or detrimental military consequences (discussed in chapters 7 and 9 to 14).

Using vignettes as a framework and analysing them by legal methodology serves several purposes. It allows an interpretation and analysis of experiences from those who have experienced them and is a recognised legal method that is utilised throughout law to analyse statutes and the doctrine of precedents that are essential to gain a proper understanding of substantive law (Manchester and Salter, 2006).

Vignettes

Vignettes are short scenes that focus on a setting or an idea to allow a researcher to explore and understand complex issues in depth (McGloin, 2008). As described by Hughes and Huby (2002), they include 'short descriptions of an event based on fact or fiction'. Vignettes are, therefore, an ideal substitute for in-situ experience and can be considered the *safest* and *best way* of obtaining information, required to determine knowledge and attitudes towards a given situation (Richman and Mercer, 2002; Callicott, 2003).

The content of each vignette, therefore, reflects legal and ethical concepts that are essential for *all* healthcare professionals to have knowledge and understanding of so that they can practice safely (Griffith and Tengnah, 2008). For example, although the following obligations are outlined in chapter 1 and discussed in specific detail in chapters 7 to 12, both the GMC and NMC respectively, state that:

(i)   A doctor and a nurse must make the patient their first concern, thereby assuming a duty of care (GMC, *Good Medical Practice, p.6* 2006; NMC, *The Code, p.1* 2008 and NMC, *Advice sheet: Duty of Care, 2008).*

(ii)   The nurse and doctor must respect the patient's dignity and promote the health and well-being of patients in their care (GMC,

Good Medical Practice 2006, *pp. 2-11* and the NMC, *The Code, p.1* 2008).

(iii) The doctor and nurse must obtain the patient's consent before giving any care or treatment (GMC, *Good Medical Practice* 2006, *p. 20;* NMC, *The Code, p.2,* 2008 and NMC, *Consent Advice Sheet,* 2008).

(iv) The doctor and nurse must allow a competent patient to refuse any medical treatment (GMC, *Good Medical Practice, Consent: Patients and Doctors Making Decisions Together, p. 19,* 2008 and the NMC, *The Code, p.2,* 2008).

(v) Where the patient is not able to give consent for him or herself, or lacks capacity to do so, then the decision about the patient's care must be made in the patient's 'best interests' (GMC, *Good Medical Practice, Consent: Patients and Doctors Making Decisions Together, 62-80,* 2008 and the NMC, *The Code, pp, 2-7,* 2008).

(vi) A doctor or nurse must respect a patient's right to confidentiality and breach confidentiality only if it is the public interest to do so (GMC, *Confidentiality, 2009, pp-36-56;* NMC, *Advice sheet: Confidentiality,* 2008 and the NMC, *The Code, p. 2* 2008).

To enhance critical analysis, problem-solving questions have been constructed at the end of each vignette. This is an acceptable approach used in law to examine case law and is now commonly used in healthcare (Parahoo, 2006). Problem-solving questions can generate analysis of pertinent issues relevant to a topic that ultimately enhance the acquisition of knowledge (Franklin et al, 2005). Furthermore, problem-solving questions, increase knowledge through enquiry by participants responding to given problems (Weigel, 2002). Therefore, they are seen as an acceptable method to solving legal problems and dilemmas (Walsh, 2010).

Concerning the context of the vignettes as explained in chapter 2, the Armed Forces operate in three distinct environments: the battlefield, operational environment and non-operational environment (Soldier Management, 2004). In addition, as the purpose of this book is to challenge if *'medical ethics in armed conflict is identical to medical ethics in times of peace'* (World Medical Association's International Code of Ethics, 2004; Hallgarth, 2007), the vignettes have been divided into those three environments which accurately reflect where army personnel work.

Accordingly, the vignettes in chapters 7, 9 and 10 refer to the **battlefield environment** and explore the ethical and professional dilemmas when a MHCP has a dual loyalty conflict in following both military orders and professional codes of practice. The vignette in chapter

11 refers to an **operational environment** and considers the ethical and professional challenges that a MHCP encounters when he/she is given a military order by a wounded senior officer not to give him treatment. The vignette in chapter 12 refers to a **non-operational environment**, when a MHCP has an ethical and professional dilemma whether to disclose patient confidentiality to the soldier's Commanding Officer. Accordingly, each chapter considers the unique ethical challenges that MHCPs face when giving care and treatment in these hostile and violent environments, compared with civilian healthcare professionals, who are often perceived to give care in a safer working environment

To enhance reality of the vignettes and explore how different soldiers from different branches or categories, known as 'Arms', are expected to react to conflict situations, the vignettes also reflect a distinct 'Arm' of the Armed Forces. As remarked by Soloman et al (2004), this method of dividing the appropriate character to each vignette makes them more realistic. Categorising in this way accurately reflects the military personnel who would actually be present in such situations that each vignette highlights. For instance, in the battlefield vignettes of chapters 7, 9 and 10 the fighting troops are part of the *Combat Arms* and are the fighting force or 'teeth' of the British Army. They consist of the infantry and the armoured units and are engaged in close action with the enemy.

Chapter 11, and the operational environment involves *Combat Support Arms,* which provide direct support to the *Combat Arms* and include the Royal Army Air Corps that pilot transport helicopters. The *Combat Service Support Arms* support and sustain the *Combat Arms* and *Combat Support Arms*. *Combat Service Support Arms* are not intended to have close engagement with the enemy, but the fluidity of the modern battlefield means that these personnel are likely to be engaged in close combat at times (Heyman, 2009). They include the Royal Army Medical Corps and the Queen Alexandra's Royal Army Nursing Corps (Queens Regulations, 1975) and as explained in chapters 1 and 2, are collectively known as *Military Healthcare Professionals* who are involved in every vignette and interaction with the other Arms.

Military Ethical Model

Although explained and analysed in context and in detail in chapters 10 to 14, Edmund Howe's (2003) model enables a logical discussion and subsequent analysis of military medical dilemmas in diverse military environments. This model allows a more precise concept of professional-military conflicts by arguing that MHCPs are governed by three role-specific ethics, which involves the person following each role strictly. These consist of **(i) a military role-specific ethic, (ii) a medical role-specific ethic and (iii) a discretionary role-specific ethic**. Howe (2003) suggests that with a military role-specific ethic, MHCPs would follow military orders above everything else. With a medical role-specific ethic, they would follow professional codes of practice and put their patients first (Howe, 2003 at pp. 333-334). Finally, the third role is where the MHCP uses some discretion in deciding when and whether the needs of the military are absolute (Howe, 2003 at p.335).

Legal Methodology

As mentioned earlier in this chapter, vignettes with problem solving questions are commonly used in law to analyse theoretical legal arguments. However, for legal problem-solving questions to be effective, it is necessary to be able to identify the relevant area of law that needs examining, use the correct legal authority and then give the legal advice (Foster, 2009). To enhance reality and reliability, each vignette is therefore analysed via a legal approach that ensures statutes and secondary legislation such as statutory instruments and subsequent regulations from a professional body i.e. the GMC and the NMC are interpreted correctly and consideration is given to judicial precedent, which is the manner in which a decision is re-enacted or applied in preceding relevant cases, according to the authority of where the original case was heard (Manchester and Salter, 2006).

Concluding Comments

In conclusion, using an ethical model and a legal methodological analysis with realistic problem solving vignettes, is the best and most appropriate method of challenging the WMAs statement is because, as suggested by Cirgin-Elleet and Beausang (2002), this type of approach has the 'ability to describe the human experience as it is lived'. Moreover, this approach illuminates the various ranges of human experience in context (Van der Zalm and Bergum 2000). It is also a beneficial way of exploring and interpreting lived experiences, as any understanding that is gained is founded on experience (Finlay, 2009). By using problem-solving questions via vignettes, it can also yield findings that are far more valuable to future practice development (Richman and Mercer, 2002). Further, since problem-solving questions are commonly used to solve and analyse legal problems, this approach appears to be the *best* and *most suitable* method of challenging the WMAs statement (Walsh, 2010).

CHAPTER SEVEN

BATTLEFIELD CONDITIONS:
DIFFERENT ENVIRONMENT
BUT THE SAME DUTY OF CARE

Introduction

This chapter offers a critique of the concept of Military Healthcare Professionals (MHCPs) owing a duty of care to wounded soldiers on the battlefield. It suggests that **(i)** medical care in the battlefield is distinctly different to civilian medical care, even in an emergency; **(ii)** such distinct differences in wartime can override normal peacetime professional ethics and **(iii)** the environment is so different that the duty of care owed by MHCPs to their patients on the battlefield should not exist or apply. This chapter also suggests that, as MHCPs have legal and professional obligations to care for the wounded on the battlefield, this obligation may conflict with following military orders, causing a dual loyalty conflict. This is because soldiers are part of the 'fighting force' and must, therefore, be fit to fight and win the battle. This makes them more of a commodity, rather than an individual with distinct healthcare needs. Drawing on analogies between battlefield and emergency civilian healthcare treatment, this chapter examines significant differences between military and civilian healthcare practice.

This chapter acknowledges that there are professional similarities between military and civilian medical practice in general. However, it is asserted that the battlefield healthcare environment is significantly different from the civilian healthcare environment, since caring for the wounded on the battlefield is detached from traditional support mechanisms (Southby, 2003).[2] This holds even when compared with administering emergency care or treatment to a casualty in a busy civilian Accident and Emergency (A&E) department in an inner city on a Friday or Saturday night, or even a localised major incident, such as a terrorist attack similar to that of the London bombings in July 2005. In such situations, the civilian healthcare professional, if they are a nurse or doctor, may be able to call on wider resources and expect, for example, the assistance of a Specialist Nurse, Modern Matron, or Senior Doctor, such as a Registrar or Consultant; although it is acknowledged that this assistance may not always be immediate. The MHCP, however, could be alone and isolated working in extreme high or low temperatures (Fry et al, 2002) and possibly could be under enemy fire, all of which make the environment extremely uncertain and dangerous (Kligman and Kupermintz, 1994). Moreover, the civilian nurse would, perhaps, be more certain of his/her medical supplies being replenished, unlike the MHCP (US Department of the Army, 1997). Accordingly, even though it is acknowledged that giving care and treatment in emergency civilian circumstances is difficult and challenging for civilian healthcare professionals (Fry et al, 2002), this chapter explores the evidence that it is unreasonable for MHCPs to owe their patients the same duty of care in the battlefield.

For clarity, this chapter starts by briefly explaining the current legal position of any civilian healthcare professional owing their patient a duty of care. Throughout the chapter, by the use of a vignette integrated within the text, legal and ethical conflicts will be highlighted, also constraints between professional regulations, military orders, ethos and command. It also explains the differences between military and civilian healthcare practice. It does this by positing that these differences are due to **(i) strategic, (ii) clinical** and **(iii) environmental criteria.** In doing so, it explains that, despite these differences, MHCPs seemingly continue to owe all their patients a duty of care. This chapter compares and contrasts this duty with a civilian nurse's duty of care and, throughout, comments upon some ethical difficulties that a MHCP can encounter on the battlefield.

The legal position

General Duty of Care

Military Healthcare Professionals are subjected to military and civilian law (Soldier Management, 2004). Concerning healthcare, the law is equally clear in explaining what the patient-healthcare professional relationship means and involves. In English law, all healthcare professionals, irrespective of whether they are military or civilian, owe their patients a duty of care, regardless of the location or the circumstances in which they give this care (General Medical Council (GMC), 2006 and the Nursing Midwifery Council (NMC) *Advice sheet: Duty of Care, 2008).* As all military personnel are governed by military law, which is embraced within

British civil law and the domestic law of whichever country they are serving in, MHCPs owe their patients a duty of care in the battlefield. Hewart, C.J. affirmed the duty of care relationship between healthcare practitioner and patient in *R v Bateman (1925 at paragraph 49)* where he stated '... If he [the doctor] accepts the responsibility and undertakes the treatment and the patient submits to his direction and treatment accordingly, he owes a duty to the patient...' The concept of owing a duty of care to a patient, therefore, provides a framework that ensures that all healthcare professionals are accountable to their patients (Witting, 2005).

The general duty of care relationship was raised further in the House of Lords in the case of *Donoghue v Stevenson (1932)*. This landmark case was the modern starting point in which Lord Atkin attempted to establish a general principle that would cover all issues of liability under negligence. In this case, which clearly focuses upon the foresight of harm, it was established that a duty of care arises between two people when one person is directly affected by the other person's *acts* or *omissions*. This is known as the *neighbour principle*, where duty is imposed if it is reasonably foreseeable that the claimant may be injured as a result of the defendant's negligence. As indicated by Allen (2009), at common law, an omission to perform an act is not unlawful in itself, as a person is not obliged to act as the Good Samaritan in the absence of a duty of care (see also *Dorset Yacht Co Ltd v Home Office, 1970 and Hill v Chief Constable of West Yorkshire, 1989)*. However, where a healthcare professional is acting in the course of their employment, they may face professional disciplinary proceedings if they fail to act accordingly (NMC, 2008, p.1). The same can be said of a doctor, as they would breach paragraph 11 of the GMCs, *Good Medical Practice Code of* Conduct (Brazier and Cave, 2007).

Although there is no legal or professional distinction between civilian and military healthcare, the law and professional guidelines are clear. This is, that if a healthcare professional gives care, treatment, or advice to a patient, they then owe that patient a duty of care (GMC 2006, and NMC Advice Sheet: Duty of Care, 2008). The duty of care and the legal responsibility begins, as earlier emphasised by Denning, L.J. in *Cassidy v Ministry of Health (1951),* '...whenever they accept a patient for treatment...' Thus, it can be argued that the duty of care concept is comprehensive and goes to the very essence of ensuring that it sets clinical boundaries for all healthcare professionals, irrespective of their being either civilian or military. This is so that they remain accountable for their acts or omissions and are liable for the consequences of careless behaviour (NMC, 2008). The duty of care concept is not as articulated by Lord Diplock in *Sidaway v Board of Governors of the Bethlem Royal Hospital and the Maudsley (1985 at paragraph 658)* to be dissected 'into a number of component parts to which different criteria of what satisfy the duty of care apply, such as diagnosis, treatment and advice'. This means that the duty of care is comprehensive, embracing and wide-ranging and cannot be separated into different compartments (Green, 2006).

As a result of the above case law, it is reasonable to suggest that for the MHCP, they owe a duty of care to a patient, irrespective of whether they give treatment in a battlefield, an operational or a non-operational environment. However, as remarked by Witting (2005) in determining if one party owed a duty of care to another, the courts need to determine if a legal relationship exists between the healthcare professional and their patient. The incremental approach to determine this arose from the House of Lords case, *Caparo Industries v Dickman (1990)*. This conceptual framework established **three factors** that need to be taken into consideration (Witting, 2005).

Firstly, the harm must be reasonably foreseeable. The test of foreseeability is that of the 'reasonable man'. Accordingly, in relation to military healthcare, the MHCP must act as the reasonable MHCP on the battlefield, operational or non-operational environment. In addition, the reasonable MHCP must realise that if they fail to give immediate medical attention to a wounded soldier on a battlefield, or the appropriate care in an operational or non-operational environment, the soldier's medical condition may deteriorate.

Secondly, there must be a relationship of sufficient 'proximity'. In a military healthcare context, this is proximity between the wounded soldier and the MHCP. Although this test can appear to be ambiguous, 'proximity' refers to legal as opposed to geographical proximity (*Muirhead v Industries Tank Specialities, 1985*). In *Donoghue v Stevenson (1932 at paragraph 580),* Lord Atkin also stated that proximity means 'close and direct relations that the act complained of directly affects a person whom the person alleged to be bound to take care would know would be directly affected by his careless act.' Thus, in a military healthcare context, if there is proximity between the MHCP and the wounded soldier, a duty of care may be assumed.

Thirdly, even when the first two factors are satisfied, it must be fair, just, and reasonable to impose a duty of care on the healthcare professional. This part is directed to public policy considerations relevant to whether there should be liability in a given situation. As remarked by Lord Pearce in *Hedley Byrne & Co Ltd v Heller & Partners Ltd (1963 at paragraph 615),* 'How wide the sphere of the duty of care in negligence is to be laid depends ultimately upon the court's assessment of the demands of society for protection from the carelessness of others'. This suggests that this third part, which is based upon policy, is flexible. Thus, as examined in chapters 8 and 9, the outcome of this case may advocate that there is some scope for a MHCP *not* to owe their patients a duty of care on the battlefield, since the demands on the MHCP owing a duty of care to a casualty in this hostile environment may be too demanding. As mentioned by Beam (2003), the battlefield is 'the antithesis of the ideal medical setting'. It is more violent than a civilian Accident and Emergency department. It is noisy, chaotic, in constant flux and unpredictable.

Professional Accountability

For MHCPs, by the very fact they are deployed on the battlefield giving medical support to soldiers, it is clear that if they come across a wounded soldier who requires treatment they have a legal and professional accountability to that patient (Tschudin and Schmitz, 2003). In such an environment, they are duty-bound to assist casualties and potential casualties (Williams, 1996). However, the difficulty posed by legal and professional accountability is, if it conflicts with military orders on the battlefield, it places the MHCP in an ethical dilemma as to what course of action to take. Thus, military orders and discipline can appear to be almost a psychological impediment for a MHCP in deciding what course of action to take.

According to Tschudin, one person can seldom solve an ethical dilemma (Tschudin, 1992). Tschudin (1992) goes further by saying that problems can be solved whereas dilemmas cannot. This scenario arises when faced with an agonising choice. For example, in consideration of the following vignette, such a conflict could occur if a MHCP driving in a light armoured tactical vehicle within a battlefield area has been given prior orders not to leave hard-packed roads due to landmines. However, they then come across a soldier lying in a dirt track five metres away who has just had a traumatic amputation of his right leg and arm caused by a landmine. Unexploded mines surround him; he is screaming out in pain and bleeding profusely. Despite the other troops in the light armoured tactical vehicle radioing for medical assistance, the MHCP, as per their training, can see the urgent need to initiate treatment by placing tourniquets around the soldier's severed limbs. The MHCP wants to start de-mining a path to reach the injured soldier by lying on their front and feeling for mines with their bare hands and gently crawling towards the soldier to treat him. (This manoeuvre would take approximately five minutes: one metre per minute). However, military orders on operations

(Armed Forces Act 2006, section 2 (3)) prevent them from doing so and state that personnel should wait until personnel with appropriate technical equipment arrive to make a safe passageway. Statistics state that there are 700,000 unexploded mines in Kuwait from the First Gulf War, so highlighting the likelihood of this threat (Bajec, 1993). The MHCPs duty to care on the battlefield, therefore, appears to be constrained by the power of military orders. However, by following military orders (because healthcare professionals must adhere to the law), MHCPs would breach the GMC, *Good Medical Practice* (2006) or the NMCs, *The Code* (2008), which gives guidance on how doctors and nurses respectively must make the patient their first concern. In addition, nurses, would not be following the guidance of the International Council of Nurses (ICN) *Code of ethics for nurses* (2000), where it advises that a nurse's fundamental responsibilities are to alleviate suffering.

Whilst a similar analogy, for example, could be drawn if a civilian healthcare professional, driving on duty in the community, witnesses a child struggling in a deep lake but is unable to help, as it is too dangerous to do so, the vignette environments are significantly different. This is because, whereas the civilian healthcare professional cannot help because they are not able to (for example, they may not be able to swim), the MHCP can help, but is ordered from a higher command not to do so. As remarked by Altun (2008), MHCPs must be unquestionably obedient to military orders, which they must follow and accept with the utmost seriousness. However, if on the other hand the MHCP disobeyed military orders and immediately de-mined a safe passage to the soldier, although there would be no conflict with professional accountability, they would have disobeyed a lawful military command and would perhaps have committed an assumed reckless act under military law that could lead to disciplinary action (Armed Forces Act 2006, section 12 (1) (a) and (b)).

Consequently, in relation to the military vignette, if the MHCP failed to act by not putting tourniquets around the soldier's severed limbs, it is likely that the soldier would exsanguinate. If the MHCP, however, disobeyed military orders and acted by de-mining a safe passageway with the intent of giving treatment to the wounded soldier, by this act they would also assume a duty of care (*Cassidy v Ministry of Health, 1951 at paragraph 586*). Thus, it appears that the law and the GMCs (*Good Medical Practice,* 2006) and the NMCs professional code (NMC, *The Code,* 2008) leave little scope for any dispute, as it is clear that the MHCP would owe a duty of care to the wounded soldier in both situations in the context of the vignette.

However, this chapter suggests that, in spite of the law and the regulations from the GMC and the NMC, MHCPs should not owe a duty of care that is subject to legal negligence when in a battlefield environment. The underpinning premise of this argument is the nature of the battlefield as a distinct hostile environment. Beam (2003) further remarks that the battlefield is the direct opposite of the model medical environment and that it is more violent than a civilian A&E department. It is noisy, chaotic, in constant flux, and unpredictable. He further remarks that, 'there are simply no comparable situations in the civilian sector, despite frequent comparisons to inner-city emergency rooms on "any Saturday night"' (Beam, 2003 at p. 371).

Military Healthcare Practice: its distinctness

Strategic differences

Gross (2006) explains that during war and on the battlefield, MHCPs treat individual soldiers as an essential part of the 'fighting force', so that they are fit to fight. Soldiers are, therefore, seen more as a commodity to win battles and wars, rather than individuals with distinct healthcare needs. As such, according to Kowtow (2006), the battlefield can force MHCPs to perform duties that are clearly not always in the patient's best interests if they have to first follow military orders. This is supported in a different article by Gross (2008) who states that 'on the battlefield, military healthcare is an adjunct of war, it does not speak of saving the lives of soldiers as an end in itself, but of salvaging their lives so they can fight'. This emphasises a clear difference between an emergency civilian situation, either within or outside a hospital, and the battlefield. This is because, unlike the MHCP, in accordance with their professional code, the civilian MHCP would need to 'make the care of people' their 'first concern' even in an emergency (GMC, *Good Medical Practice,* 2006 and the NMC, *The Code*, 2008 at p. 1). Thus, military healthcare in an organisation that is involved in fighting can seem contradictory to the values and beliefs of civilian healthcare professionals (Griffiths and Jasper, 2007).

Gross (2008) goes on to explain that in the battlefield, salvaging lives in order to maintain manpower and military capability is of paramount importance. For civilian healthcare professionals, salvaging lives is equally their goal, but for different reasons, in order to 'promote the health and wellbeing of those in their care' (GMC, *Good Medical Practice,* 2006 and the NMC, *The Code*, 2008 at p. 1). Moreover, on a wider scale, whereas civilian healthcare is directed towards saving life, military healthcare offers a legitimate framework for taking it in war (Enemark, 2008). Gross (2006) also states, 'During war, healthcare personnel do not treat individual soldiers 'qua discrete' patients but as components of a *fighting force*: a living, collective entity'. This is because in choosing a particular course of action, military personnel are governed by an enforced 'command structure', which expects its soldiers to carry out tasks that are more demanding in comparison to civilians (Sandin, 2007).

Both Gross (2008) and Kottow (2006) highlight the different ethical and moral concept that MHCPs have towards patient care when compared with civilian practice. Furthermore, they illustrate how MHCPs act differently in war when they are compared with civilian healthcare professionals. Civilian healthcare professionals caring for wounded soldiers would not consider their patients (i.e. the soldiers) as a 'fighting force'. They would 'treat people as individuals and respect their dignity' (GMC, *Good Medical Practice,* 2006 and the NMC, *The Code*, 2008 at p. 2). They would care for patients according to the severity of their wound or illness and not based on whether that individual was required to fight a decisive battle. Moreover, they would give medical and nursing care in an atmosphere that allows individualised patient care for the attainment of patient autonomy and fulfilment of self-determination (Rossow-Kimball and Goodwin, 2009).

However, the courts are keen to allow the military to remain autonomous and detached from civilian norms (Rubin, 2002). Gross's (2008) article, therefore, highlights that, for the MHCP, owing a duty of care to a patient on the battlefield may be seen as an unnecessary constraint because it is secondary to winning the battle and the war. As Tripod (2006) highlights, soldiers (this includes MHCPs) are equipped through basic training to act without later thinking of the moral or legal repercussions of their decisions. In other words, an army's existence and presence is not to adhere to normal peacetime social expectations, such as an MHCP automatically acquiring a duty of care when giving treatment to a patient on the battlefield. 'The military objective must override the interests of the individual' (*Re Post Traumatic Stress Disorder Group Litigation Multiple Claimants v Ministry of Defence, 2003 at paragraph 2. C.12)* so that they are 'fit to fight' before being accorded personal needs and individualised health care (Gross, 2006). Thus, the critical ethical difference between civilian and military healthcare practice in the battlefield is that the military need is primarily to provide care to achieve and maintain battle readiness.

Fit to fight

There are two reasons why MHCPs consider soldiers to be part of the 'fighting force', so that they are first fit to fight before being viewed as patients with individual health needs.

First, the existence of an army and its aim in a conflict is to 'fight and decisively win its nation's wars' (Westhusing, 2006). Thus, it is crucial that MHCPs ensure their soldiers are fit to fight and decisively win the battle before acknowledging any individual needs of their patients. This chapter accepts that this notion may be morally repugnant to civilian healthcare professionals and contradict the entire principles of health care (Crowe and Hardil, 1991). However, if winning the battle was not important, it can be questioned, why should an army with MHCPs exist in the first place? A state or country should not lose sight of this 'fit to fight' concept by placing constraints on those military personnel who fight and aspire to achieve this aim and those who give military medical and nursing care.

Second, as explained in chapter 4, for the British Army, wherever a service person is serving, military law and discipline must underpin Operational Effectiveness (Soldier Management, 2004), which, at its highest level, achieves the military intent of the government of the day. This could be to win the war or to maintain peace. The military Commander's intent is then mirrored in this concept. Thus, Operational Effectiveness takes precedence and is the British Army's ultimate objective before everything else. On the contrary, however, this chapter acknowledges that Operational Effectiveness is, perhaps, not a consideration or issue that frontline civilian healthcare professionals in the NHS are preoccupied with, to the extent that owing a duty of care to their patient becomes secondary. As further explained in chapter 2, Operational Effectiveness has a rather different interpretation in the NHS context: it is to ensure that civilian healthcare professionals provide equally high quality patient care while, alternatively, MHCPs high quality patient care must ensure that soldiers are 'fit to fight'. The legal mandate for providing high quality care is found in the National Health Service Act 2006.

Military Discipline

Although MHCPs owe their patients the same duty of care as civilian healthcare professionals, these healthcare professionals are different. This is because they more readily adapt their clinical skills to any situation and have a different disciplinary code (Harper, 2006), even though these differences are due to what Beam (2003) claims is a predisposition of military medical personnel to obey military orders and a closed hierarchical military rank structure that does not allow orders to be questioned by subordinates. MHCPs, by the adoption of military rank and following military orders, the wearing of combat uniform, the carrying of arms and the undertaking of general military training are 'of the military' (Bassett, 1997). This makes MHCPs soldiers first, subject to military discipline, and healthcare professionals second. Thus, discipline is the 'backbone' that promotes efficiency in the armed forces and involves MHCPs following military orders (Soldier Management, 2004 at pp. 47-50). Although it may be argued that civilian healthcare professionals have the same distinctness in terms of civilian uniform, a hierarchical structure (albeit less authoritarian than the armed forces), and an internal training structure, MHCPs nonetheless remain different as they also have diverse expectations placed upon them and more demands. (Moore and Reger, 2006). For example, MHCPs are on duty twenty-fours a day and they are sometimes ordered to attend military duties outside their normal clinical duty working hours, wearing military uniform (Queen's Regulations for the Army 1975, parts 8 and 9). For instance, a MHCP could be caring for a patient on the battlefield and then be on guard duty at a medical establishment, carrying a loaded weapon, during the night.

Furthermore, although the civilian healthcare professional must equally follow civilian orders, a civilian order is more patient-focused than a military one. Harper (2006) argues that this is one of the main differences between military and civilian medical services, as it demonstrates a significant distinction between which duty should take precedence over the other. For civilian healthcare professionals, there is no doubt that the patient's health care needs are paramount and come first (GMC, *Good Medical Practice,* 2006 and the NMC, *The Code*, 2008). However, for the MHCP, the situation is less straightforward because Operational Effectiveness takes precedence. This raises the question of the legal and ethical conflict of interest arising when MHCPs, who are soldiers first, can be acting legally and ethically in one sense only, by compromising legality and acting unethically in the other (Yeo, 1989). This is because it is legally right to follow a military order and legally wrong not to do so (Armed Forces Act 2006, parts 11-13), a dilemma, which civilian doctors and nurses do not experience because they are only accountable to the GMC and NMC respectively.

It is evident that a sword dominates military ethics, with the importance of following military orders being a priority (Toner, 2006). This means that achieving Operational Effectiveness is a feature that every

MHCP must accept and anything after that, such as an individual doctor's or nurse's autonomy or a patient's self-determination, is secondary, a concept that would be clearly unacceptable for civilian healthcare professionals. For example, one could not imagine a civilian administrator in an A&E department during an emergency ordering where and when civilian doctors or nurses must treat patients. However, in striving to achieve operational effectiveness in the battlefield, a medical obligation to treat casualties must be weighed against the military obligation to win the battle, a notion that civilian healthcare professionals would not even have to contemplate. Furthermore, in the battlefield, military orders become a 'third party', in that they can sometimes interfere with what Enemark (2008) comments on as the 'dyadic doctor–patient relationship' or nurse–patient relationship. A fundamental difference is that third-party intervention would not normally occur or affect the civilian relationship between healthcare professionals and patients, especially in an emergency environment.

Clinical differences

Gross (2008) also comments about a patient having limited rights on the battlefield. Here, he emphasises that in the American armed forces it is an offence for a soldier to refuse medical treatment, which would subsequently render him/her unfit for duty (Secretary of the Navy, 2002). In English law, '…even when his or her own life depends on receiving medical treatment, an adult of sound mind is entitled to refuse it…' (*St Georges's Healthcare NHS Trust v S, R v Collins and others, ex parte S, (1998).* Nevertheless, whilst in English law every competent adult is entitled to refuse medical treatment, even if they could die, in the British Armed Forces refusing medical treatment could equally be seen as wilful neglect of their military duty, even on the battlefield. According to the Armed Forces 2006 (Part 1 (Offences), section 16 - Malingering (1) c)), an act or omission to aggravate or prolong any injury is considered an offence. Clearly, refusing medical treatment on the battlefield would delay the soldier's return to fighting.

Other clinical differences arise from the evacuation chain of casualties. Due to the unpredictability of warfare, this chain can never be guaranteed to work. Moreover, on operations, large numbers of clinical personnel may attend the same casualty at different points in the treatment chain (Joint Medical Doctrine, 2007, paras. 120 and 122). This can make the evacuation chain longer than it would be in a civilian hospital and delay treatment (MacFarlane, 2004). In particular, this can delay critical treatment in the Golden Hour and the Platinum ten minutes (Bukowski, 2006). Although delay in emergency treatment can be equally problematic, for example when rescuing a drowning child, nonetheless, providing essential care on the battlefield is clearly deemed more dangerous. As mentioned by Callan (2005) and Murdock (2008), to prevent death, trauma patients must receive definitive care within these two crucial timescales. Moreover, as stated by Hess and Holcomb (2008), when military physicians treat patients from the battlefield 'who require massive transfusion [blood] four to five times the frequency seen in civilian practice', the situation can become more problematic. Hodgetts et al (2006) highlight this difference further when they explain that injury caused by ballistic weapons causes significantly more damage than the blunt trauma commonly seen in a civilian A&E department, and that profuse bleeding is the main cause of death on the battlefield. Consequently, the traditional ABC (airway, breathing and circulation) management is now replaced by training MHCPs to adapt to '<C>ABC management, where C stands for dealing with catastrophic haemorrhage'.

Environment differences

Localised environment differences are also significant. Unlike civilian healthcare professionals working in a stable and often relatively safe environment, MHCPs work in the battlefield, in total isolation from medical assistance. They do not have access to the same emergency facilities to summon assistance. They can be fatally injured at any time when giving treatment to their patient. They also work in extreme hot and cold conditions, without heating or air conditioning, and in harsh temporary and mobile facilities, without any reinforcements to assist or relieve them (Kraemer, 2008). Even civilian healthcare professionals and others attending major incidents outside the safety of their hospitals do not experience such conditions. If they are outside the hospital, the environment does not impede them to this extent. Although many civilian doctors and nurses work alone in the community and in isolated rural areas where mobile phone reception can be extremely poor, they are still never totally isolated in terms of communication and dangerous terrain to the same degree as MHCPs can be isolated in the battlefield. They do not, for example, ever have a minefield to circumvent before reaching a casualty. Thus, caring for the wounded on the battlefield carries 'awesome responsibility and courage' (Rajecki, 2009).

These harsh environments are not, according to Griffiths and Jasper (2009), 'ring fenced', meaning that the battlefield is no longer static;

instead, it is fluid and movable, given the use of modern weapons. For example, in the deserts of Iraq and Afghanistan, Colonel Tim Hodgetts, a military A&E consultant at the local Field Hospital, commented that 'the clinical routine was regularly interrupted by ballistic missile warnings for incoming SCUDs, or chemical attack alarms' (Hodgetts, 2004). The threat of chemical attack would have entailed all personnel wearing their nuclear, biological and chemical warfare charcoal suit and putting on their respirator within nine seconds. This makes treating casualties almost impossible, owing to the degradation (i.e. physical exhaustion) of the human body caused by the charcoal clothing.

Concluding Comments

This chapter has discussed and exposed legal and ethical dilemmas, which can create dual loyalty conflict (Coleman, 2009). It has also highlighted the difficulties for MHCPs facing this dual role conflict; that is, that of soldiers/healthcare professionals having to obey military orders while also having to follow professional codes of practice (Joint Doctrine Publication, Medical Support Joint Operations, 2007, para 112).

Military healthcare is significantly different from civilian healthcare, even more so on the battlefield (Kennedy et al 1996) because caring for the wounded in this environment is detached from traditional support mechanisms (Southby 2003). However, in spite of this distinctiveness, legally, MHCPs continue to owe a duty of care to their patients. This chapter has also highlighted that military healthcare is deemed secondary to achieving Operational Effectiveness, which is to achieve whatever military objective is given by the government of the day. This could be to win a decisive battle, the war, or to achieve peace, if deployed on a peace-keeping mission.

Best (2007) remarks that a 'medical readiness mission' supports military necessity, which is to ensure that soldiers are fit to fight. It is, therefore, clear that the primary role of MHCPs is to maintain the readiness of combat soldiers to ensure that they are fit to fight and, if necessary, to kill the enemy during war (Tricarico, 1998). As discussed, this can cause a distinct ethical dilemma for the MHCP. In one sense, they are as described by Matthews (2006), as having two roles: that of healer and that of a 'security agent' in preparing a soldier to inflict harm on another person. This dual role can be problematic. For professional bodies, such as the GMC and NMC, to have an effective code of ethics determining acceptable behaviour, it must have sole responsibility for its members (Hedahl, 2009). This, perhaps, is not possible for military doctors and nurses, because even though they are responsible and accountable to the GMC and NMC respectively and owe all their patients a duty of care (GMC, *Good Medical Practice,* 2006 and the NMC, *Advice sheet: Duty of Care,* 2008), military orders and law primarily govern their actions. However, as Witting (2005) points out in his analysis of the concept of a duty of care, the courts would be willing to examine the impact that a duty of care could have on a party as long as the argument was sufficiently robust and was in the administration of justice.

To draw a clear distinction between civilian and military healthcare it must be seen that such distinct differences in wartime can override normal peacetime professional ethics. This, however, creates ethical dilemmas for MHCPs on the battlefield. 'An action may be legal but unprofessional, exposing a healthcare professional to action by his/her Statutory Regulatory Body' (Joint Medical Doctrine, 2007, para 112) Thus, following military orders and maintaining Operational Effectiveness can make following professional codes of practice and owing a duty of care to the patient in the battlefield more difficult. This is a view shared by London (2003) who stresses that healthcare ethics very often yields to the 'acquiescence to military demands,' so acknowledging friction between achieving the military mission and adequately caring for casualties on the battlefield.

This chapter has also concluded that the limited colonisation of military law by civilian norms should remain distant (Rubin, 2992). In other words, the duty of care owed by an MHCP to his/her patient who has been injured in the battlefield is constrained and thus questionable under existing ethical and legal parameters. It could be argued that civilian norms in the battlefield cannot be colonised and are thus incompatible with the reality of war, and in particular with the battlefield environment. Perhaps, as stated by Hallgarth (2007), the 'painful truth' may be that when practising healthcare in the battlefield and 'when the stakes are sufficiently high,' to allow patients the same duty of care relationship as they would have with civilian health care professionals is not practicable or reasonable in such hostile conditions, and is too onerous a legal task and obligation for MHCPs.

A version of this chapter appeared in the Nursing Ethics journal: Kelly, J (2010) Battlefield Conditions: different environment but the same duty of care, *Nurs Ethics,* 17(5), pp. 636-645

CHAPTER EIGHT

DOCTRINE OF COMBAT IMMUNITY

Introduction

The fighting soldier in a theatre of war remains protected from any claim in negligence by the common law doctrine of combat immunity for any negligent mistake they may make when fighting. Even if a soldier negligently fires on a colleague, injuring him by 'friendly fire', he cannot be sued. By critically analysing direct quotations of the judges' comments and views from various law cases related to Crown and combat immunity, this chapter gives a legal literature review of these aged doctrines. The succeeding chapter analyses these doctrines in context to highlight the ethical complexities in decision making in the battlefield and to challenge the WMA statement that 'medical ethics in armed conflict is identical to medical ethics in times of peace'. This chapter is also a pre-requisite for the next chapter to consider whether a Military Healthcare Professional could be similarly granted combat immunity, or a modified form of it, for any negligent mistakes they make when caring for a wounded soldier on the battlefield. This chapter begins by initially exploring the historic doctrine of Crown Immunity from which combat immunity derives. It then focuses on how the courts have attempted to clarify the extent of combat immunity in modern warfare and illustrates that the courts, currently, all consider that this doctrine is a just doctrine.

Crown and Combat immunity

Historically, there is no direct English authority to confirm that a soldier in the battlefield does not owe a duty of care in tort, to another soldier. For example in *Mulcahy v Ministry of Defence (1996 at paragraph 764 (Mulcahy), Neill* L.J. stated, 'Until 1947 actions against the Crown were inhibited by two principles of ancient though doubtful origin'. These were namely:

1) To maintain the integrity of the Crown against its subjects.

2)   To allow service personnel to complete the task in hand, in
defeating the enemy in extremely dangerous and hostile environments
during war without the risk of any litigation in negligence later on.

As further stated by Windeyer J. in *Parker v The Commonwealth (1965
at paragraph 302)* [Crown] immunity was also necessary to ensure good
administration of the armed forces as '…to allow a member of the forces
to bring an action against another member for an act done in the course of
duty would be destructive to the morale, discipline and efficiency of the
service, and for that reason the common law does not give a remedy even
if the conduct complained of were malicious…' Thus, any claims against
the Crown were considered non-justiciable with the courts remaining keen
to allow the military to remain autonomous and detached from civilian
norms (Rubin, 2002).

As Hickman (2004) explains, historically Crown Immunity arose from
an inability to sue the monarch in his or her own court, since the monarch
was perceived as being a divine descendant from God and, therefore,
could do no wrong.   The Petition of Right Act 1860 allowed redress
against the Crown concerning contract, property, and probate. However,
claims in tort against the monarch were not permissible to preserve Royal
dignity.   The Crown not being subjected to scrutiny of any possible legal
wrongdoing was affirmed in the case of *Mulcahy (at paragraph 764)* when
Neill L.J. stated the 'King could not be impleaded in his own courts.'
Crown Immunity, therefore, derived from a legal doctrine where the State
or Sovereign cannot commit a legal wrong and is immune from any civil
suit or criminal prosecution. In further support of this doctrine, Lord Reid
in *Burmah Oil Company (Burma Trading) Ltd v Lord Advocate (1964 at
paragraph 354) (Burmah Oil)* stated, 'The reason for leaving the waging
of war to the King (or now the executive) is obvious.   A schoolboy's
knowledge of history is ample to disclose some of the disasters which have
been due to Parliamentary or other outside attempts at control'.   Viscount
Radcliffe in *Burmah Oil (at paragraph 364)* further added that the King
had a duty 'as the leader of the people and the chief executive instrument
for protecting the public safety'.

In England and Wales, the Crown Proceedings Act 1947 abolished
Crown Immunity. The 1947 Act made it impossible for aggrieved citizens
to sue the Crown, and in effect to sue government departments.   Prior to
this Act, there is little evidence of the rights and liabilities of servicemen
in battle. While this historic doctrine was, for most purposes, brought to
an end in the 1947 Act, section 10 of the Act provided an exception,
partially preserving Crown Immunity. From 1947 to 1987, the effect of

this section prevented any claimant from establishing a successful claim against the Ministry of Defence (MoD) in tort. For example, in *Adams v War Office (1955),* although the applicant was killed in an army exercise and the Minister of Pensions acknowledged that the death was attributable to service, the MoD successfully argued that Crown Immunity applied.

Section 10 of the Crown Proceedings (Armed Forces) Act 1947 was repealed under the Crown Proceedings Act 1987, thus removing statutory Crown Immunity for the Armed Forces. In spite of this, as was seen in *Mulcahy,* it appears that as long as military involvement can be identified, the courts will not in practice move away from the doctrine of Crown Immunity. The courts, therefore, do not see this doctrine as unjust, but instead, (1) a valuable legal instrument to protect troops when fighting the enemy and (2) also a method of retaining the dignity of the Crown from being liable for any wrongful act.

Until the decision in *Mulcahy,* 'there was no direct English authority to support the existence of combat immunity at common law' *(Re Post Traumatic Stress Disorder Group Litigation Multiple Claimants v Ministry of Defence,* 2003) *(Re PTSD).* Instead, guidance had been principally raised from the Australian case of *Shaw Savill and Albion Co Ltd v the Commonwealth of Australia, 1940) (Shaw Savill).* In this case, the notion of Crown Immunity during war was considered at great length. Starke J. fully endorsed the doctrine and strongly justified its existence. He stated that, '… the Crown has wide prerogative powers for the defence of the realm when the necessity arises…' *(Shaw Savill at paragraph 354).* Starke J. thus affirmed that Crown Immunity during war exists for the protection, safety, and security interest of the Crown during times of need. He said it is for '…the benefit of the nation as a whole…' *(Shaw Savill at paragraph 355).* He further added that in an action against the Crown the 'plea is always bad' …' *(Shaw Savill at paragraph 355)* and should be discouraged, so as not to compromise 'the safety of the realm in a national emergency' …' *(Shaw Savill at paragraph 355).* Starke J. further approved of immunity during war by adding that '…there is no doubt that the Executive Government and its officers must conduct operations of war…without the control or interference of the courts of law…' *(Shaw Savill at paragraphs 355-356)* In addition, Starke J. further stated that 'war cannot be controlled or conducted by judicial tribunals; what is necessary or reasonable in its conduct must necessarily rest with those charged with the responsibility of the operations in whatever theatre of war' …' *(Shaw Savill at paragraph 356).* Thus, Starke J. gave a clear indication that the courts should not interfere when in war with the general running of the Armed Forces, as it should be left entirely to the military.

In *Shaw Savill (at paragraph 356)*, another judge, Dixon J. endorsed the views of Starke J. by explaining that immunity in war exists in the same way that Crown Immunity exists. This is that it allows the Armed Forces to operate effectively and efficiently but also that it is for the protection of the Crown. He stated, 'To concede that any civil liability can rest upon a member of the armed forces for supposedly negligent acts or omissions in the course of an actual engagement with the enemy is opposed alike to reason and to policy' *(Shaw Savill at paragraphs 361-362)*. He further stated that, 'There is no authority dealing with civil liability for negligence on the part of the King's forces when in action...the law has always recognized that rights of ... [the]...person must give way to the necessities of the defence of the realm' *(Shaw Savill at paragraph 362)*.

Although, Dixon J. in *Shaw Savill* clearly attempted to be more specific about the scope of Crown Immunity than Starke J. his views are confusing. For instance, Dixon J. made it clear that Crown Immunity during war should not extend 'outside a theatre of war' *(Shaw Savill at paragraphs 361-362)*. 'Outside a theatre of war' *(Shaw Savill at paragraphs. 361-362)*, it rightly exposes a military person to the 'same civilian liability' *(Shaw Savill at paragraphs 361-362)* as any other person performing their daily duty. As mentioned by Richards (1902), in times of peace any claim for immunity cannot and should not succeed. However, Dixon J. has difficulty in defining the parameters of a 'theatre of war' *(Shaw Savill at paragraphs 361-362)*. He concedes that modern warfare and the mobility of the battlefield with its sophisticated weaponry systems makes it impossible to distinguish the boundaries of war, as immunity 'cannot be limited to the presence of the enemy or to occasions when contact with the enemy has been established. Warfare perhaps never did admit such a distinction' *(Shaw Savill at paragraphs 361-362)*. Regarding warfare, he then stated that 'the development of the speed of ships and the range of guns were enough to show it to be an impracticable refinement ...it has been put out of question by the bomber, the submarine and the floating mine' *(Shaw Savill at paragraphs 361-362)*. He therefore implies that a theatre of war has no boundaries and that modern warfare *should* take into account a greater geographical scope than ever before regarding the remit of Crown Immunity during war. It no longer exists in the traditionally held view of a 'soldier on the field of battle or the sailor fighting on his ship' *(Shaw Savill at paragraphs 361-362)*.

In spite of stating that immunity should not extend 'outside a theatre of war' *(Shaw Savill at paragraphs 361-362)*, Dixon J. made a further confusing statement. In giving support to immunity, he stated '...The principle must extend to all active operations against the enemy. It must cover attack and resistance, advance and retreat, pursuit and avoidance, reconnaissance and engagement...'(*Shaw Savill at paragraphs 361-362*) Here, Dixon J. seemed to give a very broad view of when immunity can apply by extending it to others not necessarily involved directly with fighting, such as non-combatants.

However, Dixon J.'s views in defining the geographical extent of combat immunity are problematic. As mentioned by Rowley (2004) in his article on combat immunity, it may allow senior military officers, who strategically plan major operational decisions in a safe environment without being exposed to hostilities themselves from the enemy and the dangers of the battlefield, to be protected also by immunity. According, to Mr Justice Elias in *Bici and another v Ministry of Defence (2004, at paragraph 87) (Bici),* immunity in war was never intended to be this wide. Thus, whilst it can be suggested that Dixon J. opened up the criteria by which immunity could be granted, he broadened its application too much. However, he did successfully establish that the theatre of war could occur anywhere in the world where there is hostile action and engagement with the enemy. As mentioned by Raiter et al (2008), terrorist attacks have become a worldwide problem and do not occur on a traditional battlefield. Nevertheless, given the lack of succinct judicial clarity regarding the scope of a theatre of war and the battlefield, there is a danger that immunity may be extended too far. This view is shared by Meierhenrich (2006), who contends that a term such as 'war' lacks true definition and meaning in modern day warfare, unless it is supported by a mission, goal, strategy and a government response in how and where the war is going to be fought.

Williams J. a third and final judge in *Shaw Savill,* took a more pragmatic approach towards when Crown immunity during war could apply. He did not expand the discussion regarding the geographical scope of immunity. Instead, he took a very narrow and precise view as to when immunity could be appropriate, but *only* in certain circumstances. He stated that service personnel should enjoy immunity when engaged in actual hostilities, but 'emphasis must be laid on the word 'solely'' (*Shaw Savill at paragraph 366).* In addition, if hostilities were taking place at the time the act was committed, then 'the alleged cause of action would not be justiciable' (*Shaw Savill at paragraph 366).*

In the later case of *Groves v Commonwealth of Australia (1982), (Groves)* Gibbs C.J. agreed with Williams J's. straightforward view of immunity from *Shaw Savill (at paragraphs 361-362)* and was less certain of Dixon J.'s broad view. Gibbs C.J. stated that 'To hold that there is no civil liability or injury caused by the negligence of persons in the course of an actual engagement with the enemy seems to me to accord with common sense and sound policy' *(Groves at paragraph 117)* . Likewise, Gibbs C.J. did not progress the scope of this aged doctrine in relation to modern warfare. Instead, he merely indicated that an action against the Crown remains non-justiciable when in 'actual engagement' fighting the enemy *(Groves at paragraph 117)*.

In *Mulcahy,* although Neill L.J. did not extend upon the word 'solely' when engaged in hostile action, he did, nonetheless; endorse some of the pragmatic views of Williams J. in *Shaw Savill (at paragraphs 364-367).* Neill L.J. stated that he did 'not find it necessary to explore the territorial limits of this immunity' *(Mulcahy at paragraph 772).* He was, therefore, careful not to expand the geographical scope of combat immunity during war, or as he referred to it, as 'battle conditions'. Instead, he emphasised 'that no duty exists where a serviceman is engaged in actual operations against the enemy' *(Mulcahy at paragraph 769)* and that 'battle conditions' exclude a 'serviceman' from being liable for a 'negligent act towards another' *(Mulcahy at paragraph 772).*

In his dictum from *Mulcahy,* Neill L.J. also remained cautious in retaining the integrity of the court's decision towards issues of combat immunity during war. Neill L.J. stated, 'in the absence of this statutory protection, one still has to consider the position at common law' *(Mulcahy at paragraph 772).* Neill L.J. thus gave greater analysis to the non-justiciable issue than the judges had done in *Shaw Savill.* Accordingly, he considered whether it was fair, just and reasonable if a duty of care can 'be imposed in such conditions so as to make one serviceman liable for his negligent act towards another' *(Mulcahy at paragraph 772).* In using the dictum from Lord Pearce in *Hedley Byrne & Co Ltd v Heller & Partners Ltd (1963),* where Lord Pearce stated, 'How wide the sphere of the duty of care in negligence is to be laid depends ultimately upon the courts' assessment of the demands of society for protection from the carelessness of others', Neill L.J. concluded that 'there is no basis for extending the scope of the duty of care so far' *(Mulcahy at paragraph 722).*

In *Mulcahy,* a further judge hearing the case, Sir Ian Glidewell, similarly agreed with his colleague, Neill L.J., in that 'public policy' *(Mulcahy at paragraph 773)* does not require soldiers to owe a duty of care to each other when engaged in the 'course of hostilities' *(Mulcahy at paragraph 772).* In the civilian case of *Hughes v National Union of Mineworkers (1991) (Hughes),* the courts were equally keen to protect public servants performing their duty. Mr Justice May stated, 'It is not, I consider, in the public interest that those decisions should generally be the potential target of a negligence claim if rioters do injure an individual officer, since the fear of such a claim would be likely to affect the decisions to the prejudice of the very task which the decisions are intended to advance'. In *Mulcahy*, Sir Ian Glidewell further added, 'If during the course of hostilities no duty of care is owed by a member of the armed forces to civilians or their property, it must be even more apparent that no such duty is owed to another member of the armed forces' (*Mulcahy at paragraph 773*). Thus, Sir Ian Glidewell in *Mulcahy* and Mr Justice May in *Hughes (at paragraph 289)* clearly advocated the notion that immunity in war should exist for a public servant when in a hostile environment. This is to ensure that both can perform the task in hand without any later claims of negligence against the Ministry of Defence through any negligent act or omission.

Sir Ian Glidewell's comments in *Mulcahy* clearly support the views currently held by the courts in that combat immunity is a fair and just doctrine. He further stated that, 'it could be highly detrimental to the conduct of military operations if each soldier had to be conscious that, even in the heart of battle, he owed such a duty to his comrade' *(Mulcahy at paragraph 773)*. In addition, he also stated that 'one soldier does not owe to another a duty of care when engaging the enemy in the course of hostilities' *(Mulcahy at paragraph 774)*. Thus, Sir Ian Glidewell makes 'engaging the enemy' the crux of when combat immunity should apply.

Mr Justice Owen, in *Re PTSD*, attempted to expand the discussion of immunity even further. He affirmed the judgment in *Shaw Savill* that 'no duty exists where a serviceman is engaged in actual operations against the enemy' *(Re PTSD at paragraph 2.C.8.)*. He also made the scope of combat immunity more specific to personnel in the Armed Forces by stating, 'The welfare of the soldier, sailor, airman must be subordinated to their combat role. The military objective must override the interests of the individual' *(Re PTSD at paragraph 2.C.12.)*. He thus intimated that if physical and psychological harm does befall a service person, 'that is the nature of warfare' *(Re PTSD at paragraph 2.C.12.)* without that harm being attributable to another person. Mr Justice Owen also questioned whether it could apply to 'anti-terrorist, policing, and peacekeeping operations' *(Re PTSD at paragraph 2.C.17)*. He concluded 'in my judgment it will apply to operations in which service personnel come under attack or the threat of attack' *(Re PTSD at paragraph 2.C.17)* He, therefore, widened the scope of combat immunity. More precisely, however, he opened up the possibility that service personnel other than combat troops could enjoy some form of immunity.

In *Bici (at paragraph 84)*, Mr Justice Elias remarked that combat immunity was not strictly a defence but a method of removing the court's jurisdiction to hear certain claims, such as injury or death, caused by a soldier to another person against the Crown. Mr Justice Elias thus re-emphasised that the doctrine of combat immunity removes the court's ability to consider whether a duty of care exists in the battlefield between one soldier and another. In *Bici,* the court also considered the possibility of a common law immunity arising from the existence of peace-keeping duties. In this case, two British paratroopers in an operational environment, but in a peace-keeping capacity, stated that they were acting in self-defence when they shot two Kosovan Albanian civilians in the Kosovan capital Pristina. This occurred in 1999 after the cessation of hostilities, after North Atlantic Treaty Organization (NATO), troops entered the province, and the Serbs had withdrawn. The court held that combat immunity did not automatically allow or grant 'full immunity' from acts committed in hostile environments. The court held that the two soldiers did have a duty of care to the claimants, which they had subsequently breached. Thus, Mr Justice Elias appeared to curtail the doctrine of combat immunity and prevent it being widely interpreted, as Mr Justice Owen has attempted to do in *Re PTSD.* However, the key to the judgment in *Bici,* as explained by King (2004), was that at the time of the shooting, there was 'no relevant aggressive action directed against the authorities at all'. Mr Justice Elias emphasised that for the doctrine to apply, the threat must be 'imminent and serious' (*Bici at paragraph 102).* He thus echoed what Williams J. stated in *Shaw Savill (at paragraph 366),* that there must be 'actual hostilities' against the enemy before it can be enjoyed. Moreover, as mentioned by Mr Justice Owen in *Re PTSD (at paragraph 2. C.13)* immunity should '...be no wider than is necessary...'

In conclusion, this chapter has highlighted the aged doctrine of Crown and combat immunity and the complexities of interpreting these statutes within a modern military context (Sainsbury, 2011). It has illustrated that the courts all believe that combat immunity is a just doctrine and that they remain keen to retain it and to continue to allow the Armed Forces to be autonomous from civilian norms (Rubin, 2002). However, as stated by Mr Justice Elias in *Bici (at paragraph 113),* 'The Queen's uniform is not a licence to commit wrong doing' and should therefore, only be enjoyed in limited circumstances. The next chapter considers combat immunity in context. In doing so, it examines whether this doctrine will also protect the Ministry of Defence for the negligent acts or omissions by a Military Healthcare Professional whose mistakes on the battlefield may have caused harm to a wounded patient. In doing so, it highlights that current professional codes of practice appear not to be helpful in solving ethical, legal, and professional conflicts in the battlefield. It also analyses the difficulties and challenges of a Military Healthcare Professional having to follow professional codes of practice when under attack from the enemy. Further, it challenges the World Medical Association's International Code of Ethics in 2004 (WMA 2004) by indicating that ethics in war is, perhaps, not the same as in a peacetime environment, as they appear to be more constrained and questionable in this violent environment.

CHAPTER NINE

BATTLEFIELD CONDITIONS: MILITARY HEALTHCARE BATTLEFIELD IMMUNITY

Introduction

Currently, as English law stands, the combatant soldier on the battlefield remains protected from any claim in negligence by the doctrine of combat immunity for any negligent act or omission he may make when fighting. In other words, the combatant soldier does not owe a fellow soldier a duty of care on the battlefield, as the duty of care is non-justiciable. However, non-combatant Military Healthcare Professionals (MHCPs), although sometimes operating in the same hostile circumstances as the fighting soldier, are unlikely to benefit from combat immunity for any clinical negligence on the battlefield. This is because they continue to owe their patient a duty of care, although this has not been tested in the courts.

Using the legal literature from the previous chapter, the aim of this chapter is to consider whether the MHCP could ever benefit from combat immunity arising from any claim in negligence, when their mistakes on the battlefield result in harm to a wounded soldier. This chapter shows that it is unlikely a MHCP could enjoy combat immunity, due to their non-combatant status. Instead, this chapter suggests that a modified form of immunity; namely, *Military Healthcare Battlefield Immunity,* could be a new and viable doctrine. However, this could only be granted in rare circumstances and to a much lesser degree than combat immunity.

The use of the vignette in this chapter does not aim to assess whether the clinical treatment was correct, or to explain in any detail the specific requirements of the clinical treatment required. In addition, although they are important legal concepts, the chapter does not also aim to discuss the International Law of Armed Conflict, civil negligence claims for clinical negligence and health care professional regulatory issues. This is because these concepts are best dealt with separately and in a different context outside the remit of this book. Instead, the objectives of the chapter are:

1)   To highlight and contextualise the unique challenges and difficulties that MHCPs face compared with civilian healthcare professionals when caring for the sick in challenging conditions and circumstances such as the battlefield (Weld and Bibb, 2009; Kelly, 2010).

2)   To help the reader appreciate and understand more readily the reality and horror of the battlefield, rather than from a pure theoretical standpoint (Moore and Reger, 2006) since this hostile environment is often described as being 'worse than Hell' (Walzer, 1978 at p. 143).

3)   To suggest that the World Medical Association's claim that 'medical ethics in armed conflict is identical to medical ethics in times of peace' is questionable (WMA, 2004).

Vignette

Corporal White, a soldier in the infantry is being treated by Captain Brown, a military doctor (known throughout the chapter as a MHCP); in the back of a light armoured tactical vehicle after being shot in the right upper arm whilst engaged in a firefight with enemy soldiers. Captain Brown is the MHCP providing medical support to the infantry section. He is wearing an upper left armband with a red cross on it, to visualise his medical status (Geneva Conventions of 1949, Additional Protocol I of 1977 (Protocol I). Private Smith is driving the vehicle from the battlefield where Corporal White's injury was sustained, on the Main Supply Route that had recently been secured due to its strategic importance to other military establishments. They are travelling to the Field Hospital, which is fifty kilometres away, in the middle of a convoy with two other military light armoured tactical vehicles, one in front and the other behind them, each carrying four infantry soldiers.

Corporal White's right arm is bleeding profusely. Captain Brown attempts to fasten a tourniquet around Corporal White's upper right arm to prevent catastrophic bleeding that will cause death. He also inserts an intravenous cannula in his left arm to start intravenous fluids to compensate for his blood loss. At the same time, Captain Brown begins to start treatment and when they are approximately ten kilometres outside the battleground, suddenly the front vehicle explodes, due to a roadside bomb. All four soldiers inside this vehicle are killed instantly. Private Smith stops his vehicle. The other vehicle also stops.

Immediately after the explosion, Captain Brown's and the rear vehicle come under intense enemy fire from approximately six insurgents lying in a ditch nearby using Kalashnikov assault rifles. The situation is perilous. The four soldiers in the rear vehicle and Private Smith all return fire. Captain Brown quickly decides to return fire, as Corporal White's life and his own are at risk. However, before firing, Captain Brown quickly finishes fastening the tourniquet around Corporal White's upper right arm to stem the bleeding and starts the intravenous infusion. As he is acting in haste, although he initially starts to fasten the tourniquet correctly, he subsequently fails to correctly complete this procedure. This results in his failing to fasten the intravenous giving-set to the cannula in the left arm securely enough when he commences the intravenous fluid. Unknown to Captain Brown at the time, this results in Corporal White not receiving adequate fluid to replenish his blood loss, as most of the intravenous fluid and blood from the where the cannula site is situated in the vein leaks from the actual cannula site. Unfortunately, Corporal White's condition deteriorates, as he continues to lose blood from his injured right arm. He starts to exsanguinate and go into shock (Hope et al, 1993). In the confusion and mayhem and due to firing at the enemy, Captain Brown does not re-fasten the tourniquet tighter to stop the bleeding, or notice that the intravenous fluid and blood is leaking from the cannula site. In addition, in the mayhem of the fire fight Private Smith accidently shoots Sergeant Jones, who is one of the soldiers from the rear vehicle in his right leg. Captain Brown, however, is unable to attend to Sergeant Jones, due to the continuing and intense enemy fire.

The fire fight is soon over, with the insurgents retreating to the distance. The dead and wounded are safely evacuated to the local military Field Hospital. When Corporal White arrives at the hospital, the medics notice Captain Brown's mistakes; the tourniquet was not tight enough and intravenous fluid and blood had been leaking from the cannula site. Unfortunately, Corporal White has to have his right arm amputated above the elbow. However, his condition improves once the bleeding has been stemmed and he is correctly given intravenous fluids. Nevertheless, although it would be unusual for military surgeons to have situational awareness of the scope of responsibility, to come to such a potentially litigious conclusion regarding Captain Brown's clinical actions, they nevertheless contend the following:

1)   Captain Brown was too enthusiastic in firing at the enemy when he had a patient to care for.

2)   Although, this is not a matter for military surgeons to rule upon, with all of the other combatant soldiers returning fire, then realistically there should not have been any need for Captain Brown to fire at the enemy as well as the combatant soldiers.

3)   Captain Brown's priority should primarily have been to his patient.

4)   Although Captain Brown acted instinctively in a soldier like manner to fight the enemy; nevertheless, he had no ethical right to fire at the enemy before fully ensuring that he had given the correct care and treatment to Corporal White.   This is because the combatant soldiers were more experienced and better skilled at giving covering fire than Captain Brown.

5)   If Captain Brown had correctly administered intravenous fluids to Corporal White in the first instance and insured that the tourniquet was sufficiently tight to prevent bleeding, then perhaps the surgeons could have saved his right arm from being amputated.

When Captain Brown realises what he has done, he acknowledges his mistakes, but argues that (1) due to the stress of the situation, (2) being under enemy fire and (3) his life being threatened, resulted in him not being able to care safely and competently for Corporal White and observe his condition more comprehensively.

Sergeant Jones, who was shot by Private Smith, the driver of Captain Brown's vehicle, survives his injuries, but unfortunately has to have his right leg amputated.   He later makes a claim against the Ministry of Defence in relation to Private Smith's alleged negligent act.   In following the principles of *Mulcahy v Ministry of Defence (1996) (Mulcahy)* discussed in chapter 8, *however*, the Ministry successfully claims combat immunity, in that the duty of care owed by Private Smith to Sergeant Jones is non-justiciable.   Meaning, that the courts will not consider whether a duty of care was owed.   Similarly, Corporal White makes a claim against the Ministry of Defence for Captain Brown's alleged negligent acts.   As Captain Brown and Private Smith were in the same incident, the same vehicle and faced the same dangers, Captain Brown also believes that combat immunity should apply, in that his duty of care to Corporal White was equally non-justiciable.   Captain Brown contends that to save all the soldiers' lives he had no option but to help his comrades fight the insurgents.

The questions that this vignette raises and which will be examined in the following discussion are:

1)   Can Captain Brown claim combat immunity for his mistakes
because of being under enemy fire when giving care and treatment to
Corporal White?
2)   If Captain Brown cannot claim combat immunity, would *Military
Healthcare Battlefield Immunity* be a new and viable doctrine to make
Corporal White's claim non-justiciable?

Combatants and Non-Combatants

Although immunity for the fighting soldier is preserved by the courts,
due to the legal distinction between combatants and non-combatants, it is
difficult to accept that a non-combatant MHCP, such as Captain Brown,
could be granted combat immunity against a claim of negligence by the
patient, Corporal White. The Third Geneva Convention defines the legal
status of combatants as either 'members of the armed forces of a
belligerent party (except medical and religious personnel)' or 'any other
person who takes an active part in the hostilities' (Geneva Conventions of
1949, Additional Protocol I of 1977 (Protocol I). Thus, according to
Mayer (2007), combatants such as Private Smith possess a military status
that legally allows them to kill the enemy during war, whereas, under the
Geneva Convention, medical personnel such as Captain Brown are non-
combatants and must not fire at the enemy unless it is in self-defence or
for the protection of their patients. If they do fire at the enemy without a
legitimate reason, they will lose their non-combatant status (Geneva
Conventions of 1949, Additional Protocol I of 1977 (Protocol I). In
addition, medical personnel must wear distinctive emblems to protect and
identify themselves as non-combatants, which also means that the enemy
should not intentionally fire at them, as to do so would constitute a war
crime (Geneva Conventions of 1949, Additional Protocol I of 1977
(Protocol I).

However, as mentioned by Kasher (2007), and as evident in the
vignette, combatants and non-combatants can be involved in the same
hostile action, yet there are different standards to their respective roles and
different outcomes to their actions. For example, when ordered to do so,
the primary concern for a combatant soldier such as Private Smith is to
engage the enemy and either kill or capture them in an attempt to win the
battle. If Private Smith does not make this his primary concern after
having been ordered to so, then he could be guilty of misconduct on
operations via the Armed Forces Act 2006, section 2(1). Nonetheless, if
Private Smith makes a mistake that is negligent during any hostilities, he
may be protected by combat immunity *(Mulcahy)*.

In contrast, for a non-combatant, such as Captain Brown, irrespective of any hostilities on the battlefield that put his or his patient's life at risk, he must make his patient, i.e. Corporal White, his primary concern. If he fails to do this or acts negligently whilst performing his clinical tasks, then he may breach his professional codes via the General Medical Council's (GMC) (*Good Medical Practice*, 2006) or the Nursing Midwifery Council's (NMC) (*The Code*, 2008) if he were a nurse and the Ministry of Defence could be sued for negligence if his patient suffered harm. Accordingly, when involved in hostile action on the battlefield, but at the same time having to care for a wounded soldier, it may be reasonable to enquire if the courts could be sympathetic to a MHCP being afforded some form of immunity against a possible negligence claim by a patient. The difficulty with this suggestion, however, is whether they could enjoy *combat immunity,* as it may suggest that the MHCP is a combatant fighting soldier as well as a healthcare professional.

As argued by Bomann-Larsen (2004), combatants and non-combatants need to maintain their distinctiveness from each other, since the word 'combat' suggests that the soldier is a combatant and legally fights the enemy. Thus, this gives him the legal right in war to kill an enemy combatant. Rogers (2004), equally comments on the importance of distinction, as it legally separates those in the military who can fight and engage in hostile actions during war and those who cannot; as further mentioned by Walzer (1978), 'War is combat between combatants'. Therefore, it allows the fighting soldier such as Private Smith to enjoy combat immunity for any claim against him if he makes a mistake that is negligent on the battlefield. However, military medical healthcare is about caring for the wounded on the battlefield, irrespective of whether they are the enemy (Kennedy et al, 1996). This, therefore, suggests that there is a clear distinction between Captain Brown's role as a MHCP on the battlefield and Private Smith's role as a combatant soldier on the battlefield that perhaps needs to be maintained. For example, NATOs Standardization Agreement (STANAG) 2449 (STANAG, 2004), regarding the Law of Armed Conflict has as one of its essential core features a clear distinction between combatants and non-combatants so, that there is clear difference between those who can and cannot legally fight in war (Prescott, 2008).

Nevertheless, there may be an argument to suggest that the distinction between combatant and non-combatant is less certain, and that further clarification of the word 'combatant' is required. May (2005) gives a broad definition of a combatant and suggests that since military personnel wear the same uniform, apart from a small emblem that legally gives them their protective status via the Geneva Convention (1949 and 1977); there is 'no clear, morally relevant line between those who fight and those who do not'. Similarly, as previously discussed by Griffiths and Jasper (2007), they contend that the battlefield is not 'ring fenced' and is no longer static due to the use of modern weapons and tactics. These perspectives (May's, 2005; Griffiths and Jasper's, 2007) suggest an extension of the meaning of the word combatant to be almost undistinguishable from that of a non-combatant. Detter (2000) equally gives a broad definition of a combatant as 'someone who distinguishes himself from the civilian population, carries arms openly and is subject to an internal disciplinary system'. Parks (1990) gives a more extreme view of a combatant as someone, including a civilian, who is involved in the nation's war effort. In the same way, Kalshoven and Zegveld (2001) state that a combatant is *any* person who contributes to the war effort such as a civilian driver transporting military equipment used in war or food to fighting troops to and from a military establishment. Likewise, Walzer's (1978) clarification of the combatant is similarly broad. Walzer (1978) implicitly distinguishes between what can happen in a battlefield and what can occur in an operational environment. In the battlefield, he explains, and as illustrated in the vignette, fighters and non-fighters (this would include a MHCP) are 'subject to attack at anytime' by the very nature of the battlefield. Therefore, according to Walzer (1978), anyone on the battlefield is a combatant. Following Detter (2000), Parks (1990), Kalshoven and Zegveld (2001) and Walzer's (1978) meaning of the word 'combatant', the distinction between combatant and non-combatant appears very narrow. Accordingly, it could be strongly suggested that there should be combat immunity for both combatant and non-combatant in the battlefield when the environment is hostile. Both are subjected to the same risk, therefore, perhaps, both should receive the same benefit of some immunity.

However, giving a broad meaning to the word 'combatant' raise concern, as it could compromise the integrity of the medical or nursing professional on the battlefield (Hedahl, 2009). This is because the existence and the role of the military healthcare profession is to address the healthcare needs of the sick and wounded with the aim of restoring them where possible to health. Annas (2008) states that the patient must always be the healthcare practitioner's first concern before any other consideration. In contrast, the existence and role of the military fighter is to conduct warfare and win the battle. This involves combatants intentionally killing other combatants during war. As mentioned previously, combatants can legally fight on the battlefield, whereas non-combatants cannot, unless they act in self-defence to protect their patients

(Farrell, 2005). Thus, the military fighter is necessary to 'fight and decisively win its nations wars' (Westhusing, 2006).

In relation to the vignette, therefore, if MHCPs such as Captain Brown were considered as combatants, there is then the danger that it could *degrade* the military healthcare profession on the battlefield from healers to a fighting force that intentionally kills enemy combatants during war (Miles, 2007). Therefore, this distinctiveness between combatant and non-combatant should continue to exist, since it could be considered as abhorrent that MHCPs on the battlefield should be classed in the same category as someone who uses violence and kills to achieve their goal, albeit legally (Madden and Carter, 2003). Thus, this creates a further difficulty for a non-combatant such as Captain Brown, who could possibly be protected by combat immunity. A more measured understanding of MHCPs comes from the views of Huntington (2003). This author explains that, despite being in the military, wearing uniform and carrying arms, they are not warriors and combatants. Instead, they are more administrative soldiers with a clearly distinguished role towards saving lives in warfare as opposed to destroying them.

In all likelihood, it is, therefore, improbable that any MHCP would be considered as a combatant. From the above discussion, it is clear that a *degraded* military medical and nursing profession would be incompatible with the Geneva Convention's legal status of non-combatants, whose primarily aim is to care for the sick and wounded during war and not kill the enemy (Geneva Conventions of 1949, Additional Protocol I of 1977 (Protocol I). It is also doubtful that NATO would create a different STANAG that considers MHCPs as combatants. Furthermore, although not a military document; without any differentiation between combatant and non-combatant, it would contravene the Dual Loyalty and Human Rights in Health Professional Practice Report (International Dual Loyalty Working Group, 2003) recommendation, which states that the 'overruling identity and priority' of a Military Healthcare Professional should be 'that of a health professional' (London et al, 2006). For the MHCP, being classed as combatant would also be incompatible with both the GMCs and NMCs Professional Codes, as it would mean that the wounded patient on the battlefield would not be the MHCPs primary concern (*Good Medical Practice,* 2006 and *The Code*, 2008).

Military Healthcare Battlefield Immunity

Notwithstanding the authors' varied views on the remit of the combatant, it is more convincing to suggest that combatants and non-combatants should remain separate from each other. Inevitably, however, this potentially makes it more difficult for negligent acts and omissions committed by a MHCP to be protected by combat immunity. However, perhaps this obstacle may enhance the possibility for a modified form of immunity in the way of *Military Healthcare Battlefield Immunity*. This is because, despite the categorisation of MHCP as non-combatants, due to the manner of the modern enemies' indiscriminate tactics via the use of roadside bombs and suicide bombers, all medical non-combatants need to be competent and ready to defend themselves and their patients via their personal weapon (Moore and Reger, 2006). In following the comments of Dixon J. in *Shaw Savill and Albion Co Ltd v the Commonwealth of Australia, 1940 at paragraph 356) (Shaw Savill)*, such indiscriminate attacks of this kind would clearly place the non-combatant in a theatre of war *(Mulcahy at paragraph 722)*. In addition, in relation to Neill L.J. comments in *Mulcahy,* there is also a strong argument to suggest that 'battle conditions' should also exclude servicemen such as Captain Brown, from being 'liable for his negligent act[s] towards another' soldier i.e. from Corporal White whilst giving medical treatment on the battlefield during hostile action *(Mulcahy at paragraph 722)*.

In further support of *Military Healthcare Battlefield Immunity*, it could be argued since non-combatants are equipped to kill the enemy, they have unintentionally made themselves targets to be attacked by that enemy (Mayer, 2007). Thus, Moore and Reger (2006) imply that the remit of the non-combatant status has extended. In such circumstances, perhaps, *Military Healthcare Battlefield Immunity* could therefore be reasonable and viable. In addition, insurgents and enemy soldiers do not often recognise the Geneva Convention's protective emblems and, irrespective of a medical personnel's non-combatant status, these insurgents and enemy soldiers readily attack *all* military personnel (Nichol and Rennell, 2009). As a result, Nichol and Rennell (2009) further suggest that for their protection, medical personnel on occasions remove or do not wear their distinguishing protective emblems. Perhaps in these hostile and violent circumstances, when being directly fired upon, medical personnel could be afforded some form of immunity if they make a mistake when caring for a patient on the battlefield.

However, an obstacle to *Military Healthcare Battlefield Immunity* can be found in the comments of Williams J. in *Shaw Savill* that were examined in detail in chapter 8. For example in the vignette, the roadside bomb placed all of the soldiers in a 'theatre of war'. Therefore, if we follow Williams J. reasoning, this alone would not necessarily grant Captain Brown, *Military Healthcare Battlefield Immunity*. The crux for

Williams J. in determining if combat immunity and *Military Healthcare Battlefield Immunity* can be granted is, '*solely*' engaged in 'actual hostilities' against the enemy *(Shaw Savill at paragraph 366)*. Although this may only be *obiter*, apart from Captain Brown, by adding this additional requirement of '*solely*', it would still allow Private Smith and all the other fighting troops in the vignette to be protected by combat immunity. This is because these fighting troops would fit Williams J.'s criteria of their *only* role being engagement with the enemy. However, the word 'solely' *(Shaw Savill at paragraph 366)* is particularly significant for Captain Brown for the following reason:

Unlike the other troops, Captain Brown is not 'solely' engaged with fighting the enemy. He is performing another task by giving life-saving medical treatment to Corporal White. Williams J. explained that although the military 'may be engaged in dangerous operations' they are not necessarily 'released from the duty to take care in war-time' *(Shaw Savill at paragraph 366)*. The vignette demonstrates that Captain Brown has a duty to take care of Corporal White's health needs as a priority before fighting the insurgents. In such circumstances, it is clear that it would be difficult to grant Captain Brown *Military Healthcare Battlefield Immunity* in this context. This is because the courts may ask the following: 'Was there a need for Captain Brown to engage in fighting the enemy when he had more experienced soldiers around him to perform the task more competently, and whose specific role is to *exclusively* engage the enemy and fight'? Captain Brown's primary role and duty of care was to save Corporal White's life and not fight *(Shaw Savill)*. Thus, in the context of the vignette and in following Williams J.'s view, perhaps *Military Healthcare Battlefield Immunity* would not be a viable doctrine or considered reasonable in these particular circumstances. This, however, is a narrower remit than deciding when combat immunity can be granted, since combat troops are not reliant on this decisive factor '*solely*' to enjoy protection from combat immunity.

In a different context, this strict position may also be equally problematic for combatant troops. For example, it could also apply to a radio operator who is not 'solely' fighting the enemy but is signalling and receiving important messages to and from his superiors. Nevertheless, for Captain Brown in particular, this criterion appears to be particularly difficult. In spite of wearing insignia that identities him as medical personnel and, therefore, a protected person via the Geneva Convention, the enemy should not fire at him. Yet, the enemy is firing at him. As mentioned by Hedahl (2009), enemy combatants or insurgents do not distinguish between who is a combatant and non-combatant. All the same, in the vignette the doctrine is weakened if it can be concluded that Captain Brown or any MHCP in the same situation did not necessarily have to fight the enemy.

In the vignette, in spite of *Military Healthcare Battlefield Immunity's* seemingly unfeasibility, if the events were different, it could be possible that this doctrine could be applied. For example, Captain Brown would have more of a convincing argument if there were no other combat soldiers to help him and Private Smith fight.

The possibility of *Military Healthcare Battlefield Immunity* being acceptable in these circumstances is enhanced by the comments of Mr Justice Owen in *Re Post Traumatic Stress Disorder Group Litigation Multiple Claimants v Ministry of Defence (2003 at paragraph 2.C.8) (Re PTSD)*. In this case, Mr Justice Owen quoted Lord Justice Neill's comments from *Mulcahy* when he said that '...no duty exists where a serviceman is engaged in actual operations against the enemy...' and '...the welfare of the soldier, sailor, airman must be subordinated to their combat role. The military objective must override the interests of the individual...' *(Re PTSD at paragraph 2.C.12)*. Thus, when actually fighting the enemy and without any help from combatant troops, it would be easier for Captain Brown to submit that he was '*solely*' engaged with the enemy. If this was the case, then it may satisfy Williams J.'s strict position that, as there was no option other than to fight, *Military Healthcare Battlefield Immunity* could be acceptable in those circumstances.

Notwithstanding this, even if the vignette changes to Captain Brown and Private Smith being '*solely*' fighting the insurgents, there is perhaps a stronger criticism against *Military Healthcare Battlefield Immunity*. For example, from the vignette, does it fail to safeguard Corporal White's normal common law rights? That is, without a duty of care, no standard of care by Captain Brown to Corporal White is owed. Although it is not the scope of this chapter, as the standard of care is analysed in depth in chapter 10, the concern with *Military Healthcare Battlefield Immunity* being viable, is that it may eradicate the standard of care that would reasonably be expected of a MHCP in this harsh and violent environment. Such an assertion could be at odds with common law principles, as without a duty of care, no benchmark for a standard of care can be ascertained (Witting, 2005). Perhaps, as mentioned by Mr Justice Elias in *Bici v Ministry of Defence (2004) (Bici),* the standard of duty is of greater importance than denying the applicability of the duty of care. Moreover, as described by Rowley (2004), when is the duty of care 'switched off'? *Military Healthcare Battlefield Immunity* would switch off the duty altogether, as it would eradicate a duty of care (or make the duty non-justiciable) and subsequent standard of care non-existent. As explained in the next chapter, if the duty of care is allowed to be switched off, then, for all MHCPs on the battlefield, this could 'dictate a very low practical standard of care in particular circumstances at the margins of the existence of the duty' (Rowley, 2004).

Concluding Comments

In conclusion, this chapter set out at the beginning to explore whether combat immunity could apply to a non-combatant, such as an MHCP in a hostile battlefield, when giving care and treatment to a wounded soldier, against a claim in negligence.   It also set out to highlight the unique challenges that a MHCP can face in a hostile environment when attempting to give care and treatment to a wounded patient.   Through an analysis of the literature and case law, it has concluded that due to the distinctiveness between the combatant and the non-combatant and the importance of both remaining separate, it is unlikely that combat immunity could be enjoyed by MHCPs.

Via a realistic vignette, this chapter then considered whether a modified form of immunity such as *Military Healthcare Battlefield Immunity* could be a viable doctrine for a MHCP against any claim by a patient treated negligently on the battlefield.   This was when the environment was particularly hostile. Here, the chapter concluded that in the context of the vignette, it might be reasonable to suggest that a MHCP could enjoy some modified form of immunity against a claim of negligence.   However, to remain compliant with the Geneva Convention's medical status of being a non-combatant and to retain the integrity of the medical and nursing professional on the battlefield, immunity may only exist as *Military Healthcare Battlefield Immunity* and not as *combat immunity.*   In addition, *Military Healthcare Battlefield Immunity* could only be enjoyed in rare circumstances, when a MHCP was *'solely'* engaged with the enemy.   As emphasised by King (2004) in his commentary about *Bici,* any immunity in war should only be used in rare situations. Mr Justice Elias in *(Bici at paragraph 90),* also stated that only in very exceptional circumstances should the 'courts recognise…the basic liberties of the citizen may have to give way to vital interests of state'. In the same case, he further stated '…the executive by reason of state necessity…' should not be '…free from any legal fetters for negligent or intentional act[s]…' *(Bici at paragraph 102).* Nevertheless, all cases are however, determined on the individual facts and it would be for a court to decide on the merits of each case and rule on whether combat immunity applies.

A version of the chapter appeared in the Journal of the Royal Army Medical Corps: Kelly, J. (2012). Military Healthcare Battlefield Immunity. *Journal of the Royal Army Medical* Corps, 158(4) pp. 308-312.

CHAPTER TEN

BATTLEFIELD CONDITIONS: STANDARD OF CARE AND DUAL LOYALTY CONFLICT ON THE BATTLEFIELD

Introduction

This final battlefield vignette considers the standard of care that should be given to a wounded soldier on the battlefield by a Military Healthcare Professional (MHCP) who:

(i)   Lacks battlefield healthcare experience.

(ii)   Is required to give emergency life saving treatment beyond his capability.

(iii)   Is a military nurse.

(iv)   Is faced with a dual loyalty conflict (Rascona, 2007) between following military orders and professional codes of conduct (NMC, *The Code*, 2008).

This chapter starts by explaining the general standard of care expected by one person to another, which is known in law as the *reasonable standard of care*.   It then considers the legal position regarding the standard of care expected by professionals such as doctors and nurses. After that, it further considers the professional standard of care that should be given by a MHCP in the hostile environment of the battlefield, and in particular, by a military nurse and also considers if military healthcare can be considered as a unique specialty requiring its own unique standard of care.

This chapter will also investigate whether the law will allow the *inexperience* of a MHCP when under attack and giving care and treatment on the battlefield to be taken into consideration and whether in all circumstances, the law will allow the standard of care in the battlefield to be variable.   This chapter will also address the difficulties in establishing 'responsible' and 'reasonable' care and treatment in this violent and hostile environment. It will also highlight the dual loyalty conflict between professional regulations and military orders that raise distinctive ethical dilemmas in war.

As explained in chapter 5, for healthcare professionals and especially those in the military, their 'moral obligations are beyond those incumbent on many other members of society' (Benetar and Upshur, 2008). In healthcare, dual loyalty occurs where the clinical role conflicts and is incompatible with professional duties to a patient and obligations to the interests of a third party such as an employer (World Medical Association, 2009). This creates inevitable ethical tensions and, on occasions, professional compromise (London et al, 2006). Thus, the healthcare professional has the problem of having 'simultaneous obligations, expressed or implied, to a patient and to a third party, often the State' (Dual Loyalty and Human Rights in Health Professional Practice Report, 2002). In the British Armed Forces, the Ministry of Defence (MoD) recognises that a MHCPs care and treatment of a patient must be 'governed primarily by medical judgement and ethics' (Joint Doctrine Publication, 2007 at Ch.1, section II, paragraph 112). However, it also states that medical treatment must be within the 'constraints of Armed Forces' medical policy' and subjected to 'military and professional constraints' (Joint Doctrine Publication, 2007 at Ch.1, section II, paragraph 112). The MoDs position therefore, places restrictions on how MHCPs should practise their healthcare profession in the military. Nevertheless, although not a military document, the Dual Loyalty and Human Rights in Health Professional Practice Report summarised that the 'overruling identity and priority' of a MHCP should be 'that of a health professional' (International Dual Loyalty Working Group-Summary in London et al 2006). The patient's clinical needs are sacrosanct (Annas, 2008). Therefore, there clearly emerges a conflict and tension created by dual loyalty for all MHCPs, who subsequently must balance that tension between patient care and military orders.

In extreme cases, such as the battlefield, the pressures of dual loyalty conflict can be more dramatic (Enemark, 2008). As explained in chapter 4, in such situations, there is a need to follow military orders to achieve Operational Effectiveness (Soldier Management, 2004). This is fulfilled by obeying orders to achieve the military intent of the government of the day, which could be to win the war or to maintain peace; the military Commander's intent then mirrors this on the battlefield. However, the importance of the standard of care given by a MHCP to a wounded soldier equally cannot be undervalued. The MoD recognise that the standard of care provided may have a permanent effect upon clinical outcomes and the effects of poor care can rarely be reversed (Joint Doctrine Publication, 2007 at Ch.1, section II, paragraph 112).   The MoD further states, 'Patients should receive the highest appropriate level of medical care in suitable clinical environments' (Joint Doctrine Publication, 2007 at Ch.1, section II, paragraph 112).

In law, the standard expected by a hypothetical reasonable man is an objective one. This means, it is not variable, as it does not allow different degrees or levels of standards. Lord Macmillan in *Glasgow Corporation v Muir (1943 at paragraph 49)*, stated that the standard does not take into account the 'idiosyncrasies of the particular person whose conduct is in question'. However, in the same case, His Lordship also stated that 'the standard of care of the reasonable man involves in its application a subjective element' (*Glasgow Corporation v Muir, 1943 at paragraph 49*). This means although the standard of care is *not* variable, it can be flexible in the sense that when determining whether a person has given sub-standard care in any given circumstance, it is a question of considering the circumstances at the time. In other words, it should be left to the court to determine if the standard in a given situation should be set very high or very low, and in judgment, whether the standard of care was 'reasonable' (Miola, 2009).

The following vignette referred to throughout this chapter was taken from the recent book by John Nichol and Tony Rennell, *Medic, Saving Lives – from Dunkirk to Afghanistan* (Nichol and Rennell, 2009). The vignette describes a real experience; however, it has been modified for the purpose of this chapter. The vignette:

1)   Gives a realistic account of the dangers faced by military nurses and all MHCPs in the battlefield when giving treatment to wounded soldiers.

2)   Highlights and contextualises the challenges, which MHCPs face when caring for the sick, in the most arduous of conditions, and circumstances (Weld, 2009).

3)   Illustrates that MHCPs have different technical skills compared with civilian healthcare professionals, which allow them to deal with combat injuries outside the traditional 'normal' civilian environment.

4)   Demonstrates that MHCPs face unique ethical challenges, compared to civilian healthcare professionals, in this violent and hostile environment due to a dual loyalty conflict (Garfield and McCarthy, 2005).

Vignette

Lieutenant Jones is a military nurse who joined the army one year ago. He qualified as a nurse two years ago. Before that, he was a 'Class 2' Combat Medical Technician in the Territorial Army. Since joining the army, he has been working as a junior nurse in a Military Defence Hospital Unit (MDHU), Accident and Emergency (A&E) department. He has some clinical experience in treating casualties in A&E under the overall supervision of more experienced nurses, but is relatively inexperienced in dealing with major trauma. He is now deployed on his first operational tour as a MHCP to Afghanistan, working at the Field Hospital. He has no previous experience on the battlefield.

Whilst a passenger in a light armoured tactical vehicle travelling to another military medical location, Lieutenant Jones, unfortunately, finds himself as the only healthcare professional giving emergency treatment to a wounded soldier, Corporal Smith. Corporal Smith, whilst on foot patrol, has just had his right arm and right lower leg blown off by a landmine. Corporal Smith is also short of breath, having sustained a penetrating chest wound, causing a right traumatic open pneumothorax. He has also sustained a left-sided tension pneumothorax from the blast of the explosion. Lieutenant Jones finds that Corporal Smith is struggling to breathe, is bleeding profusely, and is in obvious excruciating pain. He is also lying in an unmarked minefield (Nichol and Rennell, 2009 at p.345) that was previously laid by Soviet Union troops in the 1980's.

Lieutenant Jones has been given prior orders by his Commanding Officer *not* to leave hard-packed roads under *any* circumstances due, to the threat of potential landmines. Nonetheless, Lieutenant Jones instantaneously decides to disobey this lawful military order. He subsequently picks up his medical Bergen and throws it into the minefield towards Corporal Smith. When it does not trigger off another mine explosion, Lieutenant Jones jumps onto it, he then picks it up from under his feet and throws it another yard, jumps onto it again and so on, (Nichol and Rennell, 2009 at p.334) until he reaches Corporal Smith. Under constant enemy fire throughout from the Taliban and with his movement restricted due to further potential unexploded mines, Lieutenant Jones eventually reaches the wounded soldier and pushes him safely into a small ditch. In the ditch, he then administers medical treatment. Lieutenant Jones treats the pneumothorax by using a chest field dressing to seal the open chest wound to stop air from entering the chest and the lung collapsing any further. Next, as he had been trained to do so in pre-deployment training, he performs a thoracentesis, a procedure normally performed by doctors. He then places tourniquets around the blown off stumps and administers intramuscular Morphine. However, because Lieutenant Jones is (i) terrified for his own life and (ii) is giving care and treatment beyond his usual skills, knowledge, and experience; he fails to fasten the tourniquet around Corporal Smith's right leg tightly enough. Consequently, Corporal Smith loses blood rapidly and starts to exsanguinate. However, Corporal Smith's life is saved when helicopter support, with specialised medical equipment and personnel on-board, arrives shortly afterwards and eventually evacuates him to the military hospital fifty kilometres away.

By using this vignette this chapter considers the following:

1)   What is the standard of care expected by Lieutenant Jones to Corporal Smith on the battlefield?

2)   Does the dangerous environment allow Lieutenant Jones's inexperience to be taken into account when considering if the standard of care given to Corporal Smith was sub-standard?

3)   Can the standard of care given by Lieutenant Jones to Corporal Smith on the battlefield be variable?

4)   On the battleground, does a dual loyalty between following military orders and professional codes of practice, conflict with the standard of care given by Lieutenant Jones to Corporal Smith?

The legal position

General standard of care

The general standard of care expected by the reasonable man is an objective one. Thus, Lord Alderson in *Blyth v Birmingham Water Works (1843-60 at paragraph 480),* stated 'negligence is the omission to do something which a reasonable man, guided upon those considerations which ordinarily regulate the conduct of human affairs, would do, or doing something which a prudent and reasonable man would not do'. His Lordship further added, 'A reasonable man would act with reference to the average circumstances of the temperatures in ordinary years' *(Blyth v Birmingham Water Works, 1843-60 at paragraph 480).* Thus, the standard expected is not to reach perfection, but only a *reasonable* standard. However, a breach of a standard of care will occur when the defendant has not taken the steps that a reasonable man would be expected to take in the circumstances at that time.

Professional standard of care

Experts and professionals with particular skills are judged by the standards of the reasonable man with those specialist skills. The leading case of *Bolam v Friern Hospital Management Committee (1957 at paragraph 112) (Bolam)* affirms the point where McNair J. stated, it is '...not the test of the man on the top of a Clapham omnibus...' It is '...the ordinary skilled man exercising and professing to have that special skill. A man need not possess the highest expert skill...' *(Bolam at paragraph 112)* Therefore, in relation to the vignette, the standard of care that Lieutenant Jones should give on the battlefield should be that of the ordinary skilled military nurse on the battlefield. This is because, although Lieutenant Jones is collectively known as a MHCP (as explained in chapter 2), he is still a military nurse and is professionally responsible for his *own* acts and omissions (The Code, Nursing Midwifery Council, 2008, page 1). He must be judged by the standard of the reasonable, competent military nurse on the battlefield. Therefore, the question is not did Lieutenant Jones give reasonable care? Instead, it is what would a reasonable military nurse, placed in Lieutenant Jones's position have done, and did Lieutenant Jones meet the required standard when giving care to Corporal Smith?

In the later case of *Whitehouse v Jordan (1981 at paragraph 277),* Lord Edmund-Davies confirmed McNair J. point from *Bolam* more succinctly when he said, '...If a surgeon fails to measure up to the standard in *any* respect ("clinical judgment") he has been negligent...' This means that if Lieutenant Jones's standard of care when caring for Corporal Smith in the battlefield fell below that of the ordinary skilled military nurse on the battlefield in '*any* respect', he would have breached his duty of care and would be negligent. At the House of Lords, Lord Scarman in *Maynard v West Midlands Regional Health Authority (Maynard, 1985, at paragraph 639)* further endorsed McNair J.'s views by stating, '...a doctor who professes to exercise a special skill must exercise the ordinary skill of his speciality...' Therefore, this would suggest that the military nurse on the battlefield must also exercise the ordinary skill of his specialty expected in the context of his environment. Thus, Lord Scarman in *Maynard (at paragraph 639)* appeared to frame the Bolam test as a complete defence in that (i) provided a healthcare professional complied with the approved practise of the day and (ii) it was *reasonable* and *responsible,* a breach of care would not then have occurred.

In *Bolam,* McNair J. further agreed with Counsel's argument that a doctor is not guilty of negligence if he has acted '...in accordance with the standards of reasonably competent medical men at the time' *(Bolam at paragraph 112).* The *Bolam* test, as it became known, in determining whether a medical person had acted within the body of medical opinion, came under criticism and great scrutiny in *Hill v Potter (1983 at paragraph 729).* In this case, Lord Hirst stated, 'I do not accept the argument...' that '...by adapting the *Bolam* principle, the court abdicates its power of decision to doctors...' Moreover, in *Defreitas v O'Brien (1995)* there was further disharmony when it was held that a reasonable body of opinion was not substantial as a defence.

The Bolam principle was re-examined at the House of Lords by Lord Browne-Wilkinson in the case of *Bolitho v City and Hackney Health Authority (1998) (Bolitho).* His Lordship stated that if 'the professional opinion is not capable of withstanding logical analysis, the judge is entitled to hold that the body of opinion is not reasonable or responsible' *(Bolitho at paragraph 243).* Thus, this case concluded that expert evidence was no longer considered conclusive as a defence to a breach of a duty of care (Miola, 2009).

The judges, therefore, re-gained some control in deciding whether or not a breach occurred and became more questioning of professional practice (Tingle, 2002). However, it was further suggested by Browne-Wilkinson in *Bolitho* that, where medical opinion had reached a decision that was *'reasonable', 'responsible', and 'respectable'* it would only be in rare circumstances that the courts would hold a contrary view. His Lordship stated, 'it will very seldom be right for a judge to reach the conclusion that views genuinely held by a competent medical expert are unreasonable' *(Bolitho at paragraph at 244).* A view also shared by McHale (2002), who suggested that it would not be easy to be argue against a belief held by a *'responsible'* body of professional opinion.

Sub-specialties

As explained in chapters 2 and '7, giving care and treatment on the battlefield is distinctly different compared with giving emergency treatment in a civilian environment as, 'There are simply no comparable situations in the civilian sector, despite frequent comparisons to inner-city emergency rooms on "any Saturday night"' (Beam, 2003). Therefore, a difficulty the courts may have, is determining what the reasonable standard of care ought to be when on the battleground and under hostile conditions. This is because it is difficult to find an appropriate comparison, as military healthcare in general in this environment may be considered as a distinct healthcare speciality. There is also no relevant case law from which to draw guidance. Nonetheless, Otton LJ in *De*

Freitas v O'Brien (1995 at paragraph 62) (De Freitas) stated that 'a small number of tertiary specialists could constitute a responsible body of medical opinion'. He further stated that 'there is no requirement in law that the body has to be substantial' *(De Freitas at paragraph 53)*.

However, although Lords Otton and Swinton-Thomas in *De Freitas,* recognised that specialised healthcare professionals can be considered as 'specialists', this does not allow Lieutenant Jones to give care and treatment that is not considered as *reasonable* and *responsible*. In following the ruling from *Bolitho,* if the court viewed that the care given by Lieutenant Jones to Corporal Smith had no logical basis, it could, therefore, not be deemed reasonable or responsible, just because a body of opinion within their military nursing profession supported it. Thus, the body of professional opinion is not always conclusive or persuasive in determining whether a practitioner has performed below the acceptable standard of care (Heywood, 2006). This stance was earlier addressed by Sachs L.J. in the Court of Appeal case of *Hucks v Cole (1983 at paragraph 397)* when His Lordship stated if 'a lacuna in a professionals practice exists...and in the light of professional knowledge, there is no proper reason for that lacuna...and...if it is definitely not reasonable...it constitutes negligence...' Therefore, in applying the law, the care given by Lieutenant Jones must be **reasonable** and **responsible,** irrespective of him being considered a 'tertiary specialist'.

Inexperience

In *Nettleship v Weston (1971),* the court found that inexperience was not a defence and that a learner driver must exercise the same skill as an experienced driver. This is also supported by the NMC (*The Code,* 2008) in that a practitioner is expected to be competent at the point of registration. Lord Salmon in *Nettleship v Weston, 1971 at paragraph 704) (Nettleship),* stated that, '...As a rule, the driver's personal idiosyncrasy is not a relevant circumstance...' Thus, the standard of care remains objective, even for an inexperienced MHCP and for a military nurse on the battlefield. Lord Winn in *The Lady Gwendolene (1965 at paragraph 300)* demonstrated the objective reasonable man test where he stated, '...the law must apply a standard which is not to cater for [the defendants'] factual ignorance of all activities...' Thus, carelessness is not measured by ascertaining if a professional fell below their standard of conduct, but by that of the reasonable person's conduct. In affirming this, Lord Mustill in *Wilsher v Essex Area Health Authority (1986 at paragraph 814) (Wilsher)* stated '...this notion of a duty tailored to the actor, rather than

to the act which he elects to perform, has no place in the law of tort...'
Moreover, Lord Denning in *Nettleship (at paragraph 700)* when referring
to inexperience stated, 'The learner driver may be doing his best, but his
incompetent best is not good enough'.

However, this objective approach can create tensions, as clearly
recognised by Lord Mustill in *Wilsher.* When considering the
performance of the healthcare professional, His Lordship stated that the
'...proper response cannot be to temper the wind to the professional man.
If he assumes to perform a task, he must bring to it the appropriate care
and skill...' *(Wilsher at paragraph 811).* He further stated '...the standard
is not just that of the averagely competent and well-informed junior
houseman (or whatever the position of the doctor) but of such a person
who fills a post in a unit offering highly specialised service...' *(Wilsher at
paragraph 814)* This suggests that no leniency or account can be taken of
how experienced a practitioner is in his or her role, as he/she must still
perform at the standard the role dictates, and not of a lower standard.

Nonetheless, in *Wilsher* Lord Mustill was also careful to protect
inexperienced defendants in negligence cases and muddied the waters by
judging on activities of the post and the person who would normally
undertake them. He stated that as long as the professional man '...had
provided an adequate service on average, he should not be held liable for
occasions when his performance fell below the norm...' *(Wilsher at
paragraph 811).* Moreover, His Lordship implied that where treatment is
technically difficult and the chances of success are uncertain, '...the courts
can...constantly bear in mind...in those situations which call for the
exercise of judgment, the fact that in retrospect the choice actually made
can be shown to have turned out badly is not in itself a proof of
negligence, and to remember that the duty of care is not a warranty of a
perfect result...' *(Wilsher at paragraph 811).* Furthermore, '...the court
should...be particularly careful not to impute negligence simply because
something has gone wrong...' *(Wilsher at paragraph 813)*

However, Lord Mustill's position is contradictory, since at first he
rejects a subjective approach, but then almost re-introduces it via a
variable standard of care by referring to 'posts' (Jones, 2002). Lord
Browne-Wilkinson dissenting in *Wilsher* preferred a subjective approach.
His Lordship stated '... he cannot accept that the standard of care required
of an individual doctor holding a post in a hospital is an objective standard
to be determined irrespective of his experience...' *(Wilsher at paragraphs
833-834)* He further stated '...one of the chief hazards of inexperience is
that one does not always know the risk which exists...' However, in spite
of his concerns, in the same case Lord Glidwell took a more sensible

approach. His Lordship re-affirmed the objective test by stating '...the law requires the trainee or learner to be judged by the same standard as his more experienced colleagues...' *(Wilsher at paragraph 832)* Thus, the law on experience is clear, and for Lieutenant Jones it means that he must conform to the general practice of his profession and not of a lower standard irrespective of his inexperience in dealing with trauma patients on the battlefield. Consequently, in spite of Lieutenant Jones being under enemy attack, no allowance or mitigation can be given for his inexperience on the battlefield, which caused him to insecurely fasten the tourniquet around Corporal Smith's right leg.

In further consideration of the standard of care, the courts would also need to establish what the standard should be measured against; to ascertain an objective criterion, especially when nurses undertake extended roles. In the vignette for example, Lieutenant Jones took on an extended role of the nurse by performing a thoracentesis, normally undertaken by a doctor. In these situations, the courts may look at a medical standard that has to be achieved (Tingle, 2002). The leading case that deals with such situations is again *Wilsher*. In this case, the Court of Appeal reaffirmed the objective test after being questioned that the standard of care was too high. Here, Lord Mustill stated that it would be, '...a false step...' for a patient to receive care from a doctor according to their ability and not, '...a degree of skill appropriate to the task...' *(Wilsher at paragraph 814)* This therefore indicates that when undertaking a thoracentesis, Lieutenant Jones may be required to demonstrate that he has the skills, knowledge, and competency to undertake such a procedure to a medical standard. The standard should not be lowered because he is a nurse performing the procedure.

Although Lord Mustill was referring to a '... "team" standard of care, whereby each of the persons who formed the staff of the unit held themselves out as capable of undertaking the specialised procedures which that unit set out to perform...' *(Wilsher at paragraph 813)* he was, once again, being contradictory. He demonstrated a desire to protect the inexperienced professional by stating that, '...If it seeks to attribute to each individual members of the team a duty to live up to the standards demanded of the unit as a whole, it cannot be right, for it would expose a student nurse to an action in negligence for a failure to possess the skill and experience of a consultant...' *(Wilsher at paragraph 814)* In the context of the vignette, this would be problematic because Lieutenant Jones is not student nurse. He is a qualified nurse and therefore should be competent to attain the required standard. However, irrespective of Lord Mustill's contradictions, using a medical standard to judge Lieutenant

Jones actions would make sense. This is because the standard of care could be subject to a 'process of dumbing down' if inexperience was allowed to be considered (Hanson, 2005). Therefore, it appears that the dangerous environment does not allow Lieutenant Jones's inexperience to be taken into account when considering if the standard of care given to Corporal Smith was sub-standard.

Emergencies

In contrast to inexperience not being considered as mitigation for sub-standard care, in emergencies, it can be difficult for any healthcare professional to give the same standard of care that might be normally expected. The GMC, the NMC, and the law cater for such circumstances. The GMC states that 'in an emergency, wherever it may arise, you must offer anyone at risk the assistance you could reasonably be expected to provide' (*Good Medical Practice, 2001*). The NMC Code gives similar advice (NMC, *The Code,* 2008 and *Advice Sheet,* 2008). In *Wilsher (at paragraph 813),* Mustill LJ stated, 'I accept that full allowance must be made for the fact that certain aspects of treatment may have to be carried out in what one witness...called "battle conditions"' An emergency may overburden resources and, if an individual is forced by circumstances to do too many things at once, the fact that he does one of them incorrectly should not lightly be taken as negligence.' This re-affirms Lord Macmillan's dictum in *Glasgow Corporation v Muir (1943 at paragraph 49)* thus further emphasising that although the standard remains objective and is not variable, it can be flexible in an emergency.

Consequently, this may mean that although Lieutenant Jones may argue successfully that he failed to fasten the tourniquet around Corporal Smith's right leg tightly enough because he was under constant enemy fire from the Taliban and in a small ditch. He cannot argue that in those circumstances, when under fire from the enemy, he does not have to fasten the tourniquet tightly enough in the first instance. He must still act 'reasonably' and exercise the ordinary skill of a military nurse on the battlefield. Thus, the law, even in an emergency, will not allow different and variable standards of care. Nevertheless, it does, as stated by Asquith L.J. in *Daborn v Bath Tramways Motor Co Ltd and Trevor Smithey (1946, at paragraph at 337) (Daborn)* establish that 'the standard of reasonable care' that should be given is that 'which is reasonably to be demanded of him in the circumstances'. For Lieutenant Jones, the circumstances that need to be taken into account are those of a hostile battlefield environment or as Asquith LJ further stated, 'the importance of the end to be served by behaving in this way or in that' *(Daborn at paragraph at 337)*. It should, therefore, not always be deemed as the ideal care or care that was actually achieved, but the most *reasonable* care that could be achieved given the circumstances. The courts may, therefore, consider that Lieutenant Jones did not give sub-standard care when he failed to fasten the tourniquet around Corporal Jones's right leg tightly enough, which is in contrast to inexperience being considered as mitigation for sub-standard care.

Applying the objective test with a dual loyalty conflict

On finding Corporal Smith badly injured, Lieutenant Jones clearly has a dual loyalty conflict over which is the best course of action to take. As explained in chapter 7 regarding duty of care, assuming already that Lieutenant Jones owes Corporal Smith a duty of care *(Donoghue v Stevenson, 1932; R v Bateman, 1925 at paragraph 49; 1925* and Tschudin and Schmitz, 2003), Lieutenant Jones is faced with **three issues**.

Firstly, he has a professional obligation to make Corporal Smith his first concern and give him his absolute attention (NMC, 2008, page 1). This notion originally arose from the Hippocratic Oath and was later modernised by the World Medical Association's Declaration of Geneva, which stated, 'the health of my patient shall be my first consideration' and healthcare professionals must provide medical services in 'full technical and moral independence' (The World Medical Association Declaration of Geneva, 1948).

Secondly, although Lieutenant Jones has a professional obligation to give his patient his undivided attention (Rubenstien, 2003), as explained in chapter 4, Lieutenant Jones also has an obligation to follow military orders (Queen's Regulations for the Army 1975, Chapter 5, part 3, orders and duties, 5.121, a and b). Therefore, the dual conflict issues are that Lieutenant Jones can either:

(i) Disobey military orders via the Armed Forces Act 2006 (Part 1 Offences, section 2(3) Misconduct on Operations) and start giving treatment to Corporal Smith.

Alternatively,

(ii) He can follow military orders and not leave the hard packed road and thus, delay giving treatment to Corporal Smith.

Despite Lieutenant Jones's choices, whatever action he chooses he could be acting unlawfully, either professionally or militarily, and may face the respective consequences of his actions.   Thus, professional requirements and lawful military orders appear to conflict (Howe, 2003). A further compounding factor is that, if Lieutenant Jones chooses to disobey military orders and give immediate treatment to Corporal Smith, he will then be faced with having to act as the ordinary, competent, skilled military nurse on the battlefield when under fire, surrounded by mines and with little battlefield and clinical experience.   For any mistakes he may make, he would not then be able to rely as a defence on the dual loyalty conflict argument.   This is because he has already made the decision to treat Corporal Smith and disobey a lawful military order from a superior officer.   Thus, role conflict between his military duty and his professional duty can no longer support his actions.   Instead, Lieutenant Jones would need to argue successfully that, given the circumstances in which he was treating Corporal Smith, an error of judgment that he made was not necessarily sub-standard care.   Instead, it was a mistake that a reasonably competent military nurse might make, given the circumstances *(Whitehouse v Jordan, 1981).*

In contrast, if Lieutenant Jones takes the opposite course of action and omits to give care and treatment to Corporal Smith, then he may breach the NMCs Code, as he failed to make Corporal Smith his first concern (NMC, *The Code*, 2008).   Legally, this would also be an omission to act, as Lieutenant Jones would owe Corporal Smith a duty of care (*Donaghue v Stevenson, 1932).*   However, this would be difficult to substantiate, since Lieutenant Jones would have a strong argument to say that the risk of causing himself and others physical injury by entering a minefield was foreseeable and extremely high (*Bolton v Stone, 1951).*   Thus, the potential gravity of the consequences that his action may cause is a relevant consideration (*Paris v Stepney, 1951).*   Therefore, Lieutenant Jones may never have been in a position to make Corporal Smith his first concern, as the risk was too great to take.

Thirdly, it is clear that Lieutenant Jones's ethical choices are not addressed by either professional regulations or military law.   This could be regarded as being a major oversight by the professional regulators the GMC and the NMC and also the MoD as the government department governing and administering the Armed Forces.   Tobin (2005) suggests that such ethical problems that military medical personnel can face should be thoroughly addressed, prior to deployment in hostile environments. Although not within the scope of this book, this could be done via a separate professional code for military nurses and doctors via the NMC and GMC respectively.

In circumstances where there is an ethical problem, such as a dual loyalty conflict, in deciding what the correct action should be, the ethical problem should be divided between ethical dilemmas and tests of integrity (Coleman, 2009). An ethical dilemma occurs when a person is faced with several options, but has difficulty in deciding which is the correct option to take. Tests of integrity, on the other hand, occur when there are bad options and good options, but it is obvious which is the correct option to take. As mentioned in chapter 6, Howe (2003) gives a more precise concept of the professional-military conflict by arguing that military healthcare professionals are governed by three role-specific ethics, which involves the person following each role strictly. Howe suggests that with a **military role-specific ethic,** a military healthcare professional would follow a military order above everything else. With a **medical role-specific ethic,** they would follow professional codes of practice and put their patients first (Howe, 2003 at pages 333-334). Finally, the third role is where the military healthcare professional would use some **discretion** in deciding when and whether the needs of the military are absolute (Howe, 2003 at page 335). However, it is problematic to allow the MHCP to use discretion in deciding whether, and when, the needs of the military are absolute, and when those needs should become subservient to medical needs (Howe, 2003 at p.335). This is because MHCPs are not military tacticians, since they lack the military skills and knowledge to make such strategic decisions. In addition, by nature of their professional status as healthcare professionals, they are too patient focused to be the most suitable people to make these decisions objectively (Joint Doctrine Publication, 2007 at chapter 4).

In deciding to disobey military orders by attempting to circumvent the minefield to reach Corporal Smith, Lieutenant Jones may have thought that it was not an ethical dilemma, but rather a test of integrity. Moreover, following Howe's (2003 at p.333) analysis, Lieutenant Jones may have quickly concluded that this problem was best dealt with via a medical-specific role and that the patient must always come first; a view shared by Annas (2008), who argues that the patient must always be the healthcare practitioner's first concern before any other consideration. Lieutenant Jones did not appear to exhibit any difficulty in implementing his actions. He may have thought that it was overwhelmingly reasonable, obvious and a verifiable excuse to disobey military orders and leave the hard-packed road to give treatment to Corporal Smith. In doing so, Lieutenant Jones followed his professional code and made Corporal Smith his first concern (NMC, *The Code*, 2008, pg 1).

Thus, the solution to the ethical problem is clear to Lieutenant Jones. He considered that it is bad to follow military orders and good to disobey them. His duty is to the patient first. He does not appear to have a problem with duty loyalty and role conflict between following military orders and professional codes of practice. He follows a universal principle in that professional responsibility overrides all other considerations (Benetar and Upshur, 2008) and, therefore, he takes an absolutist approach by saying that 'War or not I am a doctor' (Army Doctrine Publication, 2000, Annex A to chapter 2, 2-A-1). For Lieutenant Jones, actions are right or wrong according to the balance of their good and bad consequences. Thus, the moral worth of an action should only be determined by its contribution to overall utility or the greatest good. It is, therefore, the ultimate standard between right and wrong (McLeaod, 2005). It could also be argued that Lieutenant Jones acted courageously, since he decided what was right and demonstrated the 'courage to act accordingly' (Miller, 2004).

Corporal Smith receives from Lieutenant Jones, the care and treatment that he desperately needs to survive; Lieutenant Jones's actions, however, raise three concerns.

Firstly, concerning dual loyalty, if Lieutenant Jones has acted 'instantaneously', it is questionable whether Lieutenant Jones had time enough to engage in any rational thought processes to consider the dual loyalty conflict. It is more likely that he had an overwhelming desire to protect a fellow soldier from further harm (Londen et al 2006) and not to leave any comrade behind (Rubel, 2004).

Secondly, in deciding his course of action, he has committed a military offence and disobeyed a lawful order. Moreover, he has demonstrated ill-discipline. As explained in chapter 4, military discipline is the backbone of the Armed Forces and is intrinsically linked with duty, to ensure the efficiency and effectiveness of the Commander's will (Queen's Regulations, 1975 chapter 3). It is also an essential trait that all soldiers must acquire, as it causes disharmony when absent (Lapsley and Power, 2006). Any disobedience could be considered, via the Armed Forces Act 2006 (section 6, (2) (a) (ii)), as mutinous action, as it would 'subvert discipline'.

Thirdly, Lieutenant Jones's actions show a lack of military discipline in another context. If his actions became public knowledge to other military nurses and other MHCPs, it might lead or encourage them, if faced with a similar ethical problem, to follow the same path, and to similarly disobey military orders. This in itself could cause further problems, as it could prevent further military nurses and other MHCPs from responding and following their duty appropriately (Price, 2009). On the one hand, Lieutenant Jones's actions may set a precedent that other military nurses and MHCPs may feel that they have to follow. However, on the other hand, if Lieutenant Jones faces no military consequence for disobeying orders, then his actions appear to compromise military discipline altogether. Nonetheless, 'such disobedience is a mark of professional integrity, not a sign of an incipient military coup' (Wolfendale, 2009, page 137). Therefore, it is questionable whether Lieutenant Jones's actions should be so militarily problematic as to charge him with mutiny. Moreover, if he were charged with mutiny, it would seem that there is disparity between the 'crime' and any 'consequent' punishment, when his intention was to save another's life (Coleman, 2009).

It is also useful to consider if Lieutenant Jones perceived the problem as a 'test of integrity' in a different context. However, this time, he would decide that a military specific-role would be the most appropriate way to deal with the situation. This is because; he would take a utilitarian approach and say, 'Doctor or not this is war' (Army Doctrine Publication, 2000, Annex A to chapter 2, 2-A-1). Lieutenant Jones would place the interests of the military first, abide by military law, and not compromise military discipline. This action would be a legitimate ethical response, since the interests of the State and obligations to 'serve other goods' can sometime be the overall best solution for the greater good (Enemark, 2008). Thus, if Lieutenant Jones took this decision, he would consider that duty is an action that 'we ought to do' and is an action that 'people are required to perform' (Kemerling, 2009). Gross (2006), who argues medical ethics in war has its own unique difficulties when compared to ethics in less hostile environments, equally shares this view saying that the doctor-patient relationship in war is rarely preserved intact, as it is in peacetime.

Nonetheless, if Lieutenant Jones took this cause of action, he may compromise professional codes of practice, (NMC, *The Code*, 2008, page 1) as he put following military orders before saving a human life and allowed his medical role to be limited to non-medical military superiors. Thus, he would have subordinated his clinical autonomy to military necessity (London et al, 2006). Professionally, the consequence of this is that he could breach the NMCs Code, as he would have failed to 'make the care of people' his first concern' (NMC, *The Code*, 2008, page 1). However, as mentioned earlier, this cause of action may have been a risk too far to take and, therefore, it would be unlikely that he would be disciplined, as the principle of first aid is safety for both the helper and the casualty (NMC, *The Code*, 2008).

In addition, if Lieutenant Jones had 'instantaneously' decided to obey military orders and stay on safe ground instead; as, when he disobeyed military orders, it is unlikely he would have a given any rational thought to any dual loyalty conflict. Perhaps, therefore, he should not be criticised for not making the patient his first concern. Irrespective of professional codes and dual loyalty, the risk was too great to take. For example, no healthcare professional would ever be expected to risk his or her own life by attempting to save another's in a grave situation. For instance, it would be unreasonable to expect a civilian healthcare professional to jump into an iced covered lake and attempt to rescue a person struggling in the icy water to stay afloat. If Lieutenant Jones had not decided to give treatment to Corporal Smith, irrespective of following military orders, his decision would not be condemned professionally. Moreover, because the decision was 'instantaneous', dual conflict would also not have any bearing. However, a criticism of this rationale is that soldiers are considered as a 'family' to one another (Nichol and Rennell, 2009). If Lieutenant Jones made an 'instantaneous' decision to follow military orders and not help Corporal Jones, then he may be condemned by his military comrades for abandoning his bond of loyalty to him, since his reason for doing so would be self-serving (Kleinig, 2001); although, this decision would not necessarily carry any legal consequences as he would have been following legal military orders.

Using the same analogy, that of a person struggling in icy water to stay afloat, the law would be equally sympathetic and not expect the military nurse in the minefield, or the civilian healthcare professional attempting to rescue a person struggling in icy water to give the same level of care as generally expected. Pill J in *Knight and others v Home Office and another (1990 at paragraph 244)* declared that 'the standard of care will vary with the context' and that in an emergency the standard of care cannot be expected to be the same as in a 'general practitioner's surgery' compared with a fully resourced hospital. Moreover, he further stated that 'the law should not allow and does not expect the same standard across the entire spectrum of possible situations' (*Knight and others v Home Office and another, 1990 at paragraph 244*). Thus, it is clear that, whilst there is no variable standard of care, even when giving treatment in extremely dangerous circumstances, the standard of care can be flexible to take into account the circumstances at the time.

To resolve such ethical problems as the one faced by Lieutenant Jones, perhaps the elimination of war must be an achievable goal, as this would eradicate such ethical decision-making (Beck, 1949). However, it can be argued that this view is utopian since, 'if you want peace, prepare for war' (Flavius Vegetius Renatus in Rascona, 2007). A more appropriate response, therefore, in resolving ethical problems could come from the recommendations by The Healthcare Commission (2009), on clinical governance in the British Defence Medical Services (DMS). Although the Healthcare Commission did not expand on what the standard of care should be in the battlefield, (2009, Appendix 1, Standards for Better Health, Second domain: clinical and cost effectiveness, Core standard C7, at page 95), they did suggest that Military Healthcare Professionals should respect 'human rights' by *always* making the patient their first concern (Commission for Healthcare Audit and Inspection, 2009). Therefore, as human rights, 'cannot be traded off' in the way that ethical problems have to be balanced; taking a human rights approach in *always* making the patient their first concern, perhaps, is the best way to approach any dual loyalty conflict. This is because it overrides all other criteria, such as following military orders (London et al, 2006). This view is shared by Miles (2004), who advocates that the protection of human rights to *always* make the patient their first concern is the only way to guard wounded combatants against dual loyalty conflict. The World Medical Associations Declaration of Geneva and the Physicians Oath equally place human rights and *always* making the patient their first concern above third party considerations (1948).

In the recent case of *R (Smith) v Secretary of State for Defence (2009 at paragraph 31)*, Mr Justice Collins stated that the '…the right of life of a soldier in combat is different from that of a soldier not in combat…' He thus stated that, when fighting the enemy, the 'right to life' might not exist. Mr Justice Collins further stated that these rights change when the soldier is not in combat, when he stated, '…it seems to make no sense to hold that there is a distinction between a person inside and outside premises controlled by the UK, whether he or she is a consul or a soldier…' He added that this, '…raises questions such as whether the soldier or consul is protected in a vehicle or an ambulance. If in a hospital, why not in an ambulance? If in a British base…why not in a British army vehicle? If in a vehicle, why not when the soldier gets out of the vehicle?' *(R (Smith) v Secretary of State for Defence, (2009) at] paragraph 35)*.

This subsequent reasoning by Mr Justice Collins is confusing because it might indicate that, although remaining physically in the battlefield, the right to life may become 'live' when the soldier is injured and he is no longer in close combat fighting the enemy. For instance, Corporal Smith's injuries would clearly prevent him from further engaging with the enemy. Mr Justice Collins' judgment, may therefore place obligations on military nurses and all MHCPs to 'make the patient their first concern' before following military orders on the battlefield. However, if such obligations were to be considered by the military and professional bodies, such as the GMC and the NMC, then to have any significant impact upon a military commander in this environment, they would need to be substantiated with military law and collaborated with professional guidelines via secondary legislation (London et al, 2006). Accordingly, such an approach with compatible professional and military legislation and subsequent guidelines may be help to resolve tensions between following military orders or professional codes of practice when in the battlefield. The courts may find this approach favourable, since when guidelines are followed, it allows the patient to receive evidence-based care, which can influence judges when determining if care at that time was appropriate and correct (Tingle, 2002).

Conclusion

During war it is clear that the 'exigencies of battle pose unique challenges incomparable to the civilian context because of the scale of the threats to life, unpredictability, and the level of violence' (Beam, 2003). Furthermore, in the battlefield and any military environment, it is legally right to follow a military order and legally wrong not to do so (Armed Forces Act 2006, parts 11-13).

All Military Healthcare Professionals have a 'dual loyalty conflict' between following military orders and professional codes of practice (Clark, 2006). However, not withstanding this, the vignette has shown that the standard of care expected from Lieutenant Jones to Corporal Smith on the battlefield is no different to that of any other healthcare professional attempting to rescue an injured person in an extremely dangerous situation. Moreover, whilst no account can be taken of the inexperience of the military nurse or any MHCP, the current standard of care, nonetheless, appears to be satisfactorily viable. This is due to it being sufficiently flexible to be able to protect the military nurse and MHCP in this harsh environment against a claim of a breach of a duty of care in negligence. Thus, it is argued that the law would be sympathetic and not expect the military nurse or MHCP in the minefield, or the civilian healthcare professional attempting to save a person struggling in icy water, to give the same level of care as generally expected in a more serene environment (*Knight and others v Home Office and another, 1990 at paragraph at 244*). Therefore, it is clear that whilst there is no variable standard of care, even when giving treatment in extremely dangerous circumstances, the standard of care must still be 'reasonable'. However, it can be flexible enough to take into account the circumstances at the time. As Lord Mustill stated in *Wilsher (at paragraph 811),* it is incorrect to say that, if something goes wrong, the patient '...should count himself fortunate to be alive, or that he must take the rough with the smooth...' However, as Hanson (2005) correctly points out, 'reasonable' care should not be confused with 'ideal'. Nonetheless, in support of this, Benetar and Upshar (2008) advocate that the medical professional should engage more explicitly in dialogue regarding the amount of risk any healthcare professional should place him or herself in when implementing their professional duty in a challenging and dangerous situation.

This chapter has also shown that it seems reasonable to suggest that separating ethical problems into ethical dilemmas and tests of integrity is beneficial, since it allows a person to think more critically about his/her actions and consequences (Coleman 2009). However, it is debatable whether separating them into a role-specific ethic enhances the solutions to dual loyalty conflicts. This is because MHCPs, including military nurses, will lack the military and tactical skills and knowledge relating to when and how to adopt these roles, as they are trained more to focus on patient care during war and not military strategy (Beam, 2003). A more appropriate approach to solving dual loyalty conflict appears to be recognising a wounded soldier's human rights, to *always* make the patient their first concern, supported with professional guidelines and military law (British Medical Association, 2001). This approach would then create a blueprint (Wasunna, 2003) to deal with the dual loyalty conflict that has plagued all healthcare professionals when they are involved in third party interests (Clark, 2006).

However, for the military nurse and any other MHCPs, in the context of this chapter there does not appear to be any tension between following military orders and professional codes of practice. This is because in this environment, when faced with such dire emergencies, military nurses and other MHCPs will act spontaneously. It is unlikely, therefore, that dual loyalty conflict will be dominant in their mind at that precise time of the medical emergency. This is similar to a civilian nurse at a cardiac arrest or other medical emergency, where his/her response is reflexive, instantaneous, and primarily responsive to the patient's needs before anything else. However, it is accepted that following military orders has the potential to create divided loyalties and a dual loyalty conflict with professional codes of practice (World Medical Association, 2009). Nevertheless, given the fact that decisions are made quickly on the battlefield, it is unlikely that in these situations dual loyalty conflict will create tensions in this environment, even when in the most exacting of circumstances (Coleman, 2009). As will be discussed in the vignettes of chapters 11 and 12, it remains to be investigated if in a non-medical emergency, and when not directly in combat with hostile action, the same conclusion could be drawn, in that dual loyalty conflict could have any impact on Lieutenant Jones thought processes.

Thus, this chapter suggests that dual loyalty conflict is more likely to occur in non-emergency situations, when the healthcare professional has more time to consider the consequences of their actions. Nonetheless, as the NMC and the GMC remain silent on the issue of healthcare professionals caring for the wounded on the battlefield, without professional guidelines and succinct military law for healthcare professionals in this environment, this chapter has highlighted that it remains uncertain how dual loyalty in a military healthcare context should be appropriately considered. A human rights approach to *always* make the patient the first concern could be an embryonic start, as it could be considered as a 'legitimate priority' to commence succinct military healthcare guidelines for the battlefield environment (Rubenstien, 2003). However, what the chapter has clearly highlighted is that dual loyalty and ethical difficulties are unavoidable and they are not the same when compared to civilian healthcare practice (Soloman, 2005). For all MHCPs and military nurses on the battlefield, in some circumstances, it is having the unenviable task of either obeying military orders or following professional codes of practice (Joint Doctrine Publication, 2007 at ch.1, annex 1A, 1A6).

CHAPTER ELEVEN

OPERATIONAL CONDITIONS: LEGAL CAPACITY OF A PATIENT-SOLDIER REFUSING MEDICAL TREATMENT

Introduction

This operational vignette explores the law regarding **refusal to consent** to life-saving medical treatment where the **capacity** of a patient soldier is questionable. In English law, consent to medical treatment and refusal of treatment are intrinsically linked (Carey, 2009). Using the three-dimensional ethical model explained in chapter 6 created by Edmund Howe (2003), this chapter examines the professional and ethical difficulties that a Military Healthcare Professional (MHCP) such as a doctor, nurse or medic may face when being ordered by a senior military officer *not* to give them life-saving treatment in an operational environment. This is analysed in the context of a dual loyalty conflict (Rascona, 2007) between either following military orders or professional codes of conduct (General Medical Council, *Good Medical Practice,* 2006, page 2 and the Nursing Midwifery Council, *The Code,* 2008*).* This chapter also addresses if a patient-soldier's wish to **refuse medical treatment** is compromised in an **operational environment.**

When a patient who is normally competent at making his/her own decisions, endangers his/her own and others' lives by refusing medical treatment, action from the MHCP needs to serve several purposes (Shea, 2005). This is, (1) to have environmental awareness in protecting one's own personal safety when giving care and treatment, (2) to protect the patient from further unnecessary injury and (3), to protect the healthcare professional from any legal consequences if the patient suffers harm due to treatment not being given to them (Dimond, 2006; Heron, 2009 and Jackson, 2009).

As stated previously in this book, in the renowned case of *Schloendorff v Society of New York Hospital (1914 at paragraph 126),* Justice Benjamin Cardozo, famously stated, a competent adult has a right '...to determine what shall be done with his own body...' This implies that consent is at the heart of medical law and any attempt to perform a medical procedure without consent, in any environment, could result in a negligent act (Dimond, 2006) or the tort of battery and a criminal assault (Davies, 1998). This was later endorsed in *Re MB (1997) (An Adult: Medical Treatment at paragraph 549) (Re MB)* by Lady Butler-Sloss when she stated that 'A mentally competent patient has an absolute right to refuse to consent to medical treatment for any reason, rational or irrational, or for no reason at all, even where that decision may lead to his or her own death'. This fundamental principle is subsequently reflected by the General Medical Council's (GMC) *Good Medical Practice* (2006 at page 2) and the Nursing Midwifery Council's (NMC), *The Code* (2008) professional obligations when they emphasise the importance of gaining consent from a patient prior to performing any care or treatment on them.

Apart from a hostile operational environment, where it was recently determined by the Supreme Court that fundamental human rights are different compared to soldiers not in combat, *(R (on the application of Smith) v Secretary of State for Defence, 2010),* the Mental Capacity Act 2005 and the common law is clear; that it is never permissible to give treatment to a competent patient without their consent (Heron, 2009). In addition, the common law is explicit about what gaining consent from a patient before performing any care or treatment involves (Jackson, 2009). This is (1) determination of the patient's capacity, (2) whether they voluntarily agree to the treatment and (3) if they have made an informed choice towards the treatment proposed. However, as will be discussed in this chapter, section 2(1) of the Mental Capacity Act 2005 also refers to situations where a person lacks capacity to consent to treatment themselves and section 3 of this Act where they also lack the ability to make a decision for themselves.

The following vignette referred to throughout this chapter gives a realistic account of the difficulties of obtaining lawful consent from a patient when their capacity to consent to medical treatment is questionable and where there is a dual loyalty conflict.

Vignette

A military helicopter carrying a senior officer to a military base inside hostile enemy territory crashes in the desert, 30 kilometres from the nearest military hospital. When the medical helicopter arrives with the emergency surgical team to give medical assistance, Major Scott the military healthcare professional on board, discovers that the pilot is dead.

Brigadier Peel, the senior officer, is badly wounded and in severe pain. He is also starting to go into shock as a result of bleeding profusely from his partially traumatic amputated left leg that is trapped under metalwork. He is, however, conscious. Major Scott immediately triages Brigadier Peel. He then places a tourniquet around his left leg to stop catastrophic bleeding and gives him an injection of Morphine to ease the pain. Major Scott, at the scene, judges that unless the leg is amputated completely, Brigadier Peel will die before he can be moved. As Brigadier Peel remains conscious, Major Scott explains to him that he must amputate the remaining part of his leg so that he will survive. He also explains to the Brigadier that an anaesthetist is present as a member of the emergency surgical team to anaesthetise him. However, Brigadier Peel says he would rather die before losing his leg, and therefore he refuses to consent to the procedure. Instead, as the more senior officer, he orders Major Scott to leave him to die in the desert. Major Scott informs the Brigadier that he has to act quickly because they are located in an area that is susceptible to enemy attack at anytime, and his injury is serious. The Brigadier, who is now slightly drowsy due to the Morphine, mutters incoherently to Major Scott asking him to leave him alone.

Major Scott is unsure what to do. He is aware that Brigadier Peel is a 50 year-old happily married man with two teenage children, and has been verbally expressing how much he has been looking forward to seeing his family in a fortnight's time. However, through refusal to have the remaining part of his leg amputated, the Brigadier is highly likely to die. In addition, personnel from the helicopter are in danger from enemy attack if they remain in the area longer than is necessary. Major Scott has a professional duty to allow Brigadier Peel to make his own decisions regarding whether he accepts or refuses medical treatment. However, he also has a military duty to follow military orders from the Brigadier who is a senior officer. The need to make a decision becomes more pressing when the enemy are spotted nearby.

The vignette *does not* consider whether Major Scott decides if Brigadier Peel lives or dies *but* whether Brigadier Peel, himself, is legally competent to make that decision. Though this vignette this chapter therefore considers the following:

1.   Does Brigadier Peel have the capacity to consent to medical treatment?
2.   Does Brigadier Peel have the right to refuse medical treatment?
3.   What is Major Scott's professional duty to Brigadier Peel?

4.   In the circumstances, is Major Scott obliged to follow military orders and leave Brigadier Peel to die?

Discussion

Ordinarily, it is a doctor's responsibility to amputate a limb and not a nurse's; nonetheless, war has its own unique difficulties (Southby in Beam and Sparacino, 2003). In the absence of a doctor, it is, therefore, sometimes necessary for another healthcare professional to carry out a task to save a patient's life. War, thus, places an emphasis on soldiers, including MHCPs, to perform tasks that they would not normally undertake if in a civilian environment, where generally medical help is closer at hand (Gross, 2006; Kelly, 2010). During war it is, therefore, clear that the 'exigencies of battle pose unique challenges incomparable to the civilian context because of the scale of the threats to life, unpredictability, and the level of violence' (London et al, 2006 at page 385).

As explained in chapter 6, Edmund Howe's (2003) model enables a logical analysis of professional-military conflicts. The model suggests that MHCPs are governed by three role-specific ethics, which involves the person strictly following his or her specific role. These consist of (i) a military role-specific ethic, (ii) a medical role-specific ethic and (iii) a discretionary role-specific ethic.

Options

Using Howe's three-dimensional model, Major Scott is therefore faced with four options, i.e.

Option (1). Major Scott presumes that Brigadier Peel has the capacity to refuse medical treatment and therefore can be left to die.

Option (2). Major Scott considers that Brigadier Peel no longer has the ability i.e. legal capacity to make decisions for himself. Therefore, the order that Brigadier Peel has given Major Scott, telling him to leave him to die, is an order that Major Scott *does not* have to follow. In other words, the military order given is not valid. Accordingly, Major Scott can act in Brigadier Peel's 'best interests' and amputate the remaining part of his leg without gaining the Brigadier's consent.

Option (3). Major Scott considers that Brigadier Peel no longer has the capacity to make decisions for himself and, therefore, due to the hostile environment and the potential of being attacked at any time, it is acceptable for him to overtly persuade the Brigadier to allow him to amputate his leg.

Option (4). Major Scott must obey a military order from a senior military officer, as this overrides all other considerations. Consequently, he must, therefore, not amputate the remaining part of Brigadier Peel's leg, which will inevitably cause him to die.

Options (1) and (2)

Options (1) and (2), take a medical role specific ethic approach. Here, Major Scott follows professional codes of practice and legal obligations in making Brigadier Peel his first concern (GMC, *Good Medical Practice,* 2006, page 2 and the NMC, *The Code,* 2008*).* In addition, Major Scott assesses Brigadier Peel's ability to make his own decision regarding his care and treatment (GMC, *Good Medical Practice,* 2006, page 2, GMC, *Consent: patient and doctors making decisions together*, paragraph 64, page 27, the NMC, *The Code,* 2008 and the NMC, *Consent* [Advice Sheet], 2008).

With Options (1) and (2), the first issue is to determine if Brigadier Peel is competent to make a decision over his treatment, since in order for medical consent to be valid, the patient must be capable of making the decision to accept treatment (Tingle and Cribb, 2002). The Department of Health (2009, section 1, page 9) reaffirms the law by stating that for consent to be valid; it must be informed, given voluntarily and by a person who has the capacity to give consent. Therefore, a patient with capacity must be free to make his/her own choice over whether he/she wishes to receive medical treatment without any form of persuasion from health professionals and or relatives. Consent to medical treatment should be a choice made by the patient, without any persuasion from another person (Gillon, 1986). Further, according to the GMC (2008) and the NMC (*The Code,* 2008 at page 4 and *Consent* [Advice Sheet], 2008) patients need to be supported in making their own decision over the care they receive. Thus, if Major Scott finds that Brigadier Peel is competent, then Brigadier Peel has the absolute right to refuse to have the remaining part of his leg amputated (Heron, 2009).

A fundamental aspect here is clearly one of capacity. The test for capacity is via the Mental Capacity Act 2005, which came into force in October 2007. This Act protects and empowers vulnerable people who are not able to make their own decisions (Heron, 2009). It is enhanced by the Act's Code of Practice (2007), which mirrors the Act by providing practical guidance and a 'flexible framework' for healthcare professionals involved in the decision-making process with vulnerable people. Section 1(2) of the Mental Capacity Act 2005 states, 'A person must be assumed to have capacity unless it is **established [my emphasis]** that he lacks capacity'. This presumption of capacity is not contradicted by either the Armed Forces Discipline Act 2000 or the Armed Forces Act 2006 or the GMCs or NMCs professional codes of practice. Therefore, unless 'established' otherwise, Major Scott must presume that Brigadier Peel has the capacity to make his own decisions regarding his treatment.

Whilst Brigadier Peel is likely to die unless he has his leg amputated, in accordance with the Mental Capacity Act 2005, section 1(4) 'A person is not to be treated as unable to make a decision merely because he makes an unwise decision'. Thus, Major Scott cannot automatically assume that Brigadier Peel lacks capacity simply because he believes he is making an unwise decision in refusing treatment that will result in an adverse outcome i.e. death. The principle of refusing to consent to medical treatment was affirmed in *St George's Healthcare NHS Trust v S, R v Collins, and others, ex parte S (1998 at paragraph 686) (St George's)* when Dame Butler-Sloss stated, 'even when his or her own life depends on receiving medical treatment, an adult of sound mind is entitled to refuse it'. Equally, in *Re B (Adult, refusal of medical treatment) (2002),* the court determined that a competent patient has the right to refuse treatment and their refusal must be respected, even if it results in their death. In such circumstances, the needs, beliefs, and wishes of the patient must be taken into consideration and not ignored (Fullbrook, 2007). Thus, in following the principles of the Mental Capacity Act 2005 section 1(2) outlined above, Major Scott can presume that Brigadier Peel has the capacity to refuse medical treatment and can, therefore, be left to die.

However, before a definite decision can be made in presuming that Brigadier Peel has capacity, Major Scott may also need to consider Option 2. Section 2 of the Mental Capacity Act 2005 relates to 'People who lack capacity' and section 2(1) states that, 'a person lacks capacity in relation to a matter if at the material time he is unable to make a decision for himself in relation to the matter because of an impairment of, or a disturbance in the functioning of, the mind or brain'. A 'material time 'could be due to the Brigadier being given intramuscular Morphine. Although a maternity example, Brooks and Sullivan (2002), mention the difficulties of obtaining valid consent from a woman whilst in labour, due to labour pains, and who maybe suffering from the effects of opioid analgesia such as Diamorphine or Morphine, and inhalation analgesia, such as nitrous oxide. In *Re T (adult: refusal of treatment) (1992 at paragraph 662) (Re T),* Lord Donaldson recognised the difficulty that pain or drugs may have on a person's ability to make a decision themselves. He stated '...others who would normally have that capacity may be deprived of it or have it reduced by reason of temporary factors, such as unconsciousness or confusion or other effects of shock, severe fatigue, pain or drugs being used in their treatment...' thus suggesting that a person may temporarily lack capacity to make a decision themselves in certain circumstances.

This case law is now reflected in section 3 of the Mental Capacity Act 2005 when it relates to people who have an 'inability to make decisions. Section 3(1) of the Act states that, 'a person will be unable to make their own decisions if they are unable:

(a) To understand the information relevant to the decision,
(b) To retain that information,
(c) To use or weigh that information as part of the process of making the decision, or
(d) To communicate the decision (whether by talking, using sign language or any other means).'

Thus, via sections 2(1) and 3(1) of the Act, Major Scott needs to determine if Brigadier Peel lacks capacity and is unable to make a decision for himself. Earlier, in *Re MB (at paragraph 551)*, Dame Butler-Sloss maintained that a person is not capable of having capacity if they are unable to, '...understand or retain information material to the decision...' which they have been given. These principles are now reflected in the Mental Capacity Act 2005 and the practical implications in its corresponding Code of Practice. More recently, the Royal College of Obstetricians and Gynaecologists (RCOGs) have issued best practice advice for practitioners when obtaining consent from women in labour, when they, too, could be suffering from the effects of strong opioid analgesia or pain. They advise that 'Care must be taken when obtaining consent from women who are in labour', as they may not always be able to 'recall such previously presented information during' contractions (2008). In addition, the RCOGs have also issued advise for researchers by recommending that 'Care should be taken to gain informed recorded consent at the most appropriate time' (2010), meaning that obtaining consent during painful contractions or when any patient is in severe pain is inappropriate, as the patient is unlikely to have the ability to make a decision at that particular time.

Therefore, when considering if a patient has capacity to consent to medical treatment, in the context of the vignette, Brigadier Peel needs to show that he is able to understand the issues at stake including the risks so that he is overtly able to reach a decision that is informed (Fullbrook, 2007). In *Sidaway v Bethlem Royal Hospital Governors (1985) (Sidaway)*, the court determined that information given to the patient should be judged according to reasonable professional practice from the Bolam test (*Bolam v Friern Hospital Management, 1957) (Bolam)*. However, *Sidaway* did not mean that the patient had to be informed of every possible risk. The majority of their Lordships largely endorsed the traditional test of reasonableness voiced in the case of *Bolam* nearly thirty years earlier (Brazier and Cave, 2007). Four out of the five judges in this case rejected the transatlantic concept of 'informed consent'. Even Lord Scarman, the only judge who favoured the patient's right to know, stated that a doctor has 'therapeutic privilege' (*Sidaway at paragraph 655)* thereby, allowing a doctor after conducting a 'reasonable medical assessment' to withhold information from his patient if the disclosure posed a serious threat of psychological harm to the patient.' Similarly, in *Pearce v United Bristol Healthcare NHS Trust (1999)* a 0.1% to 0.2% risk of harm occurring to a mother in childbirth was not considered relevant. This case, therefore, emphasises that *not* every possible known risk of potential harm resulting from treatment has to be discussed with the patient.

In contrast, however, in *Chester v Afshar (2004)*, the courts adopted a trend of full disclosure to a patient of risks, when they held that even a small but unavoidable risk should be discussed with the patient. This suggests that the medical practice of disclosure from the ruling of *Sidaway*, twenty-five years earlier, has moved and that the contemporary accepted practice is full disclosure to patients of 'all known risks'. In the context of the vignette, it, therefore, suggests that Major Scott should have been more explicit in informing Brigadier Peel about his injury being life-threatening if not treated immediately.

The inherent difficulty for Major Scott within this scenario is that according to section 3(1) of the Mental Capacity Act 2005, Brigadier Peel's decision may appear to be a competent one. It could be assumed that Major Scott has fully informed Brigadier Peel of the seriousness of his condition and yet he still decides to refuse treatment. Therefore, it could be considered as an unwise decision in accordance with section 1(4) of the Act. Moreover, irrespective of being drowsy from Morphine, according to section 3(3) of the Act 'the fact that a person is able to retain the information relevant to a decision for a short period **does not** [my emphasis] prevent him from being regarded as able to make the decision'. This suggests that when a person is in severe pain, or is suffering from the effects of strong analgesia, their capacity fluctuates and, therefore, that person should not *wholly* be regarded as lacking capacity. As mentioned earlier, the RGOC (2010) offer advice to practitioners on gaining consent from the patient at the 'most appropriate time' and not when they are less likely to comprehend and understand information being given to them. Thus, as previously mentioned, the Mental Capacity Act 2005 is very protective towards vulnerable adults and has a significant impact on how healthcare professionals ensure vulnerable adults' rights are protected (Griffith and Tengnah, 2008). This is in contrast to previous situations before the Mental Capacity Act 2005 when patients were in severe pain. For example, the court determined in *Rochdale Healthcare (NHS) Trust v C (1997)* that a woman in the 'throes of labour' lacked capacity to make their own decisions, thus demonstrating that the law clearly did not protect her at that time.

However, the ultimate assessment of whether a person lacks capacity depends on the clinical opinion of the clinician treating the patient at the time (Walters, 2009). Thus, an indication to Major Scott that Brigadier Peel may not have the capacity to make the decision for himself is due to the Brigadier being in severe pain, going into shock and being given a strong analgesic such as Morphine, which has caused him to become drowsy. As previously stated, in *Re T (at paragraph 662)*, Lord Donaldson recognised the difficulty of assessing capacity when a patient is normally able to make his/her own decisions. In such circumstances, it may be, therefore, be legitimate for Major Scott to determine that Brigadier Peel lacks capacity to make a decision for himself. This view would be supported by the Mental Capacity Act 2005, section 1(3), where it states that 'a person is not to be treated as unable to make a decision unless all practicable steps to help him do so have been taken without success'. Accordingly, Major Scott may argue that he has taken all the steps he possibly can, without success, in trying to persuade the Brigadier to allow him to amputate his leg. In addition, given the fact that the Brigadier has verbally been expressing how much he has been looking forward to returning home to his family, he may believe that the Brigadier is making a decision that is out of character, and he does not genuinely want to die. When a person appears to be making an irrational decision that seems to be out of character, his/her capacity can be questionable and a decision can be made in their 'best interests' without any undue influence (McHale, 2009).

Although in *Re F (a mental patient: sterilisation, 1989)* it was asserted that another person cannot consent on their behalf, section 5 (1) of the Mental Capacity Act 2005, states that if a doctor, having taken reasonable steps to ascertain that the patient lacks capacity to consent, nonetheless *may* give treatment to a patient, if via section 4, it is in the patient's 'best interests'. 'Best interests' assumes a discretionary role ethic, since it allows Major Scott to decide for himself the best course of action, given the circumstances (Howe, 2003 at page 335). In addition, 'best interests' should take into account what the patient's previous wishes and desires would be if they became unable to make a decision for themselves at a later date (Mental Capacity Act 2005, section 4).

'Best interests' in health necessitates the healthcare professional reaching the required 'standard objectives of healthcare practice' (Keown and Gormally, 1999 at page 11). Although the Mental Capacity Act 2005 does not define 'best interests' in section 4 (6) (a), (b) and (c) it states that, 'He [i.e. the medical practitioner] must consider, so far as reasonably ascertainable - (a) the person's past and present wishes and feelings, (b) the beliefs and values that would be likely to influence his decision if he had capacity and (c) the other factors that he would be likely to consider if he were able to do so. The NMC (*The Code, 2008 at paragraph 17, page 4*) states to ensure valid consent, 'you must be able to demonstrate that you have acted in someone's best interest if you have provided care in an emergency'. The GMC (*Consent: patient and doctors making decisions together, 2008 at paragraphs 62-76*) gives similar guidance. The case of *Re MB (at paragraph 555)* also emphasised that 'best interests' can also relate to fluctuating or temporary incapacity. Therefore, as long as 'best interests' is the patient's 'best interests', and not the wishes of the doctor, this provides a defence against a battery and should reduce any ethical dilemmas for healthcare professionals, such as Major Scott in the vignette (Palmer and Iverson, 1997). Major Scott may, therefore, determine that Brigadier Peel lacks capacity to consent for himself and, therefore, he can act in the Brigadier's 'best interests' and amputate his leg.

Option 3

Despite the notion of an unwise decision and 'best interests', which highlights the complexities of the decision making process for MHCPs in this type of situation, irrespective of whether they are a military nurse or doctor, in contrast to options (1) and (2), which are patient focused, Option (3) concerns undue influence by a healthcare professional over their patient. In the vignette, this would be that Major Scott assumes that Brigadier Peel no longer has the capacity to make decisions for himself and, therefore, he overtly attempts to persuade the Brigadier to allow him to amputate his leg. Lord Scott in *Bowater v Rowley Regis Corporation (1944 at paragraph 480)* stated that voluntariness is the ability of a person to '...choose freely...' In *R (Burke) (2005),* a competent patient's wishes must be respected in that they can refuse to accept medical treatment. Therefore, if Major Scott is the right person to determine that the Brigadier is competent at that particular time, then the Brigadier himself should be free to make his own choice over whether he wishes to receive medical treatment without any form of persuasion from Major Scott.

Persuasion was considered in *Re T (at paragraph 662)*, by Lord Donaldson when he highlighted a 'vitiating effect of outside influence by a third party'. His Lordship remarked that unique situations can occur and difficulties can arise for patients when they are persuaded by a third party, to such an extent that their ability to make an individual decision is overborne by the dominance of that party. His Lordship also stated whether in such a circumstance, 'the patient really means what he says, or is he merely saying it for a quiet life, to satisfy someone else' *(Re T at paragraph 663)*. If this situation were to occur, His Lordship further indicated that this could cause the patient's evidence to be manipulated, which would be in contrast to the common law standards regarding the legal principles of valid consent, and may consequently invalidate a patient's consent to medical treatment.

Choice and consent without persuasion clearly promote the concept of voluntariness, which in turn coalesces with the principle of self-determination. The Human Rights Act 1998 states that all persons have the right to self-determination and can refuse medical treatment. Article 3 states that 'No one shall be subjected to inhuman or degrading treatment (Article 3 of the Human Rights Act 1998). Moreover, in *Airedale NHS Trust v Bland, (1993 at paragrapgh 866)*, it was declared that 'the principle of the sanctity of human life must yield to the principle of self-determination'. Therefore, as stated by Lord Goff in *Re F (A Mental Patient: Sterilisation) 1989 at paragraph 564)* that 'every person's body is inviolate'; it remains unlawful, both in civil and in criminal law to force treatment upon a competent adult person (this includes a soldier) against their will. To do so, would be a battery in tort *(Scott v Shepherd, 1558-1774; Stanley v Powell, 1891; Letang v Cooper, 1965* and *Miller v Jackson, 1977)*. Hence, Brigadier Peel's *body* should not be violated through forced acceptance of treatment against his will, even *if* he could die as a consequence, since he has the right to refuse treatment *if* he has the competence to make that decision *(St George's, 1998 at paragraph 686)*.

In spite of the clear authority from case law, a further difficulty for Major Scott is that he is treating the Brigadier in hostile territory. As a consequence of the environment, Major Scott's life and his fellow soldiers' lives are at risk due to the delay in the Brigadier refusing medical treatment. It may, therefore be entirely acceptable for Major Scott to exert some undue influence over the Brigadier. Although Major Scott has other MHCPs to assist him, as explained in chapters 7, 9 and 10, he is, nonetheless, detached from traditional support mechanisms that are normally present in a civilian healthcare environment (Southby in Beam and Sparacino, 2003 at page 663). In addition, although not in a battlefield, he remains in an environment and at a location that is hostile and dangerous, and where they could be attacked at any time (Kligman and Kupermintz, 1994). Therefore, although it would be unlawful and ordinarily unethical for Major Scott to exert any undue influence over the Brigadier; however, given the circumstances of the environment, in ethical terms it may be reasonable and understandable. When ethics and law conflict, another person's rights that may be affected by a patient's decision may also need to be taken into consideration (Minkoff and Marshall, 2009). In such circumstances, the GMC (*Good Medical Practice,* 2006) and the NMC (*The Code,* 2008 at page 6) both advise that a healthcare professional must act without delay if they believe that they or a colleague maybe at risk. Therefore, in the context of the vignette, it may be ethical to exert undue influence over Brigadier Peel. However, it is accepted that this action may be morally repugnant to other health professionals working in a less hostile environment, as it would contradict the principles of healthcare ethics (Crowe and Hardil, 1991).

Option 4

The remaining option that Major Scott can consider is Option (4), which takes a military role-specific. Here, Major Scott believes that following military orders from a senior military officer overrides all other considerations and, therefore, he must leave Brigadier Peel to die as ordered. As previously discussed in chapter 4, this is underpinned by the notion that military personnel, including MHCPs, must be disciplined, and unquestionably obedient to military orders (Altun, 2008). Moreover, discipline is the 'backbone' that promotes efficiency in the Armed Forces and involves all military personnel following military orders (Soldier Management, A *Guide for Commanders*, 2004 at page 48). Accordingly, if Major Scott does not follow Brigadier Peel's orders then he may be guilty of 'Misconduct on operations' as section 2(3) of the Armed Forces Act 2006 states, 'A person...commits an offence if he fails to use his utmost exertions to carry out the lawful commands of his superiors officers'. In taking this option, Major Scott would be more influenced by the need to follow the military's organisational cultural and social expectations in obeying orders, rather than making his patient his first concern and following codes of practice (Farsides in Tingle and Crimm, 2002; GMC, *Good Medical Practice,* 2006, page 2 and the NMC, *The Code, 2008).*

However, in the context of a military role specific-ethic from the vignette, it is questionable whether Major Scott, in actuality, would follow military orders and leave Brigadier Peel behind to die, as it is acknowledged that all soldiers have an overwhelming desire to protect each other (London et al, 2006). In addition, soldiers are considered as family to one another (Nichol and Rennell, 2009), and have an unwritten code not to leave any comrade behind (Rubel, 2004). Hence, disobedience in this context could be seen as a mark of professional integrity and not a sign of an 'incipient military coup' or insubordination (Wolfendale, 2009).

In conclusion, although all military healthcare professionals have a 'dual loyalty conflict' between following military orders and professional codes of practice (Clark, 2006) in the context of the vignette, it seems unlikely that following Option (4) and Howe's military role-specific ethic would take precedence over following professional codes of practice (Howe, 2003). This is even when disobeying military orders could be seen as insubordinate (Armed Forces Act 2006, section 2(3)). It is also unlikely that Major Scott would follow Option (1) and presume that Brigadier Peel has the capacity to refuse medical treatment and, therefore, can be left to die. This is because in emergencies, patients are *less likely* to be able to comprehend the information given to them in order for the healthcare professional to obtain valid informed consent (Agerd et al, 2004). However, this does not imply that a patient can never make an autonomous decision in an emergency as a patient continues to have their 'right of self-determination' *(St George's, 1998 at paragraph 686).* Instead, it means that it is more challenging for a patient to be *fully* autonomous as their capacity to make their own decisions may be more questionable *(Sidaway v Bethlem Royal Hospital Governors, 1985).*

Consent to medical treatment is a voluntary decision made by a person who, having been given the necessary and relevant information, is able to make an informed choice over whether to accept or reject the treatment that will affect him (Gillon, 1986). Therefore, in the context of the vignette, it is more likely, however, that Major Scott would follow Option (2), and act in Brigadier Peel's 'best interests' by amputating the remaining part of his leg. Although consent must be free from any duress or coercion, must be given voluntarily and must acknowledge patient autonomy (Paterick et al, 2008), given the dangerous environment and the risk to Major Scott's safety, there is a possibility that Major Scott may instead follow Option (3). This is where he would exert some undue influence over the Brigadier regarding the necessity to proceed with this emergency treatment, thus compromising the Brigadier's right to refuse medical treatment. Accordingly, although healthcare ethics can often yield to the 'acquiescence to military demands,' in the circumstances of the vignette, this chapter has shown that dual loyalty conflict is unlikely to be problematic for Major Scott (London et al, 2006).

A version of this chapter appeared in the Nursing Ethics journal: Kelly, J (2010) Operational conditions: Legal capacity of a patient soldier refusing medical treatment, *Nurs Ethics,* 18(6) pp. 825-834.

CHAPTER TWELVE

NON-OPERATIONAL CONDITIONS: PATIENT-SOLDIER CONFIDENTIALITY AND REFUSAL OF MEDICAL TREATMENT

Introduction

This final vignette considers the ethical tensions and the dual loyalty conflict between following military orders and professional codes of conduct, concerning **medical confidentiality** of a **competent patient-soldier refusing medical treatment** in a **non-operational environment.** In the context of a vignette, this chapter suggests that dual loyalty conflict in military healthcare practice in a non-operational environment is best managed via a discretionary ethic-role (Howe, 2003 at pages 333-334). This then allows independent clinical judgment, whilst at the same time minimising ethical dilemmas, harm, and conflict to a third party, such as a military commander (Williams, 2009a). The vignette places the law in the context of a military non-operational environment (Hughes and Huby, 2002 and Williams, 2009a); this chapter also explains the law relating to refusal of medical treatment in a different context than that in chapter 11, and patient confidentiality.

In healthcare, dual loyalty occurs where the clinical role conflicts between the personal interest of the patient and the duty to another, such as an employer (World Medical Association, 2009). As mentioned in chapters 5 and 10, 'moral obligations are beyond those incumbent on many other members of society' especially Military HealthCare Professionals (MHCPs) (Benetar and Upshur, 2008). Therefore, for the MHCP, these simultaneous obligations create inevitable ethical tensions and conflict (Rascona, 2007 and Dual Loyalty and Human Rights in Health Professional Practice Report, 2002) and, on occasions, professional compromise (London et al 2006), as they need to balance the conflict between patient care and obeying military orders. For example, in the British Armed Forces, the Ministry of Defence (MoD) states that medical treatment must be within the 'constraints of Armed Forces medical policy' and medical needs must be subjected to 'military and professional constraints' (Joint Doctrine Publication, 2007 at paragraph 1A6, page 1A2). As mentioned previously in each of the vignettes, this therefore, emphasises a need for a MHCP to balance the medical needs of his/her patient with his/her military duty (Clark, 2006). It also limits how a MHCP can practise their healthcare profession in the military. On the contrary, however, the MoD also states that it recognises that 'medical judgment and ethics' cannot be ignored and compromised (Joint Doctrine Publication, 2007 at paragraph 1A6, page 1A2). Although not a military document, this view is shared by the Dual Loyalty and Human Rights in Health Professional Practice Report (2006), which summarised that the 'overruling identity and priority' of a MHCP should be 'that of a health professional', as the patient's clinical needs are sacrosanct (Annas, 2008 at page 1087).

Vignette

Sergeant Green is a serving Non-Commissioned Officer in the Coldstream Guards. He has been in the army for twenty years. He has experience of numerous operational deployments having served in Northern Ireland, the Balkans, Iraq, and more recently Afghanistan. In his last operational tour, eighteen months ago, he witnessed several of his comrades being killed and maimed by local insurgents during fire fights. His military General Practitioner, Major Smith, (a senior officer) has just recently diagnosed him with Post Traumatic Stress Disorder (PTSD) as a result of severe traumatic experiences. Major Smith recommends that he immediately start treatment to overcome this psychological illness with a military Clinical Psychologist. Sergeant Green is otherwise a fit, healthy, and competent adult.

As Sergeant Green is due to return to Afghanistan in six-weeks time, for a six-month tour, he refuses Major Smith's offer of treatment. He is worried about his future career in the army, since, if he starts treatment, he will not be able to deploy back to Afghanistan with his comrades and is unlikely to be promoted to the next rank. For the same reasons, Sergeant Green will not give Major Smith his consent to disclose his illness to his Commanding Officer (CO), a Lieutenant-Colonel. Major Smith however, has a military obligation to inform Sergeant Green's CO that he is currently unfit to deploy. However, as it will leave the CO without an experienced soldier on the operational tour, it is inevitable that the CO will want to know the exact reasons why Sergeant Green cannot deploy.

In Major Smith's medical opinion, Sergeant Green is not currently medically fit to return to Afghanistan but with his refusal to accept treatment and without his consent to disclose his illness to his CO, he is uncertain what to do. He has a professional duty to maintain Sergeant Green's confidentiality but also a military obligation to follow military orders in only allowing soldiers to deploy on operations if they are medically fit. He is also concerned if that the CO, as a higher-ranking officer, demands to know the reason why Sergeant Green cannot deploy. Major Smith is therefore concerned about possibly breaching Sergeant Green's confidentiality

By using this vignette this chapter considers the following:

1)   Does Sergeant Green have the right to refuse medical treatment?
2)   What is the duty of confidence expected by Major Smith to Sergeant Green in a non-operational environment?
3)   Does Major Smith have a legal and ethical responsibility to inform the CO of Sergeant Green's psychological illness?
4)   When there is a dual loyalty conflict between either following professional codes of conduct or military orders concerning a patient suffering from Post Traumatic Stress Disorder, what is the best solution and what is the most appropriate way to deal with this problem?

Discussion

Although not an absolute duty, the duty to safeguard medical confidentiality arises from the ethical principle of beneficence (Plambeck, 2002). However, despite soldiers subverting many of their rights in the military such as freedom of expression and speech, it remains questionable if soldiers should also subvert their healthcare rights and MHCPs should undermine their own professional autonomy (Visser, 2003). As explained in chapter 4, British service personnel are subjected to the domestic law of the country they are serving in and British military law. This is so that British service personnel are treated fairly and consistently wherever they are serving in the world (Joint Doctrine Publication, 2007 at paragraph 110). Therefore, in consideration of whether Sergeant Green could refuse the offer of medical treatment, as explained in chapter 11, guidance can be sought from Justice Benjamin Cardozo in *Schloendorff v Society of New York Hospital* (*1914 at paragraph 126*) when he famously stated that a competent adult has a right '...to determine what shall be done with his own body...' Furthermore, in English law, unless declared otherwise by a medical practitioner and as long as the patient is of 'sound mind', a competent adult is presumed to have the capacity to consent and refuse medical treatment (Mental Capacity Act 2005 ch. 9, part 1). As outlined previously in chapter 11, this is even if it that decision is considered as eccentric and the patient could die (*St George's Healthcare NHS Trust v S, R v Collins, and others, ex parte S (1998 at paragraph 174) (St George's)*. Moreover, in *Re C (Adult, refusal of treatment)(1994)* the court determined that even if a patient has a mental or psychological illness and decides to refuse medical treatment, it does not automatically call into question their capacity to make their own decisions. The General Medical Council's (GMC) *Consent Guidance* (2008) further outlines the presumption of capacity. Thus, in following the law, it therefore appears that Sergeant Green is able to refuse medical treatment for his PTSD. Being in the military and having a psychological illness does not prevent Sergeant Green from making his own decisions regarding acceptance of medical treatment (Mental Health Acts 1983 and 2007 and GMC, *Guidance of Doctors,* 2008 at paragraph 64, page 27).

The practical significance of being able to refuse treatment is that it enables a patient to have trust and confidence in their healthcare practitioner (Dimond, 2003). It also helps to maintain a successful professional relationship (GMC, *Good Medical Practice, 2008)*. In further consideration of whether if it is right for Major Smith to allow Sergeant Green to refuse medical treatment, the World Medical Association (WMA), Declaration of Geneva' (1948) stated, 'the health of my patient will be my first consideration'. I will not use my medical knowledge to violate human rights and civil liberties, even under threat'. Moreover, the WMA International Code of Medical Ethics stated, 'A physician shall be dedicated to providing competent medical service in full professional and moral independence with compassion and respect for human dignity' (1949). Accordingly, in adhering to the law and ethical principles, Major Smith must allow Sergeant Green as a competent adult to refuse medical treatment (*St George's* and *Re C (Adult, refusal of treatment), 1994)*.

The difficulty for Major Smith, however is that in the context of the vignette the refusal of medical treatment, is intrinsically linked into whether Major Smith should respect Sergeant Green's confidentiality (Carey, 2009). As such, Major Smith should warn Sergeant Green about the dangers of refusing to consent to treatment (GMC, *Confidentiality,* 2009) and the possibilities or any perceived military repercussions in doing so. The legal basis for protecting confidential information was examined in *Campbell v MGN (2004)*. This case considered the necessity to balance the right for **confidential information** to be protected with the right of **freedom of expression**. Article 8 of the ECHR protects confidential information whereas Article 10 of the ECHR protects freedom of expression, which clearly indicates that both rights conflict with one another. In *Campbell v MGN at paragraph 1012)*, Lord Hoffman concluded that '… [B]oth reflect important civilised values, but, as often happens, neither can be given effect in full measure without restricting the other…' Protecting a patient's medical data is also important as was emphasised from the case of *MS v Sweden (1999 at paragraph 41)* where the court stated that 'respecting the confidentiality of health data is a vital principle' so as to 'preserve his or her confidence in the medical profession and in the health service in general', This case further emphasises the importance of healthcare professionals not disclosing patient information unnecessarily to any other person not concerned with the patient's care (Nursing Midwifery Council, *Confidentiality Guidance Sheet*, 2009).

A significant and additional difficulty for Major Smith is that confidentiality may have to override other considerations that a doctor may have. This is because although Sergeant Green *must* be Major Smith's first concern before any other consideration (General Medical Council, 2006 and Nursing Midwifery Council, *The Code, 2008)*, which ordinarily in a civilian context would give him no other option in which way to act; as emphasised in chapter 4, on the importance of military discipline, Major Smith also has a military duty to follow military orders in only allowing fit soldiers to deploy. In the interest of the military, informing the CO of the soldier's condition may override that of maintaining the patient's confidentiality. The refusal of medical treatment however, makes it difficult for Major Smith to justify without breaching confidentiality to the CO the reason why this soldier cannot deploy. The CO as a senior officer may order Major Smith to tell him why Sergeant Green cannot deploy. As illustrated in chapter 4, following military orders and adhering to military discipline is the 'backbone' that promotes efficiency in the Armed Forces' (Soldier Management, 2004). As further illustrated in chapter 4, Murray (1921) describes following military orders as, '…the long-continued habit by which the very muscles of the soldier instinctively obeys the command; even if his mind is too confused to attend, yet his muscles will obey'. However, although military orders and discipline are evidently necessary, in the context of the vignette they become an almost a metaphorical physical impediment for Major Smith in deciding what course of action to take. This is because although confidentiality is a professional core value, it appears to be in conflict with the military core value of obeying orders (Kipnis, 2006).

As explained in chapters 7 and 11, solving ethical problems is easier than attempting to solve an ethical dilemma where one party is likely to be aggrieved of the decision that is made (Tschudin, 1992). As further explained in chapters 7 and 11, when there is a conflict in determining the correct action, ethical problems should be divided between ethical dilemmas and tests of integrity (Coleman, 2009). There are several options to choose from when faced with an ethical dilemma and a person can therefore have difficulty in deciding what the correct option is to take. With a test of integrity however, it is obvious what the correct option is, since the distinction between bad options and good options is clear. A more exact way of dealing with a situation when there is dual loyalty conflict between following professionals codes and military orders is given by Edmund Howe military model (2003) that is explained in chapter 6 and has been utilised in the vignettes of chapter 10 and 11. Using Howe's three-dimensional model, Major Smith is therefore faced with three options.

Option 1 Medical role-specific ethic

With a **medical role-specific ethic,** Major Smith would follow professional codes of practice and legal obligations and would make Sergeant Green as his patient, his first concern (Howe, 2003 and General Medical Council, 2006). He therefore would give him is undivided attention (Rubenstien, 2003). He would also respect Sergeant Green's confidentiality. Patient confidentiality arose from the Hippocratic Oath in the 4th century BC. It is now enshrined in the Declaration of Geneva where it states a physician will 'respect the secrets which are confided in me, even after the patient has died' (Declaration of Geneva, 1948). The GMC (*Good Medical Practice, Confidentiality,* 2009 at paragraph 6, page 6) also states that 'confidentiality is central to trust between doctors and patients' and that those patients have a right for their confidential medical information to be respected. This further emphasises that there must be trust and an understanding about what passes between the doctor and the patient. The NMC (*Confidentiality Guidance Sheet,* 2009) also emphasises the importance of maintaining patient confidentiality for a trustful relationship between healthcare practitioner and patient.

The difficulty however, in following a medical role-specific ethic is that although Major Smith would be practising clinical independence it would increase the tensions of the dual loyalty conflict (Williams, 2009a). This is because professional obligations that make the patient his sole concern (General Medical Council's *Good Medical Practice, Confidentiality,*

2009), which prevent him from breaching Sergeant Green's confidentiality to the CO could conflict with lawful military orders if he has to inform the CO about Sergeant's Green's condition (Howe, 2003). In such circumstances, if Major Smith decided to maintain Sergeant Green's confidentiality before military orders, he would therefore be taking an absolutist approach, as he would consider that his professional responsibility to Sergeant Green is his **first** and **only** concern above everything else (Army Doctrine Publication, 2000). As mentioned in chapter 10, Wolfendale (2009) would consider an absolutist approach, a mark of professional integrity and not military insubordination. Equally, Kipnis (2006) would assert that absolute confidentiality without any disclosure to a third party not involved with the patient's care and treatment is the only way to solely respect a patient's medical privacy.

However, although Major Smith's actions would demonstrate that confidentiality is necessary to maintain patient and professional autonomy and privacy irrespective of the environment, the effect of him taking this approach is that he fails to consider the military consequences of his actions. Hence, his failure to inform the CO why he cannot deploy may be perceived as military insubordination. Consequently, whilst Major Smith may be acting legally and ethically in one sense in upholding Sergeant Green's confidentiality, militarily he would be compromising legality and acting unethically (Yeo, 1989). In addition, in taking a medical role-specific ethic, it is also unlikely that he would allow Sergeant Green to deploy because irrespective of respecting his confidentiality, this soldier would still be medically unfit to deploy on an operational tour. Therefore, it seems likely that approach would not be the best one to take.

Option 2 Military role-specific ethic

In contrast, Major Smith may decide to follow a **military role-specific ethic**, which would dictate that MHCPs should follow military orders above everything else (Army Doctrine Publication, 2007). This approach renders Sergeant Green's healthcare needs and his confidentiality secondary to the military need. This may seem unlikely and unethical to a civilian doctor but as explained in chapter 7, in the military, although a doctor has the same degree of legal and ethical responsibility to their patients, these problems are more complex and there may be in certain circumstances, a need to place the military interest above the patient's interest (Benetar and Upshur, 2008; Kelly 2010). For example, to disclose medical information to another person to prevent an ill soldier from deploying on operational tour or within a battlefield may seem to be a reasonable action to a military doctor.

It is therefore clear that preserving patient confidentiality in the military is potentially problematic. Rogers (2006) argues that preserving confidentiality in any situation is complex since sharing information to treat and protect the patient and others from harm, often results in the widespread disclosure of personal information. As the vignette demonstrates, maintaining confidentiality becomes more challenging in the military since a caveat of a soldier voluntarily joining this type of disciplined organisation is that are aware that they will lose some of their personal autonomy in doing so (Visser, 2003). Thus, achieving medical confidentiality can be essentially flawed from the first time a patient and in particular, a military patient seeks medical treatment through their conscious decision to reveal their problem to the physician (Kipnis, 2006). Accordingly, Major Smith's actions in disclosing Sergeant Smith's PTSD to his CO may seem to be a reasonable action and justifiable. Sergeant Smith's plans to deploy on his forth-coming operational tour could not only be problematic to himself, they may also cause harm to his colleagues particularly if his symptoms were exacerbated by the operational environment (The Royal College of Psychiatrists, 2010). Therefore, under a military role-specific ethic, Major Smith would breach Sergeant's confidentiality and disclose the medical reasons why this soldier cannot deploy. It is accepted however, that this position is juxtaposed to the principles of maintaining confidentiality and may be regarded as morally repugnant to other civilian healthcare professionals (Crowe and Hardil, 1991). Professionally, such a disclosure would ordinarily in a civilian environment almost certainly lead to fitness to practise proceedings as an unjustified breach of confidentiality (GMC, *Good Medical Practice, Confidentiality,* 2009).

Option 3 Discretionary role-ethic.

It is obvious therefore; that there is no clear-cut way to deal with the problem faced by Major Smith regarding patient confidentiality. Ethical dilemmas concerning patient confidentiality are complex (Beech, 2007). However, in contrast to the medical and military role-specific ethical approaches, an alternative and superior decision could be a **discretionary role-ethic.** This role would allow Major Smith to carefully consider and determine when and whether the needs of the military are absolute (Howe, 2003 at pages 333-334). As explained in chapters 9 and 10, whilst this role is unlikely to be appropriate in a combat situation because military doctors are not military tacticians and lack the military skills and knowledge to make the best choice, where these choices are more complicated and decisions have to be made quickly (Howe, 2003 at pages 333-334); during peacetime, ethical challenges are less pressing (Simmons and Rycraft, 2010). Major Smith would also be making a decision in an environment that is safer and more familiar to him than that of a combat situation (Simmons and Rycraft, 2010). Therefore, using a discretionary role-ethic, Major Smith would still not allow Sergeant Green to deploy. Major Smith would still disclose Sergeant Green's PTSD to the CO however, unlike the military role-specific ethic; this would be for *medical reasons in the interests of the public* and *not* military reasons. Major Smith would still therefore follow a universal principle in that *professional responsibility* overrides all other considerations (Benetar and Upshur, 2008).

Whilst it might remain unacceptable to Sergeant Green for Major Smith to disclose his PTSD to his CO, nonetheless using a discretionary role-ethic has three advantages:

Firstly, Major Smith is acting professionally both to the public (see *Tarasoff v Regents of the University of California, 1976)* and his patient. He is being caring to Sergeant Green by making him his first concern (General Medical Council. *Good Medical Practice, 2006* at page 2). Furthermore, his actions are allowing for the principles of patient and professional autonomy to be respected (Seedhouse, 2001). Moreover, he is being beneficent to his patient, which is the core of medical confidentiality (Plambeck, 2002) and non-maleficent to the CO as a third party (Williams, 2009a). He is also placing accountability and responsibility to Sergeant Green's healthcare needs above all other considerations, which is more legitimate and ethical than following the orders of a powerful military individual such as a CO (Benatar and Upshur, 2008).

Thus, despite Sergeant Green refusing the offer of medical treatment from a Clinical Psychologist, Major Smith's actions are justified because it is unlikely that Sergeant Green's symptoms of PTSD will improve without treatment (NHS National Institute for Clinical Excellence, 2005). Furthermore, if deployed on an operational tour where his life and others could be at risk from enemy attacks, these symptoms may exacerbate, which in turn could potentially be harmful to himself and others if put under added stress (Sayer et al 2009; Feczer and Bjorklund, 2009). Moreover, it is more difficult to remove a soldier suffering from psychological trauma symptoms once deployed on an operational tour as liaising with the soldier's CO to have him sent back home becomes more challenging (Simmons and Rycraft, 2010). This is because a CO has many priorities and needs all the available manpower he can gather together as the evacuation of a soldier from the frontline severely depletes manpower since, it takes a fit soldier to remove an injured one (Gross, 2006). This therefore emphasises the need for MHCPs to disclose information where a patient's and other people lives could be at risk from harm before deployment (Castledine, 2010). Thus, in reaching this decision, Major Smith would have balanced the advantages and disadvantages of divulging Sergeant Green's condition to his CO with the 'level of risk at hand' (Gibson, 2006).

Secondly, confidentiality is not an absolute right and disclosure of confidential information without consent in the public interest is lawful in certain circumstances such as misconduct, illegality and gross immorality (NMC, *Confidentiality Guidance Sheet*, 2009). This was explained in *W v Egdell (1990),* where the court determined that confidentiality could be breached when it is justifiable to do so if there is the threat of serious harm to others. However, such a disclosure must only be made to the person it was intended for and not to anyone else. Thus, Major Smith should only inform Sergeant Green's CO and no one else that Sergeant Green is unfit to deploy due to PTSD. In addition, Major Smith should inform Sergeant Green that he is disclosing the information to his CO in relation to a public interest and that his reasons for disclosure will be documented in his notes (GMC, *Good Medical Practice, Confidentiality,* 2009).

The duty of confidence is thus a qualified right meaning that in certain circumstances, the law may permit Major Smith to disclose personal information about Sergeant Green if it is in the public interest to do so (McHale, 2009). For example, the GMC state personal information of a patient can be disclosed to a third party if the 'benefits to an individual or to society of the disclosure outweigh both the public and the patient's interest in keeping the information confidential' (*Good Medical Practice, Confidentiality,* 2009 at paragraph 37, page 16). Thus, it may be reasonable to Major Smith that disclosing Sergeant Green's confidentiality to his CO to prevent him deploying is justifiable. This is because it would be illegal for him as a doctor to knowingly allow a soldier to deploy on a dangerous operational tour when he is medically unfit to do so (*Tarasoff v Regents of the University of California,* 1976).

Thirdly, by Major Smith explaining to the CO the reasons why Sergeant Green cannot deploy, it minimises further potential harm to Sergeant Green if his symptoms exacerbate in a harsh environment where medical expertise from a Clinical Psychologist is less likely to be available (Simmons and Rycraft, 2010). While this may be unacceptable to

Sergeant Green, healthcare professionals should do everything they can to protect their patients from further harm (Williams, 2009b). In addition, being open and transparent to the CO, in giving him the medical reasons why Sergeant Green cannot deploy, it makes the ethical dilemma seem less problematic for Major Smith. This is because it also provides a framework to manage the dual loyalty conflict more smoothly rather than creating further tension in not giving any explanation to the CO (Annas, 2008). In addition, although Sergeant Green will not deploy and the COs manpower will be depleted, the COs interests will be met since it will prevent a psychologically unfit soldier to embark on a dangerous operational tour (Benetar and Upshur, 2008). Further, at the same time as advocating Sergeant Green's medical needs, Major Smith is also effectively communicating to the CO to avoid any negative interaction between the parties that dual loyalty can sometimes create without dialogue (Williams, 2009a). It thus prevents any undue influence from the CO as a more senior officer in ordering Major Smith to divulge personal information about Sergeant Green (Wynia, 2007). Moreover, Major Smith's actions will take into account the common interests that the CO and the Major will have in only allowing fit soldiers to deploy. A view shared by Pettrey (2003) who suggests that identification of needs and recognising common interests will minimise potential conflict between parties where there is a dual loyalty conflict.

In conclusion, the duty of confidentiality is grounded in law and medical ethics (Plambeck, 2002). This chapter has highlighted the complex nature of maintaining patient confidentiality in a military environment especially where a patient refuses to consent to medical treatment and where his personal information is divulged to a third person. This chapter has also highlighted the difficulties for a military doctor when they have a dual loyalty conflict between obeying military orders and following professional codes of practice (Benetar and Upshur, 2008). When having to follow professional codes of conduct and military orders, this role is problematic as they can be acting ethically and legally in one sense but unethically and illegally in another (Yeo, 1989). Thus, the management of military dual loyalty is challenging and can be contradictory to the values and beliefs of normal civilian ethical principles (Griffiths and Jasper, 2007).

Using Howe's (2003) three-dimensional role-specific model, this chapter has concluded that managing patient-soldier confidential information is complex and demanding. It has also concluded that to avoid further harm to a patient and an exacerbation of dual loyalty conflict in a non-operational environment (Coleman, 2009), the most appropriate method is to make the patient their first concern but also to have an awareness and appreciation that takes into consideration the interests of the third party (Williams, 2009a). For the military soldier, although they subvert some of their rights and freedoms when they join the military (Howe, 2003), they are still entitled to be treated with respect and have their private medical information kept confidential when appropriate. However, this chapter has concluded that in the context of the vignette, disclosure of confidential information about a soldier without their consent to his CO to prevent him deploying on an operational tour is both lawful and ethical when in the interests of the public (Visser, 2003).

A version of this chapter appeared in the *Online Journal of Health Ethics:* Kelly, J (2011) Using and Ethical Model to Manage Patient-Soldier Confidentiality When Medical Treatment for Post Traumatic is Refused, *Online Journal of Health Ethics,* 7(2), pp. 1-22.

CHAPTER THIRTEEN

A MILITARY-FOCUSED APPROACH TOWARDS MILITARY HEALTHCARE

Introduction

This and the subsequent chapter critically analyses and concludes the findings of each vignette in the following ways:

1) A *military-focused* approach, where a Military Healthcare Professional's *military duty* overrides all other considerations, such as patient care. This is even when following military duty is perceived not to be in the patient's best interests.

2) A *professional healthcare-focused* approach, where a Military Healthcare Professional's *professional duty* to the patient overrides all military considerations, including not following military orders.

As explained in chapter 1, the aim of this book was to challenge the World Medical Association's ascertain that **'medical ethics in armed conflict is identical to medical ethics in times of peace'** (World Medical Association, 2004; Hallgarth, 2007). As mentioned in chapter 6, this challenge was undertaken by an analysis of realistic vignettes, using a legal methodological approach and a military ethical model created by Edmund Howe (2003). This chapter concludes that medical ethics encountered by British Military Healthcare Professionals (MHCPs) on the battlefield and in operational environments are *not identical*. They are constrained and questionable under existing ethical, professional and legal parameters. Moreover, healthcare principles, such as professional autonomy, patient consent and refusal of treatment, that are ordinarily seen in civilian healthcare practice as sacrosanct when giving patient care *(St George's Healthcare NHS Trust v S, R v Collins, and others, ex parte S, 1988)*, are, by contrast, generally interpreted differently in military healthcare practice, especially in the battlefield and operational environment (Gross, 2006).

Although a dichotomy exists between the dual roles of MHCPs and soldiers in unique environments, such as the battlefield and operational areas (Kelly, 2010), this and the next chapter suggests the following:

1)   The need for MHCPs to follow *both* lawful military orders and professional codes of practice remains problematic in the hostile environments of the battlefield and operational areas.

2)   As explained in chapter 12, although the conflict of following *both* lawful military orders and professional codes of practice are more problematic in hostile environments; nevertheless, in non-operational environments the situation remains challenging.

3)   Military law conflicts with common law principles in the battlefield, operational and non-operational environments that ordinarily, in a civilian healthcare context, are afforded unquestionably to all patients.

4)   The need to follow *both* lawful military orders and professional codes of practice is unable to ease the dual loyalty conflict between the military need to obtain Operational Effectiveness and the MHCP's legal requirement to follow professional codes of practice via the General Medical Council (GMC) or the Nursing Midwifery Council (NMC).

5)   A *military-focused approach* towards healthcare is unable to help solve ethical and professional conflicts and dilemmas in the battlefield and operational environments.

6)   Equally, a *professional healthcare-focused* approach is similarly unable to help resolve ethical and professional conflicts and dilemmas for MHCPs in the battlefield and operational environments.

7)   Edmund Howe's (2003) model, utilised in the vignettes, is a useful method in attempting to resolve professional, ethical, and military medical conflicts and dilemmas.   However, although the model suggests that MHCPs are governed by three role-specific ethics: a *military role-specific ethic,* a *medical role-specific ethic* and a *discretionary role-specific ethic;* as will be explained in this chapter, this model, nonetheless, has some limitations in the battlefield, operational and non-operational environments. This is because it does not appear to give clear answers to ethical and professional problems and dilemmas. This chapter, therefore, suggests that the model should be seen as a guide, rather than a definitive problem-solving tool.

A Military-Focused Approach towards Military Healthcare

Chapter 4 explained the importance of military discipline and soldiers obeying military orders above all other considerations; soldiers have certain duties that they ought to or ought not to perform (Noble-Adams, 1999; Orend, 2004). If they violate this approach, they could then be disciplined via the Armed Forces Discipline Act 2000. Consequently, concerning the vignettes and healthcare from a *military-focused* approach, MHCPs would have to obey military orders that override all other considerations, such as patient care. This, according to Edmund Howe's (2003) model, would be following a *military role-specific ethic,* where a military duty and order is followed before everything else; it considers military healthcare from a purely military position and is *not* patient focused. As mentioned in chapter 2, although the NHS view Operational Effectiveness in a different context, which is to ensure that it provides high quality patient care, by striving to make people healthy through providing the most effective diagnostics and subsequent treatments to detect diseases earlier (National Service Act 2006 and High Quality Care For All, 2008), perhaps it could be said that it is not a consideration or issue that civilian frontline personnel in the NHS are preoccupied with to the same extent as military frontline personnel. Nevertheless, achieving Operational Effectiveness in the Armed Forces and following military orders is critical, and it is the British Army's ultimate purpose and objective before everything else (Soldier Management, 2004).

Accordingly, in chapter 7, using the *military-focused* approach to healthcare, where the MHCP was a passenger in a light armoured tactical vehicle driving within a battlefield area and, when coming across a wounded soldier, ignored prior orders not to leave hard-packed roads due to landmines; however, the MHCP then decided to give treatment to the soldier lying in a dirt track five metres away. This could be seen as **not** a military ethical action; since from a military focused position, the MHCP disregarded his military duty, and instead started to give immediate care and treatment to a soldier screaming in pain. Consequently, it involved the MHCP disobeying a lawful military order, and perhaps compromising Operational Effectiveness by his ill-discipline (Warbuton, 2009).

Similarly, in chapter 10, where the soldier was also ordered not to leave hard-packed roads due to landmines, but instead rushed to give treatment to a fellow soldier, this could also be seen as **not** a military ethical action for the same reasons. Equally, concerning the operational vignette in chapter 11, where an injured senior officer refused life-saving treatment and the MHCP considered that undue influence could be a solution to his dilemma in treating the officer to save his life, this could also be considered as an action that was not a military ethical one, as he disobeyed military orders from the senior officer. Thus, with a *military-focused approach* towards healthcare, a person following this approach would view that the MHCP's actions in chapters 7, 10 and 11 were militarily unethical, as the soldiers disregarded the needs of the military, which as explained in chapter 2, is to be operationally effective at all times (Paley, 2002). However, in using a *military-focused approach* towards healthcare there are **six** main difficulties that highlight that ethics in war is *different* and is *not* identical to ethics in peace. These are as follows:

1. Professional codes of practice are compromised and professional autonomy diminishes

A criticism of a *military-focused approach* towards healthcare, that following military orders should take priority over giving treatment and care to wounded patients, is that professional codes of practice would be compromised (Gross, 2006). This is because the *military-focused approach* questions whether a MHCP should have a duty to treat and act freely when they are commanded to follow another duty in a particular way that ultimately may compromise patient care (Bailey et al, 2008). In addition, although the patient must always be the MHCP's first concern, before any other consideration including following military orders (Annas, 2008), the consequences of the MHCPs in chapters 7 and 10 following a *military-focused approach,* in contrast to the actions they actually took, would not have made the wounded soldier their first concern. Thus, professional codes of practice would have been compromised (GMC, 2006 and the NMC, 2008).

In a *military-focused approach,* in the context of chapters 7, 10 and 11, the MHCP's first concern should have been to follow military orders. However, it may be argued that this *military-focused approach* position could compromise the integrity of the medical or nursing professional on the battlefield, as MHCPs would fail to address the healthcare needs of the sick and wounded with the aim of restoring them, where possible, to health (Hedahl, 2009). In addition, in relation to chapters 10 and 11, this action would contravene the Dual Loyalty and Human Rights in Health Professional Practice Report recommendation, where it is stated that the 'overruling identity and priority' of a MHCP should be 'that of a health care professional' (London et al, 2006). Moreover, this *military-focused approach* position is, perhaps, incompatible with the Geneva Convention's legal status of non-combatants, whose primary aim is to care for the sick and wounded during war (Geneva Conventions of 1949, Additional Protocol I of 1977 (Protocol I).

Following a *military-focused approach* on a battlefield is clearly problematic for MHCPs, since in healthcare ethical reasoning; if following military orders takes priority over following codes of practice, it diminishes professional autonomy (Gross, 2006). Autonomy may be seen as giving the greatest satisfaction for the MHCP, rather than following military orders, as it enables the MHCP to work more independently without being constrained by military rules and regulations (Thorgen and Crang-Svalenius, 2009). Moreover, it may be argued that as autonomy is a person's ability to maximise and act within the scope of their professional practice, according to their knowledge, skills and judgment, it is the best approach towards achieving an optimum outcome for the patient (Weston, 2009). In addition, it allows a healthcare professional to make decisions that are free from third party interference, such as following military orders (Weston, 2010) with the expectation that they will give their patient the best care available that is clinically evidence-based (Kramer and Scmalenberg, 2003). Faris et al (2010) suggests that a lack of professional autonomy can also be a barrier to not giving the patient optimum treatment and care. Thus, it is evident that following a *military-focused approach* on a battlefield is problematic and challenging for the MHCP, as he/she do not have the same ability to practice autonomously as their civilian counterparts. Subsequently, this could compromise patient care in this environment, as healthcare professionals may be impeded from having full control over how they should care for their patients (Burns, 2009).

2. Achieving Operational Effectiveness remains problematic and challenging

In the context of chapter 12, where a soldier refused medical treatment for a psychological injury, although (i) dual loyalty conflict and a *military-focused approach* in this non-operational environment is less problematic than on a battlefield and operational environment and (ii), the doctor's decision to not allow the soldier to deploy was clearly not a *military role-specific* ethic or a *medical role-specific* ethic, but a *discretionary role-ethic;* nonetheless, the constant need for the MHCP to achieve Operational Effectiveness remains problematic and challenging, even in a less hostile environment. This is because, although the MHCP in chapter 12 made professional interests a priority before military interests, the doctor could nevertheless still compromise Operational Effectiveness if he allowed an unfit soldier to deploy. As explained in chapter 12, the reason for this is that it can become more difficult to remove an unfit soldier from the battleground and operational environment than from a non-operational environment, as a Commander's priorities are more stretched in a hostile setting (Simmons and Rycraft, 2010) and it reduces manpower by a fit soldier medically evacuating an unfit one (Gross, 2006).

In the context of chapter 12, therefore, it may be argued that to be fully autonomous a healthcare professional requires not being overburdened with rules and regulations, as it is the outcomes of the actions that are more important (Bahadori and Fitzpatrick, 2009). However, it is evident that having to constantly follow military orders and continuously achieve Operational Effectiveness becomes almost a 'physical' impediment and a restriction to allowing empowerment of autonomous practice and giving optimum patient care (Timmons and Ridenour, 1994). Therefore, in *military-focused approach* reasoning, if it is correct that following military orders should take priority over following professional codes of practice; by contrast, in the context of chapters 11 and 12, it may be reasonable to suggest that it does not allow the MHCP to make the ultimate assessment of whether a wounded or ill soldier, **(i)** in actuality, lacks capacity to consent and refuse medical treatment (Walters, 2009) and **(ii)** can have their medical information kept private from third parties who are not healthcare professionals. In addition, it also does not allow the MHCP to make the wounded or ill soldier their first concern (GMC, 2006; NMC, 2008).

3. The 'best interests' and wishes of the patient are diminished

As illustrated in chapter 11, if a MHCP uses undue influence over a patient to accept medical treatment, then it may be argued that the consequences of this are that, not only is this unlawful, but it also does not take into account the 'best interests' and wishes of the patient (NMC, The Code, 2008). This is especially where the patient's capacity to accept and refuse medical treatment is questionable (Griffith and Tengnah, 2008). As explained in chapter 12, although the Mental Capacity Act 2005 does not define 'best interests', the situation of exerting any undue influence over a patient and making following military orders a priority over following professional codes of practice is clearly not compatible with this Act. In accordance with sections 4 (6) (a), (b) and (c) of the Mental Capacity Act 2005 the medical practitioner *must* consider, where possible, factors such as the patient's past and future beliefs, values and wishes that could affect his/her decision-making. Clearly, a *military-focused approach* does not to take into account the patient's 'best interests'.

Accordingly, if the best interests and wishes of the wounded patient in the battlefield and operational environment are subordinated to military interests, towards achieving Operational Effectiveness, then as explained in chapters 7, 10 and 11, it is reasonable to suggest that a *military-focused approach* may be seen as morally repugnant to civilian healthcare professionals and to contradict the entire principles of healthcare ethics (Crowe and Hardil, 1991). However, in contrast to chapters 7, 10 and 11 in chapter 9, where the MHCP started firing at enemy soldiers who were attacking him, this can be considered as a military ethical action in *military-focused approach* terms. This is because the MHCP followed military orders in achieving Operational Effectiveness. Yet, in healthcare terms, this action caused the greatest harm to the patient. Accordingly, to consider the MHCP's actions in chapter 9 as an ethical action would deny the principles of beneficence, which consider and promote the best interests of the patient (Davis et al, 1997) and non-maleficence, which is to prevent harm (Vocye, 2009). Clearly, in chapters 7, 10 and 11 if the military duty came before the duty to follow professional codes of practice, all the wounded soldiers would have died.

4. Sub-standard patient care

Chapter 9 considered if combat immunity, and if not, whether a modified form of combat immunity, namely *Military Healthcare Battlefield Immunity,* could protect a MHCP for any negligent acts or omissions in the battlefield. As explained in chapter 9, combatant troops remain protected from any claim in negligence by the common law doctrine of combat immunity for any negligent acts or omissions they may make against a fellow soldier when fighting. In this vignette, as the MHCP fired at the enemy, and by doing so, failed to give the wounded soldier the correct clinical treatment, resulting in the loss/amputation of the soldier' right arm, the MHCP did nonetheless perform an ethical *action* within a *military-focused approach.* This is because the MHCP followed the military duty of ensuring Operational Effectiveness by firing at the enemy who were attacking them. However, the difficulty with this is that, although this action may be considered an ethical one in *military-focused healthcare* terms, nonetheless, the professional standard of care, as explained in chapter 10 as being '…the ordinary skilled man exercising and professing to have that special skill…' (*Bolam v Friern Hospital Management Committee, 1957 at paragraph 112)* would have been below the legal standard expected of a professional person, and of a MHCP, in those circumstances. Therefore, although the existence and aim of an army in a conflict is to 'fight and decisively win its nation's wars' (Westhusing, 2006), by following military orders before following codes of practice, it would seem to disregard the notion that soldiers must be 'fit to fight' (Gross, 2006). In addition, it discounts the common law position of what the reasonable professional standard of care ought to be in the battlefield. This is because, in chapter 9, the MHCP put fighting the enemy *before* patient care.

5. Blurring of the role of the combatant and non-combatant

The Geneva Conventions of 1949 and Additional Protocol I of 1977 requires strict separation between combatants and non-combatants. This means that medical personnel must not fire at the enemy, unless it is in self-defence, or for the protection of their patients. Nonetheless, chapter 9 highlights a blurring of the role of the combatant and non-combatant in the battlefield, when a MHCP may feel he is required to leave his patient to fire at the enemy. Even though this book acknowledges that giving care and treatment in emergency civilian circumstances is difficult and challenging for civilian nurses (Fry et al, 2002; Kelly, 2010), it is unlikely that they would ever leave their patient, as the MHCP did in chapter 9, either temporarily or for a longer period, to fight or perform another task, and especially one that was not a clinical task. This is especially so when, as in chapter 9, other soldiers were at hand to perform that task in fighting back at the enemy. As mentioned by Kasher (2007), although combatants and non-combatants can be involved in the same hostile action, there are different standards as to their respective roles and different outcomes to their actions. From a pure healthcare position, a MHCP *must* make the patient their first concern (GMC, 2008; NMC, 2008), which according to Annas (2008) must be 'First, Last' and 'Always'. Thus, it may be argued that the consequences of the MHCP's actions in chapter 9 eroded the distinction between combatant and non-combatant (Sidel and Levy, 2003). Moreover, as mentioned in chapter 9, as the word 'combatant' suggests that a soldier can legally kill in war, it is, perhaps, important to have clearer distinction regarding the roles of combatants and non-combatants (Bomann-Larsen, 2004) and those who can legally kill in war and those who cannot (Rogers, 2004). 'War is a combat between combatants' it is not between *combatant* and *non-combatant* (Walzer, 2005) thus suggesting that a MHCP should never engage in fighting.

6. Failing to make the patient their first concern.

With *a military-focused approach* towards healthcare, in relation to chapter 9, where a MHCP left his patient to fire at the enemy before giving him the correct care and treatment, this may be seen as the correct decision at that time, since the MHCP helped save other soldiers' lives. However, in contrast to this argument, the MHCP may have elevated group needs above an individual patient's needs, to the detriment of patient care, when, in reality, there was no need to do so. This is because the other 'combatant' soldiers were probably more capable of defending themselves against enemy attack than a 'non-combatant' medic (Robertson et al, 2007). Consequently, in professional terms, the MHCP's actions would be unethical because they failed to make the patient their first concern (GMC, 2006 and NMC, 2008, p.1). In addition, due to this MHCP's clinical mistake, he did not act as 'the reasonable MHCP' in giving the wounded soldier the appropriate care and treatment (*Bolam v Friern Hospital Management Committee, 1957*). In professional terms, therefore, in the context of the vignette in chapter 9, as there were (a) several experienced combatant troops to perform the task more competently than the MHCP of shooting at the enemy and (b) whose specific role as a combatant is to *exclusively* engage the enemy and fight (*Shaw Savill and Albion Co Ltd v the Commonwealth of Australia, 1940 at paragraph 366*), for this MHCP in chapter 9 to shoot at the enemy was, perhaps, the wrong action. This is because it caused further harm to the patient and it was, perhaps an unnecessary action for a MHCP to perform.

CHAPTER FOURTEEN

A PROFESSIONAL HEALTHCARE-FOCUSED APPROACH TOWARDS MILITARY HEALTHCARE

In contrast to the preceding chapter and a *military-focused approach,* a **professional healthcare-focused approach** would, according to Howe's model, be following a *medical role-specific ethic,* as MHCPs would follow professional codes of practice and put their patients first before following military orders. It would also be following a *discretionary role-specific ethic,* as the MHCP would examine the consequences of any future decision he/she makes. This would then allow the MHCP to use some discretion in deciding when, and whether, the needs of the military are absolute, before professional codes of practice (Howe, 2003 at p.335). With a *discretionary role-specific ethic,* a MHCP would judge whether an action is right or wrong, based on the consequences of the action. However, it accepts that it can only deal with *possible* consequences, as it is impossible to predict the exact outcome of an action (Pieper, 2008). This, ultimately, makes it difficult to ascertain what is the right action to take, since determining whether it was the right decision can only be made retrospectively. Nonetheless, this approach would argue that autonomy, beneficence, non-malificence and justice should form the basis of moral principles when dealing with ethical dilemmas in healthcare (Griffith and Tengnah, 2008). Nevertheless, in relation to a **professional healthcare-focused approach** and by using a *medical role-specific ethic* and a *discretionary role-specific ethic,* this book concludes that there are five main difficulties with this approach that highlight that ethics in war is *different* and *not* identical to ethics in peace. These are as follows:

1) **Operational Effectiveness** is compromised on the battlefield and in an operational environment, as military interests become subordinated to medical interests towards achieving optimum patient care.

2)   **Military discipline** and **strict obedience** in following military orders without question is also compromised.
3)   **Professional codes of practice** by the GMC and the NMC seem to be incompatible with military law in the three environments.
4)   The MHCP may place him or herself at **unnecessary risk** in following professional codes of practice before military orders.
5)   The **dual loyalty conflict** issue, between either following military orders or following professional codes of practice, remains unresolved.

1. Disobeying lawful military orders

Disobeying lawful military orders is a military offence, as it is legally right to follow a military order and legally wrong not to do so (Armed Forces Act 2006, part 1, section 12). Therefore, in chapters 7 and 10 the military ethical action would have been for the MHCPs to have followed military orders and not leave the hard-packed roads to give care and treatment to the wounded soldiers. Similarly, in chapter 11, the military ethical action would have been for the MHCP to obey the military order given by the wounded senior military officer and not give him any treatment, thereby allowing him to die.

However, in contrast, it could also be argued that, in chapters 7 and 10, although the MHCPs' disobeyed military orders, it could be suggested that the MHCPs' *did* perform an ethical action in healthcare terms since they saved the soldiers' lives and thus acted in a beneficent manner (Robertson et al, 2007). They also made the wounded patient their first concern (GMC, 2006 and NMC, 2008). Likewise, in chapter 11, it could be argued that, although undue influence over a patient is considered unlawful and can invalidate a patient's consent to medical treatment *(Re T (adult: refusal of treatment), 1992),* in the circumstances of that vignette, as explained in chapter 11, it may be considered understandable and an ethical action for the MHCP to consider undue influence in persuading the wounded soldier to accept medical treatment, as other soldiers' lives were at risk by the wounded soldier refusing treatment. However, it is accepted that this reasoning of medical ethics in war would not be acceptable in peacetime ethics (Crowe and Hardil, 1991).

2. Operational Effectiveness and military discipline is compromised

As suggested in chapter 4, military discipline and following military orders to achieve Operational Effectiveness is the primary aim and function of any army. Thus, military effectiveness can only succeed when soldiers are unquestionably obedient to military commands (Jackson, 2007). Concerning the soldiers in chapters 7 and 10, therefore, who did not follow military orders, and instead left hard-packed roads to give treatment to wounded soldiers; as mentioned earlier, with a *military-focused approach, any* action that the soldiers performed *should* have been for the *motive* of following military orders to achieve Operational Effectiveness (Soldier Management, 2004). However, by following professional codes of practice and disobeying military orders to give treatment to wounded soldiers, they subsequently compromised Operational Effectiveness and military discipline (Purtilo, 1999). Therefore, as a consequence of their actions, it may be argued that disobeying lawful military orders could be considered as insubordinate and a mutinous action according to section 6 (2) (a) (ii) of the Armed Forces 2006, Part 1 (Offences), if a soldier 'disobeys authority in such circumstances as to subvert discipline'. In addition, the MHCP's actions could also be considered as 'Disobedience to lawful commands' if a soldier via section 12, 1(a) of this Act, 'disobeys a lawful command; and (b) he intends to disobey, or is reckless as to whether he disobeys, the command'.

3. Unnecessary risk, incompatibility of professional codes of practice with military law and exacerbation of dual loyalty conflict

In chapters 7 and 10, where the soldiers ignored military orders not to leave hard packed roads due to potential landmines, a person disposed in favour of following *military-focused approach,* instead of a *professional healthcare-focused approach,* would have regarded the MHCP's decision to ignore military orders as being reckless. This is because there was a genuine risk that the MHCP could have caused themselves and other soldiers nearby harm. This was especially so if it had led to further landmines being detonated. The *military-focused* MHCP may also argue that the risk of the soldiers causing themselves physical injury by entering a minefield was foreseeable and extremely high (*Bolton v Stone, 1951*). In addition, the advocate of *military-focused* healthcare may also assert that the potential enormity of the consequences that their action may cause in terms of further injury is a relevant concern that needs to be taken into consideration when deciding what the best possible course of action is to take (*Paris v Stepney, 1951*).

In the context of all the vignettes, it could also be argued that, where there is an unsafe working environment, it is unlikely that any healthcare professional would ever be expected and able to give the appropriate care and treatment, compared to a more peaceful environment (Roche et al, 2010). For the MHCP, this becomes more problematic, since, as mentioned in chapter 7, despite frequent comparisons to inner-city emergency rooms on "any Saturday night"' being the equivalent of the battlefield (Beam, 2003 at p. 371), a civilian healthcare professional generally works in a safer environment. As mentioned by Southby (2003) in chapters 7 and 10, the battlefield is detached from traditional support mechanisms. This, therefore, seems to suggest that, in spite of being an occupational hazard for MHCPs, being exposed to dangerous and threatening situations in the battlefield (Wallenius et al, 2004), healthcare professionals are, nevertheless, not obliged to place themselves in any unnecessary risk that could cause them further harm when giving care and treatment to a patient. It also suggests that following military orders should always take precedence before following codes of practice on the battlefield since, 'Doctor or not, this is war' (Army Doctrine Publication, 2000 at paragraph 112).

Similarly, in chapters 11 and 12, it may also be argued that, as a consequence of following professional codes of practice before military orders, professional codes of conduct via the GMC (*Good Medical Practice*, 2006) and the NMC (*The Code*, 2008 *and NMC, Consent Advice Sheet*, 2008) and case law regarding consent and refusal of medical treatment, appear to be incompatible with the Armed Forces Act 2006. Moreover, it may also be argued that dual loyalty conflict is exacerbated, since the MHCP's clinical role conflicts with military obligations (Rascona, 2007). For example, **(i)** although in the famous case of *Schloendorff v Society of New York Hospital (1914 at paragraph 126),* Justice Benjamin Cardozo, famously stated, a competent adult has a right '…to determine what shall be done with his own body…' **(ii)** moreover, in *St George's Healthcare NHS Trust v S, R v Collins, and others, ex parte S (1998 at paragraph 174) (St George's)* Dame Butler-Sloss stated, 'even when his or her own life depends on receiving medical treatment, an adult of sound mind is entitled to refuse it' and **(iii)**, equally, in *Re B (Adult, refusal of medical treatment) (2002), it was held that* a competent patient has the right to refuse treatment and their refusal must be respected, even if it results in their death; nevertheless, in adhering to professional guidelines and common law principles, if a soldier refused medical treatment and prolonged his injury, the soldier may have committed a military offence. This is because according to the Armed Forces 2006, Part 1 (Offences), s.16 - Malingering (1) c, 'A person subject to service law commits an offence if, to avoid service – by any act or omission he aggravates or prolongs any injury of his'. Thus, this re-iterates the incompatibility of professional codes of practice with military law.

As explained in chapter 10, despite **(i)** the Ministry of Defence stating that 'Patients should receive the highest appropriate level of medical care in suitable clinical environments' (Joint Doctrine Publication, 2007 at Ch.1, section II, para 112), **(ii)** the GMC (2006) and the NMC (2008) both stating that the patient should be the healthcare professional's first concern and **(iii),** the professional obligation for MHCPs, irrespective of their environment, is to give their patients their complete attention (Rubenstien, 2003), soldiers have a contractual agreement to protect their State above all other considerations 'on the assumption that the deaths of some will saves the lives of many' (Gross, 2006). This is a view supported by Sarikonda-Woitas and Robinson (2002), who argue that weighing what is the greatest good i.e. between either following military orders or following professional codes of practice, is the one that overall produces the best outcome.

Thus, in further consideration of chapter 7, in the context of military healthcare, perhaps the overall 'best outcome' is to defeat the enemy and minimize pain to as many people as possible. This is because, as mentioned in chapter 7, the existence of an army and its aim in a conflict is to 'fight and decisively win its nation's wars for the protection of everyone in the State (Westhusing, 2006). Moreover, the severely wounded soldiers, who are likely to die anyway, irrespective of the treatment they receive, may not derive any benefit from a MHCP following professional codes of practice before following military orders (Stein, 2002). However, it is clear that this position would not only exacerbate dual loyalty conflict, as following military orders would supersede professional codes of practice, causing harm to the patient, which in itself would be incompatible with both the GMC's and NMC's professional codes, but also an advocate of following professional codes of practice before military orders would, perhaps, find such a position objectionable and morally unacceptable in healthcare practice (Crowe and Hardil, 1991). Nevertheless, as the vignettes of chapters 9, 10 and 11 have shown, dual loyalty conflict between following military orders or following professional codes of practice are more problematic in environments such as the battlefield and operational areas, where the environment necessitates that decision have to be made more quickly (Enemark, 2008). Therefore, in the battleground and operational environments, a *military-focused* MHCP would assert that it might be acceptable for professional codes of practice to yield to military orders if it is considered the 'best for the general good' (Williams, 2009).

In conclusion, although the patient's needs are sacrosanct (Annas, 2008), this and the previous chapter have highlighted the conflicts and tensions that dual loyalty creates for MHCPs in balancing between following military orders or following professional codes of practice. Thus, these two chapters have also illustrated that dual loyalty conflict is more problematic on the battlefield and operational environment than in a non-operational environment. In doing so, it has also illustrated that medical ethics in war is *not* identical to medical ethics in peace. This is because the principles of military necessity, that ultimately will help to preserve the welfare of the state including its citizens, take precedent over normal civilian healthcare principles such as professional and patient autonomy and the right to accept and refuse medical treatment (Gross, 2006).

Both this and chapter 13 have highlighted that neither a *military-focused approach* nor a *professional healthcare-focused approach* can confidently help to resolve ethical conflicts and dilemmas and tensions in military healthcare practice on the battlefield and operational environment. It has also demonstrated, in parts, where military law seems to be incompatible with normal civilian healthcare ethics (Gross, 2006) and the common law *(St George's)*. Thus, the decision to follow either military orders or professional codes of practice, when MHCPs are faced with ethical dilemmas, remains problematic. When analysing both a *military-focused* approach and a *professional healthcare-focused* approach, there are counter arguments to assert that neither approach is the best one to take. For example, even though professional autonomy allows healthcare professionals to work more independently, instead of being overly restricted by rules and regulations (Thorgen and Crang-Svalenius, 2009), Martinelli-Fernandez (2006) suggests that autonomy is misinterpreted, as it does not allow a person to do as they please. Instead, it is the basis of morality and duty that allows a person to govern themselves via certain laws. In addition, it is more important to evaluate why and how a rule is followed, instead of not whether it is followed (Warbutton, 2009).

Both chapters have also highlighted that the military's goal is to defeat the enemy (Howland, 1999) and to send its soldiers into battle to win the war (Westhusing, 2006). It has also demonstrated that in a military environment, and especially in the battlefield, it is critical that military orders are followed, to avoid insubordinate acts, such as disobeying a lawful command, which could compromise Operational Effectiveness (Soldier Management, 2004). Thus, from a *military-focused approach*, soldiers should follow their military duty without question (Price, 2009). However, both chapters conclude by suggesting that solving ethical and professional dilemmas in war is distinctly different than in peace, and perhaps cannot be considered purely from either a *military-focused approach* or a *professional healthcare-focused approach.* This is because for MHCPs, unlike their civilian counterparts, their 'moral obligations are beyond those incumbent on many other members of society' (Benetar and Upshur, 2008).

CHAPTER FIFTEEN

CONCLUDING COMMENTS AND REFLECTIVE NOTES

This final chapter summarises the aim of the book, and draws attention to its constraints, limitations, and boundaries. It also highlights the uniqueness and originality of the book and indicates some implications for future practice and research.

Via a legal methodological approach explained in chapter 6, using real life vignettes, the main aim and requirement of the book was:

> 'To challenge the World Medical Association's statement and establish that medical ethics in British Military Healthcare Practice during armed conflict is *not identical* to medical ethics in times of peace'

To challenge the main requirement, this book has successfully substantiated the four sub-requirements stated in chapter 6, which were as follows:

1) Although there are similarities between civilian and military healthcare practices, the hostile and diverse environments that Military Healthcare Professionals work in is significantly different to a civilian healthcare environment, even in an emergency (discussed in chapter 7).

2) Although, a dual loyalty conflict may exist in other areas of healthcare apart from the military, it is not as problematic as it is in diverse military environments (discussed in chapters 7, 9, 10, 11 and 12).

3) Professional codes of practice by the General Medical Council and the Nursing Midwifery Council are not a sufficient solution to the existing and emerging ethical and professional conflicts in battlefield and operational environments.

4) Medical ethics in armed conflict are constrained and questionable under existing ethical, professional, and legal parameters. Therefore, although not within the scope of this book, new professional regulatory solutions to solve these ethical conflicts are required.

The Vignettes, as opposed to more traditional empirical methods used in nursing and healthcare research produced a meaningful and effective substitute for real life experiences in war zones and were the *safest* and *best way* of obtaining information to address the World Medical Association's assertion that **'medical ethics in armed conflict is identical to medical ethics in times of peace'.** This approach was enhanced, as the author had extensive knowledge and experience of nursing both in civilian and diverse military environments. This allowed the author to draw on their own experiences in the construction of the vignettes and challenge the WMA's statement. However, although as explained in chapters 13 and 14, the vignettes successfully challenge the WMAs claim, research is never perfect, as it can be biased and thwarted with subjectivity and misinterpretations (Parahoo, 2006). Therefore, the following five points are illustrated as the main limitations, constraints, and boundaries of the book.

Main limitations, constraints and boundaries of the book

Firstly, although case law in legal academia is considered as primary research (Manchester, 2006), it may be difficult to convince professionals outside the legal field that the information obtained from case law equates to primary data from traditional empirical or qualitative research undertaken in healthcare. Therefore, the analysis obtained from the vignettes may be questionable to readers who have limited understanding and knowledge of the law.

Secondly, although the author has followed the strict principles of interpreting law, some readers may not have the legal skills and legal knowledge to interpret the case law. Understanding legal terms such as *judicial precedent* and *obiter dictum* are challenging, even for those well acquainted with legal terminology. **Thirdly,** with the absence of personally interviewing soldiers, who may have experienced firsthand ethical and professional dilemmas and conflicts in combat, it leaves some uncertainty as to the accuracy, reality, and reliability of the vignettes and their outcomes. Accordingly, each vignette may not necessarily be representative of Military Healthcare Professionals' (MHCPs) actions and responses to combatant situations as a whole. Therefore, it leaves some uncertainty as to the accuracy of whether each MHCP would have reacted in the manner in which the author has indicated they would in each vignette.

Fourthly, while it is reasonable to expect other MHCPs to have had similar experiences to the author's and each other when deployed on operational tours; nevertheless, given **(i)** the undefined nature of the role between that of a soldier and the other of a healthcare professional; compounded with **(ii),** the unpredictability and fluidity of war, this cannot be assumed. As well as this, a commander's decision not to allow a MHCP to follow professional codes of practice *before* military orders can also not be assumed, as on occasions, given the context of the situation and the environment, a commander may yield military orders in favour of professional codes of practice. However, the new understanding offered within the book provides some indication of how MHCPs may experience ethical and professional dilemmas in diverse and sometimes hostile environments, and where a commander may not be sympathetic to the advice of a MHCP regarding patient care.

In keeping with the nature of a legal interpretation, as explained in chapter 6, the conclusions, as highlighted in chapters 13 and 14 do not provide, nor are they designed to provide, specific or general indications of key implications for future practice in military healthcare. However, the descriptive and interpreted accounts of each vignette demonstrate the uniqueness and originality of this area of study, which are empathised further in the following five points.

Uniqueness, originality, and strengths of the study

Firstly, the legal methodology used in the study has been proven to be **(i)** a viable, creative, innovative and a unique qualitative methodological approach to examine complex professional issues in challenging military healthcare environments, **(ii)** a way of interpreting the law, legal concepts, and professional issues simultaneously in these challenging military environments and **(iii)** a new qualitative method to address ethical, professional and legal challenges in other areas of healthcare outside military environments.

Secondly, the book has provided new ways of understanding MHCPs' difficulties in having to follow both professional codes of practice and military orders in diverse and challenging military environments, where a dual loyalty conflict can become almost a physical and psychological impediment in being to act in one way or the other.

Thirdly, the book has shown the complexity and variations in decision-making by MHCPs in the battleground and operational environments when in hostile and violent circumstances.

Fourthly, the book has successfully highlighted the need for the development of professional regulatory solutions from the General Medical Council and the Nursing Midwifery Council to solve ethical and professional conflicts in diverse military environments. This is so they can ease the burden of a MHCP experiencing a dual loyalty conflict between either following military orders or professional codes of practice.

Fifthly, with its underpinning theory, this study has illustrated that further study in this area is necessary. This can be at a practical level, i.e. in the specific military environments that this research has highlighted, to explore more succinctly the relationship between military law, where immediate obedience to military orders are expected, and professional codes of practice.

In conclusion, the influencing factors on MHCPs' decision-making appear to be between the on-going struggle to following either **military orders** or **professional codes of practice.** Decision-making in military healthcare, therefore, appears to be dependent on these two factors. This is because of the constant dual loyalty conflict, and when a MHCP decides which choice to take, there may be a detrimental consequence for themselves or their patient (Williams, 2009). As highlighted in chapter 7, the unique nature of military healthcare in diverse and sometimes hostile military environments explains the variation in practice seen between civilian healthcare and military healthcare (Beam, 2003).

It is apparent that healthcare decisions also appear to be informed by the constant desire to achieve Operational Effectiveness, which is not an issue that civilian nurses are concerned with to the same extent. As explained in chapter 2, Operational Effectiveness for civilian nurses is considered in a different context. However, it may be possible, as a result of this book, that guidelines may be developed which instil and embrace both Operational Effectiveness and professional codes of practice, which are able to solve battlefield and operational ethical and professional problems more smoothly than before, without conflict (Robinson, 2007). Nonetheless, this book has clearly identified the important and influential role played by MHCPs in the battlefield and operational environments, and that ethics in war *is* different than in peacetime, as they are more constrained by military law and the need to continuously achieve Operational Effectiveness.

In relation to contextual features of ethical decision making in the battleground and operational environments, this book raises awareness among MHCPs of the powerful influence of both military law and professional codes of practice from either the General Medical Council or the Nursing Midwifery Council. In addition, whilst recognising the individual nature of care for a wounded soldier, it is important that MHCPs recognise the contextual constraints placed on their practice, particularly the diverse military environments, where the need to achieve

Operational Effectiveness is dominant (Baumann, 2007). Once recognised, perhaps MHCPs can work towards diminishing dual loyalty conflict by working towards guidelines where professional autonomy is recognised but also where Operational Effectiveness is not compromised.

EXPLANATORY NOTES

Chapter 1

1. Doctors, nurses, midwives, dentists, physiotherapists, combat medical technicians, radiographers, and healthcare assistants are all considered as Military Healthcare Professionals in the British Armed Forces. However, for the purpose of this book, it mainly concerns military doctors and nurses.

2. For this book, the battlefield is defined as an environment from the following circumstances. Where direct contact with the enemy takes place due to hand-to-hand fighting, or more commonly, where the soldier and enemy are engaged in firing rounds, rockets and grenades at each other. As explained in chapter 9, Military Healthcare Professionals are considered via the Geneva Convention of 1864 as non-combatants. They, therefore, would be located in this environment to treat wounded soldiers only, and not fight unless in self-defence, for the protection of themselves, and or their patients.

3. An operational environment equates to being on an operational tour but not directly on the battlefield. This is specifically referred to in chapter 11, to highlight that a soldier can be deployed on an overseas tour that is operational, but not necessarily on the battlefield.

4. A non-operation environment examined in more detail in chapter 12, equates to a civilian hospital or a Military Defence Hospital Unit (MDHU).

5. Military Defence Hospital Units are located within the National Health Service hospitals (NHS Trusts). Service personnel are integrated throughout the trust, working alongside NHS staff, to provide medical, nursing, and other clinical treatment to NHS and military patients. There are currently five Military Defence Hospital Unit's at:

   - MDHU Portsmouth (Queen Alexandra Hospital, Portsmouth Hospitals NHS Trust)
   - MDHU Derriford (Derriford Hospital, Plymouth Hospitals NHS Trust)
   - MDHU Frimley Park (Frimley Park Hospital NHS Foundation Trust)
   - MDHU Northallerton (Friarage Hospital, South Tees Hospitals NHS Trust)
   - MDHU Peterborough (Peterborough and Stamford Hospitals NHS Foundation Trust). At http://www.parliament.the-stationery-office.co.uk

/pa/cm200708/cmselect/cmdfence/327/32707.htm (last visited 20 November 2012).

6. Royal Centre for Defence Medicine (Birmingham). The Defence Medical Services also run a number of other units, which include Defence Services Medical Rehabilitation Centre (Headley Court), and the Duchess of Kent's Psychiatric Unit (Catterick). There are also two military hospitals, one in Cyprus, and the other in Gibraltar. In total, there are 15 rehabilitation units across the UK and Germany, and 15 military run Departments of Community Mental Health. At: http://www.mod.uk/DefenceInternet/MicroSite/DMS/ (last visited 20 November 2012).

Chapter 2

1. Military Annual Training Tests (MATTS) for the Army Medical Services and troops other than infantry soldiers (infantry troops have a more arduous training regime) includes the following:

a. Weapon handling test, live firing on a range at 100 metres, 200 metres, and 300 metres.

b. A physical fitness test which includes in one session, 2 minutes of press-ups followed by 2 minutes of sit-ups, 1/2mile run in a squad immediately followed by a 1 ½ mile run in which a person has to run according to their specific age and gender.

c. A Combat Fitness Test where irrespective of age, gender, weight or height every person has to carrying 15kgs over 6 miles in 1½ hours or prior to deployment, 15kgs over 8 miles in 2 hours.

d. Battlefield Casualty Drill Training, which includes basic first aid training in the battlefield.

e. Chemical, Biological, Radiological, and Nuclear training, which includes performing set drills such as eating, drinking, and decontamination of patients having suffered a chemical or radiological injury. This is achieved whilst being exposed to CS gas in a gas chamber wearing full protective clothing and a respirator.

f. Map reading, which involves orientation of maps, navigation to set locations and use of compasses.

g. Values, Standards, Health Living, Substance Misuse, Equality and Diversity, which involves educating soldiers that the Army does not tolerate any discrimination regarding sex, gender, sexual orientation. Training and alcohol or drug misuse.

h. Law of Armed Conflict, which involves educating soldiers on the Geneva Convention, who are legitimate targets during war and who are protected personnel when wearing their protective emblems (Murphy, 2009).

Chapter 3

1. 'The International Committee of the Red Cross (ICRC) is an impartial, neutral and independent organization whose exclusively humanitarian mission is to protect the lives and dignity of victims of armed conflict and other situations of violence and to provide them with assistance'. At: http://www.icrc.org/HOME.NSF/060a34982cae624ec12566fe00326312/125ff e2d4c7f68acc1256ae300394f6e?OpenDocument (last visited 20 November 2012).

2. Named after the German-American jurist and political philosopher Francis Lieber, the Lieber Code was an instruction signed by President Abraham Lincoln for the Union Forces during the American Civil War on the 24 April, 1863. It is also known as Instructions for the Government of Armies of the United States in the Field. Its function was to direct the Union Forces on how soldiers should conduct themselves in wartime principally in the following areas:
    *   Martial Law
    *   Military jurisdiction
    *   Treatment of spies and deserters
    *   The treatment of Prisoners of War

3. 'The St Petersburg Declaration of 1868 is the first formal agreement prohibiting the use of certain weapons in war. It had its origin in the invention, in 1863, by Russian military authorities of a bullet which exploded on contact with hard substance and whose primary object was to blow up ammunition wagons. In 1867, the projectile was so modified as to explode on contact with a soft substance. As such the bullet would have been an inhuman instrument of war, the Russian Government, unwilling to use the bullet itself or to allow another country to take advantage of it, suggested that the use of the bullet be prohibited by international agreement.' At http://www.icrc.org/ihl.nsf/INTRO/130?OpenDocument (last visited 20 November 2012).

4. Banning the use of nuclear weapons took place at the Seventeenth International Red Cross Conference, meeting in Stockholm in August 1948.

5. The Geneva Conventions comprised of four treaties as follows:

    (i)   First Geneva Convention - for the Amelioration of the Condition of the Wounded and Sick in Armed Forces in the Field, 1864. At: http://www.icrc.org/ihl.nsf/INTRO/365?OpenDocument (last visited 20 November 2012).

    (ii) Second Geneva Convention - for the Amelioration of the Condition of Wounded, Sick and Shipwrecked Members of Armed Forces at Sea,

1906. At: http://www.icrc.org/ihl.nsf/INTRO/370?OpenDocument (last visited 20 November 2012).

(iii) Third Geneva Convention - relative to the Treatment of Prisoners of War, 1929. At: http://www.icrc.org/ihl.nsf/INTRO/375?OpenDocument (last visited 20 November 2012).

(iv) Fourth Geneva Convention - relative to the Protection of Civilian Persons in Time of War, 1949. At: http://www.icrc.org/ihl.nsf/INTRO/380 (last visited 20 November 2012).

6.   The Additional protocols of the Geneva Conventions are as follows:

(v) Protocol Additional to the Geneva Conventions of 12 August 1949, and relating to the Protection of Victims of International Armed Conflicts (Protocol I), 8 June 1977. At: http://www.icrc.org/ihl.nsf/INTRO/470 ((last visited 20 November 2012).

(vi) Protocol Additional to the Geneva Conventions of 12 August 1949, and relating to the Protection of Victims of Non-International Armed Conflicts (Protocol II), 8 June 1977. At: http://www.icrc.org/ihl.nsf/INTRO/475?OpenDocument (last visited 20 November 2012).

(i) Protocol additional to the Geneva Conventions of 12 August 1949, and relating to the Adoption of an Additional Distinctive Emblem (Protocol III), 8 December 2005. At: http://www.icrc.org/ihl.nsf/INTRO/615?OpenDocument (last visited 20 November 2012).

Chapter 4

1.   Currently the army uses a document called, the Army General and Administrative Instructions (AGAIs) which allows various departments in the army and also each regiments and Corps to manage and administrate their everyday affairs and to use in the administration of discipline in conjunction with the Armed Forces Discipline Act 2000 and the Armed Forces Act 2006. At: http://www.amca.org.uk/resources/20081016_AGAI+67_Edn3+1_U.doc (last visited 20 November 2012).

2.   The Strategic Defence Review was a British policy document produced by the Labour Government than came to power in 1997. It reviewed all aspects of the British Armed Forces such as manpower, equipment and the future role of the military for future operations. At: http://www.armysearch.mod.uk/query.html?qt=strategic+defence+review&charset=iso-8859-1&style=test2&col=armyweb and at: http://www.army.mod.uk/21129.aspxs (last visited 20 November 2012).

3. Under the provisions of the Naval Discipline Act 1957, the Army Act 1955 and the Air Force Act 1955, when members of one Service are co-operating with one or both of the other Services they enjoy like power of command over members of another Service as the members of that Service of 'corresponding rank' insofar as power of command depends upon rank or rate.

4. 'Delegated or secondary legislation allows the Government to make changes to the law using powers conferred by an Act of Parliament. Statutory instruments form the majority of delegated legislation'. At http://www.parliament.uk/business/bills-and-legislation/secondary-legislation/ (last visited 1 December 2011). 'Statutory Instruments, also known as SIs, are a form of legislation which allow the provisions of an Act of Parliament to be subsequently brought into force or altered without Parliament having to pass a new Act. They are also referred to as secondary, delegated or subordinate legislation'. At http://www.parliament.uk/business/bills-and-legislation/secondary-legislation/statutory-instruments/ (last visited 20 November 2012).

5. 'NICE was set up as a Special Health Authority for England and Wales on 1st April 1999. It is an independent organisation responsible for providing national guidance on treatments and care for those using the NHS in England and Wales. NICEs remit is to develop authoritative guidance on the clinical and cost effectiveness of treatments. This guidance is intended to provide information on best practice for frontline NHS staff'. NICEs recommendations were initially persuasive and not binding. However, since January 2002, this guidance is now equal to the status of 'Directives' (Grubb, 2004).

6. 'National Service Frameworks (NSFs) set national healthcare standards. They are designed to improve the quality of health services and ensure that everyone gets the same level of care. The two main roles of NSFs are setting clear quality requirements for care based on the best available evidence, and offering strategies and support to help health organizations achieve these standards. Each NSF sets a target for improving the standard of care and the associated healthcare outcomes related to that care' (Grubb, 2004).

7. The Army Act 1955, the Naval Discipline Act 1957, and the Air Force Act 1955 were all repealed via the Armed Forces Act 2006, which received Royal Assent in November 2006.

8. 'T was injured in a car accident when she was 34 weeks pregnant. She was admitted to hospital and the possibility of her requiring a blood transfusion arose. T had been brought up by her mother, who was a Jehovah's Witness, but she was not herself a member of that religious sect. After a private conversation with her mother, T told the staff nurse that she use to belong to a religious sect, which believed blood transfusion to be a sin and a bar to eternal salvation, that she still maintained some beliefs of the sect and that she did not want a blood transfusion. Shortly afterwards she went into labour and because of her distressed condition it was decided that delivery should be by Caesarean section. After being alone with her mother, T again told medical staff that she did not want a blood transfusion and was informed that other solutions to expand the blood could be used and that blood transfusions were not often necessary after a Caesarean section. T then blindly signed a form of refusal of consent to blood transfusions but it was not explained to her that it might be necessary to give a blood transfusion to save her life. After undergoing an emergency Caesarean operation her condition deteriorated and she was transferred to an intensive care unit where, given a free hand, the consultant anaesthetist would unhesitatingly have administered a blood transfusion but felt inhibited from doing so in the light of Ts expressed wishes. T was instead put on a ventilator and paralysing drugs were administered. Ts father and boyfriend applied to the court for assistance and following an emergency hearing the judge authorised the administration of a blood transfusion to T and declared that, in the circumstances then prevailing, it would not be unlawful for the hospital to do so, despite the absence of her consent, because a blood transfusion appeared manifestly to be in her best interests. At a second hearing, the judge held that T had neither consented to nor refused a blood transfusion in the emergency, which had arisen, and accordingly that it was lawful for the doctors to treat her in whatever way they considered, in the exercise of their clinical judgment, to be in her best interests'. (*Re T (Adult: Refusal of Medical Treatment) (1992)*.

9. In *Ahmed v Austria (1996)*, 'The applicant, a Somali national, was granted refugee status in Austria on the grounds that his involvement in the activities of an opposition group gave rise to the risk that if he were to return to Somalia he would suffer persecution. The applicant was subsequently convicted of attempted robbery and sentenced to two and a half years imprisonment. The Federal Refugee Office ordered the forfeiture of the applicant's refugee status. The applicant appealed to the Minister of the Interior and his appeal was dismissed. The Administrative Court set aside the decision to expel him. The Minister of the Interior again ordered the forfeiture of the applicant's refugee status and the Administrative Court upheld that decision. The applicant complained that his expulsion to Somalia would expose him to a serious risk of being subjected to treatment contrary to art 3 of the European Convention on Human Rights. It was determined that the expulsion of an alien by a contracting state might give rise to an issue under art 3, and hence engage the responsibility of the state under the Convention, where substantial grounds had been shown for believing that the person in question, if expelled, would face a real risk of being subjected to treatment contrary to art 3 in the receiving country. In those circumstances, art 3 implied the obligation not to expel the person in question to that country. Article 3 prohibited in absolute terms torture and inhuman or degrading treatment or punishment, irrespective of the victim's conduct'

Chapter 5

1. The European Parliament resolution of 15 January 2009 on Srebrenica reiterated that 'The Srebrenica massacre refers to the July 1995 killing of more than 8,000 Bosniak men and boys, as well as the ethnic cleansing of another 25,000–30,000 refugees, in and around the town of Srebrenica in Bosnia and Herzegovina, by units of the Army of Republika Srpska (VRS) under the command of General Ratko Mladić during the Bosnian War. In April 1993, the United Nations had declared the besieged enclave of Srebrenica in the Drina Valley of north-eastern Bosnia a 'safe area' under UN protection. However, in July 1995 the United Nations Protection Force (UNPROFOR), represented on the ground by a 400-strong contingent of Dutch peacekeepers, failed to prevent the town's capture by the VRS and the subsequent massacre by the Bosnian Serbs of more than 8,000 civilians and prisoners, mostly men and boys'. At http://www.europarl.europa.eu/sides/getDoc.do?pubRef=-//EP//TEXT+TA+P6-TA-2009-0028+0+DOC+XML+V0//EN&language=EN (Last visited 1 December 2011).

2. 'NATO is an alliance of 28 countries from North America and Europe committed to fulfilling the goals of the North Atlantic Treaty signed on 4 April 1949. Its role is to safeguard the freedom and security of its member countries by political and military means' The United Kingdom is a member of NATO. At http://www.nato.int/cps/en/natolive/what_is_nato.htm (last visited 20 November 2012).

3. The United Nations is an international organisation whose stated aims are facilitating cooperation in international law, international security, economic development, social progress, human rights, and the achieving of world peace. The UN was founded in 1945 after World War II to replace the League of Nations, to stop wars between countries, and to provide a platform for dialogue. It contains multiple subsidiary organizations to carry out its missions. At http://www.un.org/en/index.shtml (last visited 20 November 2012).

Chapter 6

1. The rank structure of officers in the British Army are as follows: Junior Officers - Second Lieutenants', Lieutenants' (collectively known as subalterns) and Captains'. Senior Officers include Majors', Lieutenant Colonels', Colonels', Brigadiers', Major Generals', Generals', Lieutenant-Generals' and Field Marshalls'. A senior medical officer would hold the rank of Major and above or equivalent in the other two services.

2. Military operations are the employment of military resources to achieve a specific objective set by the Government of the day. Operation Telic refers to Iraq and Operation Herrick to Afghanistan. The British Military on 30th April 2009 formally ended combat operations in Iraq after more than six years of fighting. At: http://www.telegraph.co.uk/news/worldnews/middleeast/iraq/5250764/British -troops-to-leave-Iraq.html (last visited 20 November 2012).

3. The General Medical Council was created originally by the Medical Act 1858 and now amended via the Medical Act 1983. The Nursing Midwifery Council is controlled via the Nurse, Midwives and Health Visitors Act 1997 and the Nursing Midwifery Order 2001 (Grubb, 2004). In 1902, the Midwives Registration Act established the state regulation of midwives. The Nurses Act 1919 established the General Nursing Council and the state regulation of nurses. In 1983, the United Kingdom Central Council for Nursing, Midwifery and Health Visiting (UKCC) was established. In 2002, the UKCC ceased to exist and the Nursing & Midwifery Council (NMC) was created.

4. Although, the International Law of Armed Conflict, civil negligence claims for clinical negligence and personal injury claims against the Ministry of Defence are important and relevant legal concepts, in the context of the vignette, chapter 9 does not intended to focus on these issues as they are outside the remit of the book.

5. Secondary legislation (also called 'subordinate legislation') is made under authority contained in primary legislation (Martin, 1997).

6. These are instruments made under authority contained in Acts of the UK Parliament. There are three main types of Statutory Instrument. They are 'Orders', 'Regulations', and 'Rules'.

Chapter 7

1. The battlefield is where direct contact with the enemy takes place due to hand-to-hand fighting or where the soldier and enemy are closely engaged in firing bullets, rockets, and grenades at each other.

2. For ease of clarity, medical care also refers to nursing care.

3. Light armoured tactical vehicles have now replaced the traditional Land Rover

4. 'The first 60 minutes following a serious injury is known as the "Golden Hour". Seriously injured casualties correctly resuscitated and treatment begun in a definitive care facility during this vital time will be given the best

chance of survival with minimum long-term disability. Of those victims of major trauma who die, two-thirds will have suffered major head or other central nervous system injuries about which little could have been done that would have altered the inevitable outcome. However, two-thirds of the remaining fatalities would be preventable if the casualty were to receive appropriate medical management in this "Golden Hour". The majority of preventable deaths at the scene occur because of inadequate airway management.   The rest occur because of inadequate management of ineffective breathing or inadequately treated shock following haemorrhage.' At: http://www.haworth21.karoo.net/The%20Golden%20Hour.htm   (last visited 20 November 2012).

5.   The Platinum 10: 2nd BCT, 101st Airborne improves medical training to help save lives, *Infantry Magazine*, July-August 2006.   'Recently, the Army medical community rediscovered that even more important than the Golden Hour was the first 10 minutes after a traumatic injury. The first 10 minutes is now being called the "Platinum 10"' At:
http://findarticles.com/p/articles/mi_m0IAV/is_4_95/ai_n17154164/   (last visited 20 November 2012)

6.   A tactical ballistic missile developed by the Soviet Union during the Cold War and exported widely to other countries.

Chapter 8

1.   The battlefield is defined where direct contact with the enemy takes place due to hand-to-hand fighting or, as more commonly is the case, where the soldier and enemy are closely engaged in firing bullets, rockets, and grenades at each other.   Such a battlefield could be those currently in Afghanistan where British soldiers are fighting the Taliban.

2.   In *Mulcahy v Ministry of Defence (1996) a* serving soldier in the Artillery Regiment was serving in Saudi Arabia in the course of the Gulf war. He was injured when he was part of a team managing a Howitzer, which was firing live rounds into Iraq; he was standing in front of the gun when the gun commander negligently fired it. The Ministry of Defence sought to have the application struck out as disclosing no cause of action. The judge held at first instance that there should be a trial but on appeal the Court of Appeal held that even on the facts pleaded, the plaintiff did not have a cause of action in negligence against the defendant. No duty of care can be owed by one soldier to another on the battlefield.

3.   In *Burmah Oil Company (Burma Trading) Ltd v Lord Advocate (1964),* case installations belonging to the appellant companies near Rangoon had been destroyed by the army in order to prevent them falling into the hands of the

enemy. It was held that as the demolitions had taken place otherwise than in the course of actual military operations compensation was payable.

4.   *Re Post Traumatic Stress Disorder Group Litigation Multiple Claimants v Ministry of Defence,* 2003 Lord Owen stated there was no direct English authority to support the existence of combat immunity at common law'. This group action case involved over 1800 ex-service Claimants who alleged that they were traumatised through exposure to traumatic events on front line tours in Northern Ireland, The Falklands War, the first Gulf War, and the Balkan Wars.

5.   In *Shaw Savill and Albion Co Ltd v the Commonwealth of Australia (1940)* a collision at sea occurred off the Australian coast between the Merchant Vessel, the *Coptic* and the Australia military navy vessel the *HMAS Adelaide,* a warship owned by the Commonwealth of Australia, which caused damage to the *Coptic*. The owners of the *Coptic* sued the Commonwealth of Australia for negligence. The action failed due to *HMAS Adelaide* being involved in military operation against the enemy during WWII.

6.   In *Groves v Commonwealth of Australia (1982),* an airman in the Royal Australian Air Force was injured when he was leaving a stationary aircraft being used to transport civilians in a time of peace. The accident occurred when a folding ladder collapsed beneath him because of the absence of locking pins. The High Court held that as the case arose out of routine duties in time of peace the plaintiff was entitled to the same protection of the common law as would protect other members of the community, and that the Commonwealth were vicariously liable for the negligence of other members of the crew.

7.   In *Hughes v National Union of Mineworkers (1991),* Anthony Hughes was a serving police officer in the Lancashire Constabulary, and the action arises from injuries, which he suffered on 6 September 1984 during mineworkers' disturbances at Kellingley Colliery in North Yorkshire.

8.   An operational environment is within a theatre of war but outside of the battlefield where direct fighting is occurring.

Chapter 9

1.   A Corporal is a junior non-commissioned officer in the British Army below the rank of Sergeant.

2.   Infantry soldiers are fighting frontline soldiers

3.   A Captain is a junior officer in the British Army

4. A light armoured tactical vehicle is a commonly used wheeled vehicle to transport troops that replaced the traditional Land Rover.

5. A fire fight is the military terminology for a localised small battle.

6. A section compromises of 10-12 men

7. The Main Supply Route or MSR is a road that the military secure in order to transport troops and equipment to various locations within a battle zone.

8. A Field Hospital is the equivalent to a NHS Trust Hospital in the UK.

9. A tourniquet is a constricting or compressing device used to control venous and arterial circulation to an extremity for a period of time. It is considered as a lifesaving piece of medical treatment in the Army.

10. An intravenous cannula is a flexible tube which when inserted into the body is used to either withdraw fluid or insert fluid to replenish any fluid lost by a patient.

11. In this circumstance, intravenous fluid is inserted directly into the vein via the intravenous cannula to replace the blood lost due to the injury sustained.

12. A Kalashnikov assault rifles is an automatic assault rifle capable commonly used by insurgents.

13. A 'giving-set' is a long flexible tube that connects a bag of intravenous fluid to a cannula.

14. The fatal process of total hypovolaemia (blood loss). It is most commonly known as 'bleeding'to death

15. Shock in clinical terms is a life-threatening medical emergency. The patient's blood pressure falls so that vital organs are not perfused correctly. Eventually the tissues and the major organs around the body stop working and if left untreated the patient will die.

16. A Standardization Agreement (STANAG) is term used to describe common military or technical procedures or common equipment between the member countries of the alliance. Each NATO state ratifies a STANAG and implements it within their military organisation. The purpose is to provide common operational and administrative procedures and logistics, so one member nation's military may use the stores and support of another member's military.

17. The aim of STANAG 2449 is to standardize training in the Law of Armed Conflict (LOAC) by establishing a minimum standard of training in the LOAC to ensure that military operations are conducted in accordance with international law.

18. An operational environment is within a theatre of war but outside of the battlefield where direct fighting is occurring.

19. *Obiter* is a remark or observation made by a judge in a case, and although included in the body of the court's opinion, it does not form a necessary part of the court's decision or is given material consideration.

Chapter 10

1. A Lieutenant is a junior officer in the army.

2. Combat Medical Technicians are unique to the British Army and serve in the Royal Army Medical Corps (RAMC) only. They are similar to civilian paramedics but do not acquire a recognisable qualification that can be transferred to a civilian environment. They are classed in order of seniority as either a CMT 1, 2, or 3. Class 3 CMT's are familiar to the Territorial Army branch of the RAMC only and not the regular part of the Corps. Training of each class takes 10 weeks of clinical and theoretical training. They give emergency treatment, evacuate casualties, and deal with the routine medical needs of soldiers both in conflict and in times of peace. Combat Medical Technicians are employed within Medical Regiments and Medical Centres in a support role, working under the guidance of Medical Officers. At http://www.armyjobs.mod.uk/jobs/pages/jobdetail.aspx?armyjobid=med300/309+&category= (last visited 20 November 2012).

3. An open pneumothorax is a medical emergency where air or gas is present in the pleural cavity resulting in collapse of the lung on the affected side. This makes the lung collapse, causing chest pain and makes breathing difficult. If untreated the patient can die due to a lack of oxygen. An open pneumothorax develops when penetration injury to the chest allows the pleural space to be exposed to atmospheric pressure.

4. A tension pneumothorax is when air within thoracic cavity cannot exit the pleural space. It is fatal if not diagnosed and treated immediately.

5. A Bergen is a haversack but can be used as a first aid bag that as well as containing usual first aid equipment, it also contains airways, tourniquets, and possibly intravenous fluid and the equipment necessary to administer it.

6. An armed radical Islamist movement that operate in the area of Afghanistan and Pakistan. They are currently engaged in fighting British soldiers and other Western forces.

7. A thoracentesis is an invasive procedure to remove fluid or air from the pleural space. A cannula, or hollow needle, is carefully introduced into the thorax, generally after administration of local anaesthesia.

8. Morphine is an opioid analgesic to relieve severe pain.

9. In *Bolam v Friern Hospital Management Committee (1957)*, John Bolam suffered a depressive illness. He was advised by a doctor to have electro convulsive therapy. He was not told of the risk of bone fractures nor was he given relaxant drugs. He suffered several injuries during his therapy and sued the doctor.

10. In *Bolitho v City and Hackney Health Authority (1998)*, 'Patrick Nigel Bolitho was being treated for croup at St. Bartholomew's Hospital on 16 and 17 January 1984 when he was two years old. Patrick suffered catastrophic brain damage as a result of cardiac arrest induced by respiratory failure. Patrick was admitted into the hospital for respiratory difficulties and was placed under the care of the doctor. The Doctor did not come to see Patrick when the nurse had called her, and on a second occasion, the Doctor delegated the care to another doctor, her junior. This doctor did not also visit and see Patrick. This led to further complications in the patient and then severe brain damage from which he eventually died.

11. The defendants argued based on *Bolam v Friern Hospital Management Committee [1957]* that their decision not to have intubated him earlier could be confirmed by a reliable and respectable body of opinion. The House of Lords held that there would have to be a logical basis for the opinion not to intubate. This would involve a weighing of risks against benefit in order to achieve a defensible conclusion. This means that a judge will be entitled to choose between two bodies of expert opinion and to reject an opinion, which is 'logically indefensible'. On the facts, it was decided that not intubating the child in the particular circumstances at hand was not a negligent way to take, even though the expert opinion on the matter was divided.' *Bolitho v City and Hackney Health Authority* [1998] AC 232.

12. Whether a body of medical opinion needs be a substantial body was considered by Lord Swinton-Thomas in *Defreitas v O'Brien* (1995) 25 BMLR 51 in agreeing with the judge when the case was first heard.

13. The Healthcare Commission is the commission for Healthcare Audit and Inspection.

14. The Defence Medical Services consists comprising of the Royal Navy, the British Army and the Royal Air Force but a single service medical directorates, the training agency, dental services, and its headquarters the Defence Medical Services Department (DMSD). It is headed by The Surgeon General (SG) and The Deputy Chief of Defence Staff (Health).

15. In *R (Smith) v Secretary of State for Defence (2009)*, 'Private Jason Smith joined the Territorial Army in 1992, when he was 21 years old. In June 2003, he was mobilised for service in Iraq. On 26 June 2003, after a brief spell in Kuwait for purposes of acclimatisation, he arrived at Camp Abu Naji, which was to be his base in Iraq. From there he was moved to an old athletics stadium some 12 kilometres away, where about 120 men were billeted. By August, temperatures in the shade were exceeding 50 degrees centigrade. On 9 August, he reported sick, saying that he could not stand the heat. Over the next few days, he was employed on various duties off the base. On the evening of 13 August, he was found collapsed outside the door of a room at the stadium. He was rushed by ambulance to the medical centre at Camp Abu Naji but died almost immediately of hyperthermia or heat stroke'. *R (Smith) v Secretary of State for Defence (2009 at paragraph 1)*

16. A condition in which the heart suddenly and unexpectedly stops beating.

Chapter 11

1. An operational environment equates to being in an area that is not on the battlefield but is subject to attack by the enemy at any time.

2. In *Re MB (1997) (An Adult: Medical Treatment,* 'The patient, aged 23, was the mother of one child, and was carrying another. She did not attend an antenatal clinic until she was some 33 weeks pregnant. The baby was found to be in the breach position and at 50 *per cent* risk of serious injury during vaginal delivery. The patient was admitted to hospital where she agreed to delivery by Caesarean section. However, because of a needle phobia she was not prepared to allow blood samples to be taken nor to undergo anaesthesia by way of injection. She was seen by a consultant anaesthetist and agreed to anaesthesia by mask without injection. She went into labour and was taken to the operating theatre. However, when she saw the mask she refused to consent to anaesthesia. Later that evening the hospital obtained a declaration from the court that it would be lawful for the gynaecologist to operate. The patient appealed. Held - dismissing the appeal: (1) The relevant principles to be applied were: (a) in general, physically invasive medical treatment without the patient's consent was a tortious and a criminal assault (b) a mentally competent patient had an absolute right to refuse medical treatment even when this might lead to the patient's death (c) in an emergency medical treatment could be given if, through lack of capacity, there was no consent,

provided it was essential and no more than was reasonably required in the patient's best interests'. *Re MB (1997) (An Adult: Medical Treatment)*.

3. An autojet intramuscular injection of 10mgs of Morphine is carried by every military person in the field for their own personnel use if wounded. This is to be administered by another military person or themselves.

4. *St George's Healthcare NHS Trust v S, R v Collins, and others, ex parte S (1998) 'A* single woman born in June 1967, working as a veterinary nurse, sought to register as a new patient at a local NHS practice in London. She was approximately 36 weeks pregnant. She had not sought antenatal care. Pre-eclampsia was rapidly diagnosed. She was advised that she needed urgent attention, with bed rest and admission to hospital for an induced delivery. Without this treatment, her health and life and the health and life of her baby were in real danger. She fully understood the potential risks but rejected the advice. She wanted her baby to be born naturally.

5. She was seen by Louise Collins, a social worker approved under the Mental Health Act 1983, and two doctors, Dr Caroline Chill and Dr Siobhan Jeffreys, a duly qualified practitioner registered under s 12(2) of the Act. They repeated the advice she had already been given. She adamantly refused to accept it. An application was made under s 2 of the Act by Louize Collins for her admission to Springfield Hospital 'for assessment'. Dr Chill and Dr Jeffreys signed the necessary written recommendations. That evening (25 April) S was admitted to Springfield Hospital against her will.

6. Shortly before midnight, again against her will, she was transferred to St George's Hospital. In view of her continuing adamant refusal to consent to treatment, an application was made ex parte on behalf of the hospital authority to Hogg J sitting in the Family Division in chambers, who granted a declaration, which in summary terms, dispensed with S's consent to treatment. Later that evening appropriate medical procedures were carried out and at 22.00 S was delivered of a baby girl by Caesarean section. When she recovered, she developed strong feelings of revulsion and at first rejected her baby.

7. On 30 April, she was returned to Springfield Hospital. On 2 May, her detention under s 2 of the Act was terminated, and against medical advice, she immediately discharged herself from hospital.

8. During the period when she was a patient, no specific treatment for mental disorder or mental illness was prescribed.' *St George's Healthcare NHS Trust v S, R v Collins, and others, ex parte S [1998] 3 All ER 673 at 678.*

9. Re B (Adult, refusal of medical treatment) *(1999)* 'the claimant, who was then 41 years old, suffered a haemorrhage of the spinal column in her neck.

She was admitted to a hospital run by the defendant NHS trust. Although the claimant recovered sufficiently to return to work, her condition deteriorated at the beginning of 2001. She was readmitted to the hospital after suffering an intramedullary cervical spine cavernoma. As a result of the cavernoma, she became tetraplegic and suffered complete paralysis from the neck down. She was transferred to the hospital's intensive care unit and began to experience respiratory problems. She was treated with a ventilator, upon which she had been entirely dependent ever since. After neurological surgery to remove the cavernous haematoma, she was able to move her head and articulate words. She gave formal instructions to the hospital through her solicitors that she wished artificial ventilation to be removed, even though she realised that that would almost certainly result in her death. She was assessed by two consultant psychiatrists at the hospital. They initially concluded that she had capacity to make a decision in respect of the withdrawal of treatment, and preparations were put in hand to turn the ventilator off. However, those preparations were called off after the psychiatrists changed their minds as to the claimant's capacity'. *Re B (adult: refusal of medical treatment) [2002] two All ER 449 at 450.*

10. In *Re T (adult: refusal of treatment) (1992),* T was injured in a car accident when she was 34 weeks pregnant. She was Jehovah Witness patient refusing to consent to a blood transfusion. This case is explained in detail in chapter 2, footnote 37, page 35.

11. In *Rochdale Healthcare (NHS) Trust v C (1997),* 'The patient was in hospital for the birth of the child. The consultant obstetrician was of the opinion that a Caesarian section was necessary. She refused to give consent to the treatment saying that she would prefer to die. The obstetrician was of opinion, and told the patient, that without the operation both she and the child would die. As the patient was in the throes of labour with all that involved in terms of pain and emotional stress and who, in those circumstances could speak in terms which seemed to accept the inevitability of her own death, was not a patient who was able properly to weigh-up the considerations that arose so as to make any valid decision'. *Rochdale Healthcare (NHS) Trust v C* [1997] 1 FCR 274.

12. Fluctuating capacity can occur when the patient is drowsy after being given a drug such as Morphine.

13. Temporary capacity can occur when the patient is administered with a general anaesthetic or is sedated.

Chapter 12

1. A Major is a senior office in the British Army, above a Captain but below a Lieutenant Colonel.

2. Post-Traumatic Stress Disorder is a psychological disorder in response to severe traumatic experiences. It is diagnosed in accordance with the *Diagnostic and Statistical Manual of Mental Disorders* (DSM IV) (1995), which is a categorical classification system. At http://www.psych.org/MainMenu/Research/DSMIV.aspx (last visited 20 November 2012).

3. A Lieutenant-Colonel is a higher ranking senior officer than a Major.

4. In *Campbell v MGN (2004),* the supermodel Naomi Campbell was photographed leaving a meeting of Narcotics Anonymous. The photograph was published in the Daily Mirror, which lead to Naomi Campbell suing for breach of confidence. In a majority decision, the court determined that even though Ms Campbell had brought into the public domain that she was being treated for a drug addiction, she was however still entitled to have certain information kept confidential such as the place where she was being treated and the type of treatment she was being given.

5. The European Convention of Human Rights and Fundamental Freedoms protect both the right for confidential information and the right of freedom of expression.

6. In *Tarasoff v Regents of the University of California (1976)* Prosenjit Poddar killed Tatiana Tarasoff. Tatiana's parents, alleged that two months earlier Poddar confided his intention to kill Tatiana to Dr. Lawrence Moore, a psychologist employed by the Cowell Memorial Hospital at the University of California at Berkeley. They allege that on Moore's request, the campus police briefly detained Poddar, but released him when he appeared rational. They further claimed that Dr. Harvey Powelson, Moore's superior, then directed that no further action be taken to detain Poddar. No one warned Tatiana's or her family of his intention to kill. *Tarasoff v Regents of the University of California* 17 Cal 3d 425, 551 P2d 334 [Cal 1976].

References

A Moral Profession, (2003), *Military Medical Ethics*, Washington, DC Borden Institute, vol. 1, ch. 10, pp. 269-291.

Adams v War Office [1955] 1 WLR 1116.

Agan, J. Koch L.C and Rumrill, Jr (2008) The use of focus groups in rehabilitation research, *A Journal of Prevention, Assessment and Rehabilitation*, 31(2), pp. 259-269.

Agerd A. Herlitz J. and Hermeren G. (2004) Obtaining informed consent from patients in early phase of acute myocardial infarction: physicians' experience and attitudes, *Heart*, 90(2), pp. 208-210.

Ahmed v Austria [1996] ECHR 25964/94.

Airedale NHS Trust v Bland [1993] 1 All ER 821 at 866.

Air Force Act 1955. At: http://www.legislation.gov.uk/ukpga/1955/19/pdfs/ukpga_19550019_en.pdf (last visited 20 November 2012).

Akander, D and Sangeete, S (2010) Immunities of State Officials, International Crimes, and Foreign Domestic Courts, *The European Journal of International Law*, 21(4), pp. 815-852.

Algasse, R.C. (1977) Protection of civilian lives in warfare: a comparison between Islamic law and modern international law concerning the conduct of hostilities, *Military law and Law of War Review*, pg. 246.

Altun I. (2008) Innovation in behaviour patterns that characterize nurses, *Nurs Ethics*, 15(6), pp. 838-40.

American Psychiatric Association (1995) Post Traumatic Stress Disorder at: http://www.psych.org/Resources/DisasterPsychiatry/APADisasterPsychiatryResources/WhenDisasterStrikes.aspx (last visited 20 November 2012). Also at: http://www.nhs.uk/Conditions/Post-traumatic-stress-disorder/Pages/Introduction.aspx (last visited 20 November 2012).

Annas, J. (2008) Military Medical Ethics - Physician First, Last, Always, *The New England Journal of Medicine*, 359, pp. 1087-1090.

Appiah, K.A. (2006) *Cosmopolitanism. Ethics in a World of Strangers*, New York/London: Norton.

Arber, S. (1993) The research process. In: Gilbert, N. (ed.) *Researching Social Life*, London, Sage.

Army Act 1955. At:

http://www.legislation.gov.uk/ukpga/1955/18/pdfs/ukpga_19550018_e
n.pdf (last visited 20 November 2012).

Army Doctrine Publication (2000), *Logistics, Medical Supplement,* (3),
annex A to chapter 2, 2-A-1. Ministry old Defence.

Armed Forces Discipline Act 2000. At:
http://www.legislation.gov.uk/ukpga/2000/4/pdfs/ukpga_20000004_en
.pdf (last visited 20 November 2012).

Armed Forces Discipline Act 2000. At:

Armed Forces Act 2006. At:
http://www.legislation.gov.uk/ukpga/2006/52/pdfs/ukpga_20060052_e
n.pdf (last visited 20 November 2012).

Armed Forces Act 2006, (c.52) Part 1 (Offences), mutiny, section 6, (2)
(a) (ii). At:
http://www.legislation.gov.uk/ukpga/2006/52/pdfs/ukpga_20060052_e
n.pdf (last visited 20 November 2012).

Armed Forces Act 2006. Part 1, section 12. At:
http://www.legislation.gov.uk/ukpga/2006/52/pdfs/ukpga_20060052_e
n.pdf (last visited 20 November 2012).

Armed Forces Discipline Act 2000. At:
http://www.legislation.gov.uk/ukpga/2000/4/pdfs/ukpga_20000004_en
.pdf (last visited 20 November 2012).

Armed Forces Discipline Act 2000. At:
http://www.legislation.gov.uk/ukpga/2000/4/pdfs/ukpga_20000004_en
.pdf (last visited 20 November 2012).

Army General Administrative Instructions and Material Regulations For
The Army (1998), chapter 67, Crown Copyright.

Badaracco, J. (1997) *Defining Moments. When Managers Must Choose
between Right and Wrong,* Cambridge, MA: Harvard University Press.

Bahadori, A. and Fitzpatrick, J.J. (2009) Level of Autonomy of Primary
Care Nurse Practitioners, *Journal of the American Academy of Nurse
Practitioners*, 21, pp. 513-519.

Bailey, T.M.Rosychuk, R.J. Yonge, O. and Marrie, T.J. (2008) A Duty to
Treat During a Pandmoc? The Time for Talk is Now, *The American
Journal of Bioethics,* 8(8), pp. 29-31.

Bakas, T. Farran, C.J. Austin, J.K. Given, B.A. Johnson, E.A. and
Williams, L. S (2009) Content Validity and Satisfaction with a Stroke
Caregiver Intervention Program, *Journal of Nursing Scholarship*,
41(4), pp. 368-375.

Bajec, I. (1993) Post-Gulf War explosive injuries in liberated Kuwait,
Injury, 24(8), pp. 517-520.

Barter, C and Renold, E. (1999) The use of vignettes in qualitative research, *Social Research Update*, 25, pp. 1-6.

Barter, C and Renold, E. (2000) 'I Wanna Tell You A Story' Exploring the application of vignettes in qualitative research with children and young people, *International Journal of Social Research Methodology*, 3(4), pp.307-323.

Bassett, A. (1997) *Guns and Brooches: Australian Army Nursing from the Boer War to the Gulf War,* Oxford University Press Australia, Oxford.

Beam TE (2003) Medical Ethics on the Battlefield: the Crucible of Military Medical Ethics, 2003; in TE Beam & L.R Sparacino (Eds) *Military Medical Ethics*, 2, pp. 369-402, Washington, DC Borden Institute, Falls Church, Va.: Office of the Surgeon General

Beck, L.W. (Ed) (1949) *Critique of Practical Reason and other Writings in Moral Philosophy,* Chicago, University of Chicago Press, pp. 346-350.

Beech, M. (2007) Confidentiality in health care: conflicting legal and ethical issues, *Nursing Standard*, 2(21), pp. 42- 46.

Bendelow, G. (1993) Using visual imagery to explore gendered notions of pain. In *Researching Sensitive Topics* (Renzetti, C.M. and Lee, R.M. edns) Sage, London, pp. 212-228.

Benetar, S.R. and Upshur, R.E.G. (2008) Dual Loyalty of Physicians in the Military and in Civilian Life, Public Health and the Military, *American Journal of Public Health*, 98(12), pp. 2131-2165.

Best, R. (2007) *CRS Report for Congress, military medical care questions and answers*, March 7. At: http://vrb.homestead.com/2008_CRS_Report_on_Increase_in_TRICA RE_Costs.pdf (last visited 20 November 2012).

Bianchi, A (2007) Assessing the Effectiveness of the UN Security Council's Anti-terrorism Measures: The Quest for Legitimacy and Cohesion, *The European Journal of International Law,* 17(5), pp. 881–919.*Bici and another v Ministry of Defence* [2004] EWHC 786 (QB).

Bici and another v Ministry of Defence [2004] EWHC 786 (QB).

Bloche, M.G. and Marks, J.H (2005) Doctors and Interrogators at Guantanamo Bay, *New England Journal of Medicine*, 353(1), pp. 6-8.

Blyth v Birmingham Water Works [1843-60] All ER Rep 478 at 480.

Bolam v Friern Hospital Management Committee [1957] 2 All ER 118

Bolitho v City and Hackney Health Authority [1998] AC 232

Bolton v Stone [1951] 1 All ER 1078

Bomann-Larsen, L. (2004) Licence to kill? The question of just vs, unjust combatants, Journal *of Military Ethics,* 3(2), pp. 142-160.

Bowater v Rowley Regis Corporation [1944] KB 476

Boyd, J.W Himmelstie, D.U. Lasser, K, McCormick, D, Bor, D.H. Cutrona, S.L. and Woolhandler, S. (2007) U.S. Medical Students' Knowledge about the Military Draft, the Geneva Conventions, and Military Medical Ethics, *International Journal of Health Studies*, 37(4), pp. 643-650.

Brazier, M and Cave, E (2007) *Medicine, Patients and the Law*, 4th edn, Penguin, England.

Brooks, H and Sullivan, WJ. (2002) The importance of patient autonomy at birth, *International Journal of Obstetric Anaesthesia*, v.11, pp.196-203.

British Medical Association (2001) *The medical profession and human rights, handbook for a changing agenda. London: BMA publications, 247.*

Burmah Oil Company (Burma Trading) Ltd v Lord Advocate [1964] 2 All ER 348

Bradley, A.W. and Ewing, K.D. (2007) *Constitutional and Administrative Law*, 14th edn., Pearson Education Limited.

Bryman, A. (2004) *Social Research Methods*, Oxford University Press, Oxford.

Bugnion, F (1995) Remembering Hiroshima, *International Review of the Red Cross*, 35 (306), pp. 307-313.

Bukowski, C.W. (2006) The Platinum 10: 2nd BCT, 101st Airborne improves medical training to help save lives, *Infantry Magazine,* July-August. At: http://findarticles.com/p/articles/mi_m0IAV/is_4_95/ai_n17154164/ (last visited 20 November 2012).

Burns, D. (2009) Clinical Leadership for general practice nurses, 2: Facilitating Factors, Practice Nursing, 20(10), pp. 519-523.

Burns, N. and Grove, S. (2003) *Understanding nursing research*, 3rd edn. WB Saunders, Philadelphia.

British Armed Forces At: http://en.wikipedia.org/wiki/British_Armed_Forces (last visited 1 December 2011).

Callicott, K. (2003) Culturally sensitive collaboration within person-centred planning, *Focus on Autism and Other Developmental Disabilities*, 18, i1, pp. 60-69.

Callan, V. (2005) Extrication of the seriously injured road crash victim, *Emergency Medicine Journal,* Nov, 22(11), pp. 817-21.

Campbell v MGN [2004] 2 All ER 995.

Carey B. (2009) Consent and refusal for adolescents: the law, *British Journal of Nursing,* 18(22), pp. 1366-1368.

Carney, E. (1996) Macedonians *and Mutiny: Discipline and Indiscipline in the Army of Phillip and Alexander,* Classical Philosophy, 89, pp. 19-44.

Cassidy v Ministry of Health [1951] 1 All ER 574 at 586.

Castledine, Sir George. (2010) Limitations of confidentiality, British Journal of Nursing, 19(2), p. 135.

Chang, K.H. and Horrocks, S. (2008) Is there place for ontological hermeneutics in mental-health nursing research? A review of a hermeneutic study, *International Journal of Nursing Practice,* 14, pp. 383-390.

Chester v Afshar [2004] UKHL 41.

Cirgin-Elleet, M. and Beausang, C.C. (2002) Introduction to qualitative research, *Gastroenteral Nurs,* 25, pp. 10-14.

Clarke, P. A. (2006) Medical Ethics at Guantanamo Bay and Abu Ghraib: The Problem of Dual Loyalty, *Journal of Law, Medicine and Ethics,* Fall, pp. 570-580.

Clarke, K.A. (2009) Uses of a research diary: learning reflectively, developing understanding and establishing transparency, *Nurse Researcher,* 17(1), pp. 68-76.

Cluett, E. and Bluff, R. (2006) *Principles and Practice of Research in Midwifery,* p 6, Churchill Livingstone, Edinburgh.

Coleman, S. (2009) The Problems of Duty and Loyalty, *Journal of Military Ethics,* 8(2), pp. 105-115.

Commission for Healthcare Audit and Inspection, (2009) *Defence Medical Services: A review of the clinical governance of the Defence Medical Service in the UK and overseas,* Summary, p. 14 and Appendix 1, Standards for Better Health, Second domain: clinical and cost effectiveness, Core standard C7, e), p. 95.

Crowe, C and Hardil, K. (1991) Nursing and War: transforming our legacy. *The Canadian Nurse,* 87, pp. 291-302.

Crowe, C. and Hardil, K. (1991) Nursing and War: transforming our legacy. *The Canadian Nurse,* 87, pp. 291-302.

Crown Proceedings Act 1947. At:
http://www.legislation.gov.uk/ukpga/1947/44/pdfs/ukpga_19470044_e n.pdf (last visited 20 November 2012).

Crown Proceedings Act 1987. At:
http://www.legislation.gov.uk/ukpga/1987/25/pdfs/ukpga_19870025_e n.pdf (last visited 20 November 2012).

Curtis, E. and Redmond, R (2007) Focus Groups in Nursing Research, *Nurse Researcher*, 14(2), pp. 25-37.

Cutcliffe, J.R, Joyce, A. Cummins, M. (2004) Building a case for understanding the lived experiences of males who attempt suicide in Alberta, Canada, *Journal of Psychiatric and Mental Health Nursing*, 11, pp. 305-312.

Daborn v Bath Tramways Motor Co Ltd and Trevor Smithey [1946] 2 All ER 333 at 337

Davis, A.J., Aroskar, M.A., Liaschenko, J. and Drought, T.S. (1997) *Ethical Dilemma and Nursing Practice*, 4th edn, New Jersey, Prentice-Hall, Inc.

Davies M. (1998) *Textbook on Medical Law*, Blackstone Press Limited, 2nd edn, ch 6 & 7.

Declaration of Geneva (1948) Adopted by the 2nd General Assembly of the World Medical Association, Geneva, Switzerland. At: http://www.wma.net/en/30publications/10policies/g1/index.html.pdf?print-media-type&footer-right=[page]/[toPage] (last visited 20 November 2012).

Defence about defence. At: http://www.mod.uk/DefenceInternet/AboutDefence/WhatWeDo/Legal/ArmedForcesAct/ArmedForcesAct2006.htm (last visited 20 November 2012).

Defence Medical Services At http://www.mod.uk/DefenceInternet/microsite/dms (last visited 20 November 2012).

Defreitas v O'Brien (1995) 25 BMLR 51.

Delivering Our Armed Forces' Healthcare Needs: A Concordat between the UK Departments of Health and the Ministry of Defence (2005). At: http://www.dh.gov.uk/prod_consum_dh/groups/dh_digitalassets/@dh/@en/documents/digitalasset/dh_4134564.pdf (last visited 20 November 2012).

Department of Health (2009) Reference guide to consent, 2nd edn, section 1, p. 9. Crown Copyright. At: http://www.dh.gov.uk/prod_consum_dh/groups/dh_digitalassets/documents/digitalasset/dh_103653.pdf (last visited 20 November 2012).

Department of Health (2010), *Equity and excellence: Liberating the NHS*, White paper, Presented to Parliament by the Secretary of State for Health by Command of Her Majesty, Crown Copyright.

Deslauriers, M. (2002) *How to Distinguish Aristotle's Virtues*, In: Koninklijke Brill, NV Lieden, Phronesis, XLV11/2, 47(2), pp. 101-126.

Detter, I (2000) *The Law of War,* 2nd edn, Cambridge University Press, pp. 151-154.

Dicey, A.V. In: Loveland, I. (1996) *What is the prerogative? A Definitional Controversy, The Royal Prerogative*, Constitutional Law, Blackstone, ch. 4, p. 10.

Dimond, B. (2003) Legal aspects of consent, *British Journal of Nursing Monograph*, Mark Allen Publishing, London.

Dimond B. (2006) *Legal Aspects of Midwifery*, 3rd edn, Elsevier, Philadelphia.

Donaghue v Stevenson [1932] AC 562

Dual Loyalty and Human Rights in Health Professional Practice Report (2002) *Physicians for Human Rights and School of Public Health and Primary Health Care,* University of Cape Town, Health Sciences Faculty.

Duggleby, W. (2005) What about focus group interaction? *Qualitative Health Research,* 15(6), pp. 832-840.

Ellis, P. (2010) *Understanding Research for Nursing Students*, Learning Matters, Exeter

Enemark, C. (2008) Physicians at War: The Dual-Loyalties Challenge, *Journal of Military Ethics,* 7(4), pp. 320-322.

Erle, R.H. (1902) Martial Law, *18 L. Q. Rev.* pp. 133.

Enemark, C. (2008) Physicians at War: The Dual-Loyalties Challenge, *Journal of Military Ethics,* 7(4), pp. 320-322.

Erle, R.H. (1902) Martial Law, *18 L. Q. Rev.* pp. 133.

Ellis, P. (2010) *Understanding Research for Nursing Students*, Learning Matters, Exeter

Employment Rights Act 1996. At: http://www.legislation.gov.uk/ukpga/1996/18/section/192 (last visited 20 November 2012).

Enemark, C. (2008) Triage, Treatment, and Torture: Ethical Challenges for US Military Medicine in Iraq, *Journal of Military Ethics*, (7)3, pp.187-201.

—. (2008) Physicians at War: The Dual-Loyalties Challenge, *Journal of Military Ethics,* 7(4), pp. 320-322.

Erle, R.H. (1902) Martial Law, *18 L. Q. Rev.* pp. 133.

Eskelinen L. and Caswell D. (2006) Comparison of social work practice in teams using video vignette technique in a multi design, *Qualitative Social Work*, 5(4), pp.489-503.

European Convention of Human Rights (1950).

Explanatory Notes to Armed Forces Discipline Act 2000, Chapter 4. At:

http://www.legislation.gov.uk/ukpga/2000/4/notes/contents   (last visited 20 November 2012).

Employment Rights Act 1996. At:
http://www.legislation.gov.uk/ukpga/1996/18/section/192 (last visited 20 November 2012).

Faris, J. A. Douglas, M.K. Maples , D.C. Berg, L. R and Thrailkill, A (2010) Job satisfaction of advanced practice nurses in the Veteran's Health Administration,   *Journal of the American Academy of Nurse Practitioners*, 22, pp. 35-44.

Farrell, T. (2005) *World Culture and Military Power*, July-September, *Security Studies*, 14(3), pp. 448-488.

Farsides B. In: Tingle J and Crimm A (2002) *An ethical perspective-consent and patient autonomy*, Nursing Law and Ethics, 2nd edn, Blackwell Publishing, ch 8, p. 122.

Feczer, D. and Bjorklund, P. (2009) Forever Changed: Posttraumatic Stress Disorder in Female Military Veterans, Case Report, Perspectives in Psychiatric Care, 45(4), pp. 278-291.

Fenrick, W, J (2001) Targeting and Proportionality during the NATO Bombing Campaign against Yugoslavia, *The European Journal of International Law*, 12 (3), pp. 489-502.

Finlay, L. (2009) Exploring lived experience: principle and practice of phenomenological research, *International Journal of Therapy and Rehabilitation*, Sept, 16(9), 474-481.

Fleischmann, S.T. (2006) Teaching Ethics More Than an Honor Code, *Sci Eng Ethics*, 12, pp. 381-9.

Foster, S (2009) *How to Write Better Law Essays*, Pearson, Longman, London.

Franklin, G.F. Coleman A.M. Shumpert, K.D. and Medley, M.B. (2005) The use of problem-based learning in rural special education preservice training programs, *Rural Special Education Quarterly* 24(2), pp. 28-32.

Friedenberg, J. Mulvihill, M. and Caraballo, L.R. (1993) From ethnography to survey: some methodological issues in research on health seeking in East Harlem, *Human Organizational*, 52, pp. 151-161.

Fry S Harvey, Hurley, R.M and Foley, B.J. (2002) Development of a Model of Moral Distress in Military Nursing, *Nursing Ethics,* 2002, 9(4), pp. 373 – 387.

Fullbrook S. (2007) Consent and capacity; principles of the Mental Capacity Act 2005, *British Journal of Nursing,* 16(7), pp. 412 - 415.

Ganz, G (1997) Delegated Legislation: A Necessary Evil or a Constitutional Outrage?' In Leyland, P and Woods, T (eds) *Administrative Law Facing the Future: Old Constraints and New Horizons,* pp. 63–64.

Garfield, R and McCarthy, C.F. (2005) Nursing and nursing education in Iraq: challenges and opportunities, *International Council of Nurses,* 52(3), pp. 180-5.

General Medical Council (GMC). (2006). *Good Medical Practice.* pp. 2. At: http://www.gmc-uk.org/static/documents/content/GMP_0910.pdf (last visited 1 December 2011).

—. (2006), *Management for Doctors, Regulating Doctors, Ensuring Good Medical Practice,* p. 4 para. 4, London.

—. (2008). *Consent: patient and doctors making decisions together.* At: Retrieved from http://www.gmc-uk.org/static/documents/content/Consent_0510.pdf (last visited 20 November 2012).

—. (2008). *Supplementary Guidance: Conflicts of interest,* paragraph 2. At http://www.gmc-uk.org/static/documents/content/Conflicts_of _interest. pdf (last visited 20 November 2012).

—. (2009). *Confidentiality: Guidance of Doctors.* At http://www.gmc-uk.org/static/documents/content/Confidentiality_0910.pdf (last visited 20 November 2012).

—. (2011). Consent guidance: Legal Annex- Common Law. At http://www.gmc-uk.org/guidance/ethical_guidance/consent_guidance _common_law.asp. (last visited 20 November 2012).

General Sir Mike Jackson (2007) Soldier, The Autobiography of General Sir Mike Jackson, pp. 12-13.

Geneva Convention of 1864, Protocol I, Art 41, para 3 and Geneva Conventions of 1949, Additional Protocol I of 1977 (Protocol I).

Geneva Conventions of 1949, Additional Protocol I of 1977 (Protocol I), Art. 43 chapter VII, article 38. At: http://www.icrc.org/ihl.nsf/WebART/470-750053?OpenDocument and http://www.icrc.org/ihl.nsf/WebART/470-750047?OpenDocument (last visited 20 November 2012).

Geneva Conventions Act 1957. At: http://www.legislation.gov.uk/ukpga/1957/52/pdfs/ukpga_19570052_e n.pdf (last visited 20 November 2012).

Geneva Conventions (Amendments) Act 1995/ At: http://www.legislation.gov.uk/ukpga/1995/27/pdfs/ukpga_19950027_e n.pdf (last visited 20 November 2012).

Gerrish, K. and Lacey, A. (2006) *The Research Process in Nursing*, Blackwell Publishing, 5th edn.

Gibson, E. (2006) Medical Confidentiality and Protection of Third Party Interests, *American Journal of Bioethics*, 6(2), pp. 21-22.

Gillon, R. (1986). *'Philosophical Medical Ethics'*, Chichester, John Wiley and Sons, pp, 100-105.

Glasgow Corporation v Muir [1943] 2 All ER 44

Goodnough, K. (2005) Issues in Modified Problem-Based Learning: A Self-Study in Pre-Service_Science-Teacher Education, *Canadian Journal of Science, Mathematics and Teaching Technology Education*, 5:3 July, pp. 289-306.

Goodwin, V, and Happell, B. (2009) Seeing both the forests and the trees: a process for tracking individual responses' in focus group interviews. *Nurse Researcher*, 17(1), pp. 62-67.

Gould, D. (1996) Using vignettes to collect data for nursing research studies: how valid are the findings? *Journal of Clinical Nursing*, 5(4), pp. 207-212.

Gourney, K. and Ritter, S. (1997) Commentary: What future for research in mental health nursing, *Journal of Psychiatric and Mental Health Nursing*, 4, pp 441-446.

Government to Slash NHS Targets. At: http://news.bbc.co.uk/1/hi/health/3912933.stm   (last   visited   20 November 2012).

Green, S. (2006) Coherence of Medical Negligence Case, *Med Law Review*, 14(1)1 March, pp. 1-14 at p. 5.

Grey, I.M. McClean,B. and Branes-Homes,D. (2002) Staff attributions about the causes of challenging behaviours; effects of longitudinal training in multi-element behaviour support, *Journal of Learning Disability*, 6(3), pp. 297-322.

Griffiths, L. and Jasper, M. (2007) Warrior nurse: duality and complementarity of role in the operational environment, *Journal of Advanced Nursing*, 61(1), pp. 92-99.

Griffith, R. and Tengnah, C. (2008) *Law and Professional Issues in Nursing*, Learning Matters Ltd, Exeter.

Griffith R. and Tengnah C (2008) Mental Capacity Act 2005: statutory principles and key concepts, British Journal of Community Nursing, 13(5), pp. 233-237.

Gross, M. (2004) Bioethics and armed conflict: mapping the moral dimensions of medicine and war. *Hastings Cent Rep,* 34, pp. 22-20.

Gross, M. (2006) *Bioethics and Armed Conflict, Moral Dilemmas of Medicine and War*, ch. 3, p 71, The MIT Press Cambridge, Massachusetts, London, England.

Gross, M.L. (2008) Why Treat the Wounded? Warrior Care, Military Salvage, and National Health, *The American Journal of Bioethics*, 8(2), pp 3-12 at p. 4

Groves v Commonwealth of Australia (1982) 150 C.L.R 113 at 117.

Grubb, A. (2004) *Principles of Medical Law*, 2nd edn., Oxford University Press

Gump, L.S. Baker, R.C. and Roll, S. (2000) The Moral Justification Scale: Reliability and Validity of a New Measure of Care and Justice Orientations, *Adolescence*, 35(137), pp. 67-76

Hackett, General Sir John (1963) *The Professional of Arms*, London, Times Publishing Company.

Hallgarth, W.M. (2007) Bioethics and Armed Conflict: Moral Dilemmas of Medicine and War, *Journal of Military Ethics*, 6(1), pp. 83-84.

Hanks, R.G. (2010) Development and testing of an instrument to measure protective nursing advocacy, *Nursing Ethics*, 17(2), pp. 255-267.

Hansen, J. (2006) Using Problem-Based Learning in Accounting, *Journal of Education for Business*, March/April pp. 221-224.

Hanssen, I. (2004) An international nursing perspective on autonomy, *Nursing Ethics* 11(1) pp. 29-41.

Hanson, T. (2005) Case Comment, Delivery by caesarean section: the difference between a national standard and negligence, *Medical Law Review*, 13(2), pp. 268-272.

Happell, B (1996) Focus group interviews as a tool for psychiatric nursing research, *Australian and New Zealand Journal of Mental Health*, 5(1), pp. 40-44

—. (2007) Focus groups in nursing research: an appropriate method or the latest fad? *Nurse Researcher*, 14(2), pp.18-24.

Harper, P. (2006) Different skills, different attitude, same duty of care, *British Journal of Nursing*, (15)10, pp. 537-539.

Hedahl, M (2009) Blood and Backwaters: A Call to Arms for the Professional of Arms, Journal *of Military Ethics*, 8(1), pp. 19-33.

Hedley Byrne & Co Ltd v Heller & Partners Ltd [1963] 2 All ER 575 at 615.

Hek, G. (1994) The research process, *Journal of Community Nursing*, 8 (6), pp 4-6.

Helvetius In: Cramer, S. (1921) *Disciplining Americans*, North American Review, 214, July/Dec, p. 774.

Heron J. (2009) *Medical Law*, ch.3, Pearson Education Limited, Dorset.

Hess, J.R and Holcomb, J.B. (2008) Transfusion Practice in Military Trauma, *Transfusion Medicine,* 18(3), pp. 143-150.

Heywood, R. (2006) The Logic of Bolitho, *Professional Negligence,* 22(4), pp. 225-235.

Heyman, C. (2008) *The British Army: A Pocket Guide 2008 – 2009,* Crown copyright.

Hickman, T. (2004) The "uncertain shadow": throwing light on the right to a court under Article 6(1)", *ECHR, Public Law,* pp. 1-14.

High Quality Care For All (2008) *NHS Next Stage Review Final Report,* Department of Health, Crown Copyright.

Hill v Potter [1983] 3 All ER 716 at 729.

Hitchings, E. (2008) Everyday Cases in the Post-*White* Era, [2008] Fam Law 873

Hodgetts, T.J. (2004) Personal view: a day in the life of an emergency physician at war, *Emergency Medical Journal,* 21, 129-130.

Hodgetts, T.J. Mahoney PF. Russell MQ. Byers M. (2006) ABC to <C> ABC: redefining the military trauma paradigm, *Emerg. Med. J.* 23(10): 745-746.

Hucks v Cole [1983] 4 Med. L.R. 393, CA at 397

Hughes, R. (1998) Considering the vignette technique and its application to a study of drug infecting and HIV risk and safer behaviour, *Sociology of Health and Illness,* 20(3), pp. 381-400.

Hughes, R. and Huby, M. (2002) The application of vignettes in social and nursing research, *Methodological Issues in Nursing Research,* 37(4), pp. 382-386.

Hughes v National Union of Mineworkers [1991] 4 All ER 278 at 289.

Huntington, S.P. (2003) The military mind: Conservative realism of the professional military ethic. In: War, Morality and the Military Profession. Boulder, Colo: Westview Press. In W. Madden and B.S. Carter, Physician-Soldier.

International Committee of the Red Cross (2002) *International Humanitarian Law-Answers to your Questions,* Geneva, Switzerland. At: http://www.icrc.org/eng/assets/files/other/icrc_002_0703.pdf (last visited 20 November 2012).

—. (2011) *Health Care in Danger-Making the Case.* At: http://www.icrc.org/eng/assets/files/publications/icrc-002-4072.pdf (last visited 20 November 2012).

—. (2011) *How Does Law Protect In War? Outline of International Humanitarian Law,* vol. 1. At http://www.icrc.org/eng/assets/files/publications/icrc-0739-part-i.pdf (last visited 20 November 2012).

International Council of Nurses. *Code of Ethics for nurses.* Geneva: ICN, 2000.

International Dual Loyalty Working Group-Summary. (2006) In: L. London, L.S. Rubenstein, L. Baldwin-Reagaven and A. Van Es, 'Dual Loyalty among Military Health Professionals: Human Rights and Ethics in Times of Armed Conflict', Cambridge Quarterly of Healthcare Ethics, 15, pp. 381-391.

Jackson, M. (2007) *Soldier,* The Autobiography of General Sir Mike Jackson, Bantam Press, London, pp. 12-13.

Jackson E. (2009) *Medical Law: Text, Cases and Materials,* 2nd edn., Oxford University Press.

Jasper, M.A (2005) Using reflective writing within research, *Journal of Research in Nursing,* 10(3), pp. 247-260.

Johnson, J.T. (1999*) Morality and Contemporary Warfare,* New Haven, CT: Yale University Press, p. 212.

Jones, M.A. (2002) *Textbook on Tort,* Oxford University Press, 8th edn.

Jones, M. and Irvine, B. Civitas (2003) Health Briefing, NICE or NASTY: Has NICE Eliminated the 'Postcode Lottery in the NHS'? At: http://www.civitas.org.uk/pdf/NICE.pdf (last visited 20 November 2012).

JSP 383, The Joint Service Manual of The Law of Armed Conflict (2004) *Historical and General Background,* para 1.1 - 1.2. Also at: http://www.mod.uk/NR/rdonlyres/82702E75-9A14-4EF5-B414-49B0D7A27816/0/JSP3832004Edition.pdf (last visited 20 November 2012).

Kelly JC. (2010) Battlefield Conditions: different environment but the same duty of care, *Nurs Ethics,* 17(5), pp. 636-645.

Kasher, A. (2007) The Principle of Distinction, *Journal of Military Ethics,* 6(2), pp. 152-167.

Kennedy, T.E., Hill, E., Adams, N.R., and Jennings, B. (1996) A conceptual model of army nursing practice, *Nursing Management,* 27(10), pp.33-36.

Kemerling, G. (2009) Philosophy Pages. At http://www.philosophypages.com/dy/d9.htm#duty (last visited 20 November 2012).

Keown, J and Gormally L. (1999) Human dignity, autonomy and mentally incapacitated patients: a critique of 'Who Decides', *4 Web JCL.*

King, S. (2004) Case Comment Personal injury, negligence, armed forces, service personnel, *Journal of Personal Injury Law,* 3, C107-112.

Kinicki, A.J. Hom, P.W. Trost MR (1995) Effects of category prototypes on performance-rating accuracy, *Journal of Applied Psychology*, 80(3), pp. 354-370.

Kipnis, K. A. (2006) Defense of Unqualified Medical Confidentiality, *The American Journal of Bioethics*, 6(2), pp. 7-18.

Kligman A and Kupermintz H. (1994) Response style and self-control under SCUD missile attacks: the case of the sealed room situation during the Gulf War, *Journal of Trauma Stress*, 7, pp. 415- 426.

Kleinig, J. (2001) The Blue Wall of Silence: An Ethical Analysis, *International Journal of Applied Philosophy*, 15, pp, 1-24.

Koch, T. (2006) Weaponising Medicine, *Journal of Military Ethics*, 32, pp. 249-255.

Kohlberg, L. (1964) *Development of moral character and moral ideology*. In: M. L. Hoffman & L.W. Hoffman, Eds., Review of Child Development Research, Vol. I, pp. 381- 431 New York Russel Sage Foundation.

—. (1981) Essays on Moral Development, vol. 1 *The Philosophy of Moral Devlopment: Moral Stages and the Idea of Justice* (New York: Harper and Row). In Verweij, D. Hofhuis, K. and Soeters, J. (2007) Moral Judgement within the Armed Forces, *Journal of Military Ethics*, 6(1), pp. 19-40.

—. (1984) *The meaning and measurement of moral judgment*. In L. Kohlberg, *Essays on moral development*, Vol. II, The psychology of moral development, pp. 395-425 San Francisco, CA Harper & Row (Original 1981).

Kottow, M.H. (2006) Should medical ethics justify violence, *Journal of Medical Ethics*, 32(8), pp. 464-467.

Knight and others v Home Office and another [1990] 3 All ER 237 at 244

Kramer, M. and Schmalenberg, C. (2004) Essentials of a Magnetic Work Environment: Part 2, *Nursing,* 34(7), pp.44-47.

Kraemer, L.A. (2008) A Military Twist to the Profession of Nursing, *MEDSUNG Nursing,* August, (17), 4, pp. 275-277.

Krueger, R.A and Casey, M.A. (2000) *Focus Groups. A practical Guide for Applied Research,* 3rd, Sage, London.

Lamp, N. (2011) Conceptions of War and Paradigms of Compliance: The 'New War' Challenge to International Humanitarian Law, *Journal of Conflict $ Security Law,* 16 (2), pp. 225-262.

Lantz, G. (2005) Comment, War, nursing and morality, *Nursing Ethics*, 12(2), pp. 193-195.

Lapsley, D.K and Power, F.C. (2006) Character Psychology and Character Education, *Journal of Military Ethics,* (50)1, pp. 77-78.

Last, J. (2001) *International Epidemiology Association; a dictionary of Epidemiology*, 4th edn., New York, Oxford University Press.

Law, R. (2004) From Research Topic to Research Question: A Challenging Process, Nurse Researcher, 11(4), pp. 54-66.

Lere, J. C. & Gaumnitz, B. R. (2003) The Impact of Codes of Ethics on Decision Making: Some Insight from Information Economics, *Journal of Business Ethics,* 48(4), pp. 265-379.

Letang v Cooper [1965] 1 QB 232.

Letwin, O. (2001) Implementation of The Third Pillar (Hansard), *HC Deb 21 November 2001, vol 375 cc419-32. At:*
http://hansard.millbanksystems.com/commons/2001/nov/21/implement
ation-of-the-third-pillar (last visited 20 November 2012).

Link, B.G. Phelan, J.C. Bresnahan, M, Stueve, A. and Pescosolido, B.A. (1999) Public conceptions of mental illness: labels, causes dangerousness and social distance, *American Journal of Public Health,* 89, pp. 1328-1333.

Lipowski, E.E. (2008) Developing great research questions, *American Journal of Health Systems Pharmacy*, Sep 1, 65(17), pp.1667-70.

London, A.J. (2003) Threats to the common good, *Hastings Cent Rep 33*, pp. 17-25.

London L. Rubenstein LS. Baldwin-Reagaven L and Van Es A. (2006) Dual Loyalty among Military Health Professionals: Human Rights and Ethics in Times of Armed Conflict, *Cambridge Quarterly of Healthcare Ethic,* 15, pp. 381-391.

Loveland, I. (1996) *What is the prerogative? A Definitional Controversy, The Royal Prerogative*, Constitutional Law, Blackstone, ch. 4, p. 10.

Lind, G. (1999) Scoring of the Moral Judgment Test (MJT). Unpublished manuscript, University of Konstanz, Konstanz. In: Verweij D Hofhuis, K and Soeters J (2007) Moral Judgement within the Armed Forces, *Journal of Military Ethics*, 6(1), pp. 19-40.

Lutzen, K. (2004) Editorial comment: some reflections on the morality of war, *Nurs Ethics,* 11(6), pp. 541-2.

MacFarlane, C. (2004) Emergency Thoracotomy and the Military Surgeon, *ANZ J Surg,* 74, pp. 280-284.

McGloin, S. (2008) The trustworthiness of case study methodology, *Nurse Researcher*, 16(1), pp. 45-55.

McHale, J.V. (2009) Patient confidentiality and mental health. Part 2: dilemmas of disclosure, *British Journal of Nursing,* 18(6), pp. 996-997.

McKinstry, B. (2000) Do patients wish to be involved in decision making in the consultation? A cross sectional survey with video vignettes, *British Medical Journal*, 321, pp. 867-871.

Matthews, R.S. (2006) Indecent Medicine: In Defense of the Absolute Prohibition again Physician Participation in Torture, *American Journal of Bioethics*, 6(3) pp. W34-W44.

Madden, W. and Carter, B. S. (2003) 'Physician-Soldier: A Moral Profession', In T.E.Beam and L.R. Sparacino, eds., *Military Medical Ethics*, vol. 1, ch. 10, 269-291, Textbooks of Military Medicine, Washington, DC: Office of the Surgeon General, Borden Institute.

Manchester, C. and Salter, D. (2006) *Exploring the Law*, 3rd edn, Thomson and Sweet and Maxwell.

Mapp, T. (2008) Understanding phenomenology: the lived experience, Research and Education, *British Journal of Midwifery*, 16(5), pp. 308-11.

Martin, E. (1997) *Oxford Dictionary of Law*, Oxford University Press, p 242.

Martinelli-Fernandez S (2006) Educating Honorable Warriors, *Journal of Military Ethics*, (5)1, pp. 55-66.

Mastaglia, B. Toye, C, and Kristjanson L.J. (2003) Ensuring content validity in instrument development: challenges and innovative approaches, *Contemporary Nurse*, 14, pp. 281-291.

May, L. (2005) Killing Naked Soldiers: Distinguishing between Combatants and Non-combatants, *Ethics & International Affairs*, 19(3), pp. 39 – 53.

Mayer, L. (2007) Nonlethal Weapons and Noncombatant Immunity: Is it Permissible to Target Noncombatants? *Journal of Military Ethics*, 6(3), pp. 221-231.

McHale, J. (2002) Quality in health care: a role for the law? Quality and Safety in Health Care, *BMJ Publishing Group Ltd*, 11, pp.:88-91.

—. (2009) Capacity to consent-health care and adult patients, *British Journal of Nursing*, 2009; 18(10), pp. 639-641.

McLeod, I. (2005) *Theories of Justice,* chapter 10, Legal Theory, 3rd edn, Palgrave, Macmillan.

Medical Support to Joint Operations (2007) *Joint Doctrine Publication,* 4-03, 2nd edn, ch.1, annex 1A, 1A6, ch.1, s.II, para. 112. Ministry of Defence.

—. (2007) *Joint Doctrine Publication,* 4-03, 2nd edn, ch.1, annex 1A, 1A6, ch 4. *Command, Control, Communications, and Information.*

—. Joint Doctrine Publication (2007), 4-03, 2007; 2nd edn., ch.1, annex 1A, paragraph 1A6, page 1A2.

Meierhenrich, J (2006) "Analogies at War", *Journal of Conflict and Security Law*, C&S Law 11 (1), 1 March.

Mental Capacity Act 2005. At:

http://www.legislation.gov.uk/ukpga/2005/9/pdfs/ukpga_20050009_en
.pdf (last visited 20 November 2012).

Mental Capacity Act 2005 ch 9, part 1, 1 The principles. At:
http://www.legislation.gov.uk/ukpga/2005/9/pdfs/ukpga_20050009_en
.pdf (last visited 20 November 2012).

Mental Capacity Code of Practice 2007. London, The Stationery Office.

Mental Health Act 1983. At:
http://www.legislation.gov.uk/ukpga/1983/20/pdfs/ukpga_19830020_e
n.pdf (last visited 20 November 2012).

Mental Health Acts 2007. At:
http://www.legislation.gov.uk/ukpga/2007/12/pdfs/ukpga_20070012_e
n.pdf (last visited 20 November 2012).

Mierson, S. and Freiert, K. (2004), Problem based Learning, *ASTD*,
October 2004, pp. 15 - 17.

Miles, S.H. (2004) Abu Ghraib: its legacy for military medicine, *The
Lancet*, 364, pp. 725-729.

—. (2007) Medical Ethics and the Interrogation of Guantanamo 063, The
American Journal of Bioethics, 7(4), pp. 5-11.

Miller v Jackson [1977] QB 966.

Miller, J.J. (2004) Squaring the Circle: Teaching Philosophical Ethics in
the Military, *Journal of Military Ethics,* (3)3, pp. 199-215.

Minkoff H and Marshall MF (2009) Government-Scripted Consent: When
Medical Ethics and Law Collide, *Hastings Centre Report*, 2009; 39(3),
pp. 21-23.

Maynard v West Midlands Regional Health Authority [1985] 1 All ER 635
at 639.

Ministry of Defence (2007). *Medical Support to Joint Operations, Joint
Doctrine Publication 4-03 (Second Edition)* (ch.1, annex 1A,
paragraph 1A6, 1A2 and 112). At:
http://www.mod.uk/NR/rdonlyres/C0D56BC1-731B-4062-B509-
4EBFA4AD49F8/0/JDP4032Ed. (last visited 20 November 2012).

Ministry of Defence v Griffin [2008] EWHC 1542 (QB).

Miola J. Negligence and the legal standard of care: what is 'reasonable'
conduct? *British Journal of Nursing* 2009; 18(12), pp 756-757.

Molan, M.T. (2001) *Minsters powers: prerogative power, Constitutional
Law*, The Machinery of Government, Old Bailey Press, 3rd edn., ch. 8,
p. 226.

Moore, B and Reger, G (2006) Clinician to Frontline Soldier: A Look at
the Roles and Challenges of Army Clinical Psychologists in Iraq,
Journal of Clinical Psychology, 62(3), pp. 395- 403.

Montgomery, B. (1958) The memoirs of Field-Marshall the Viscount Montgomery of Alamein, K.G. London: Collins, 1958 In: Soldier Management: A Guide for Commanders (2004), Discipline, ch 2, p. 45.

Moreno, J.D. (2008) Embracing Military Medical Ethics, *The American Journal of Bioethics,* 8(2), 1-2.

Morris, M. Perry, A. Unworthy, C. Skeat, J, Taylor, N. Dodd, K. Buncombe, D. and Docket, S. (2005). Reliability of the Australian Therapy Outcome Measures for quantifying disability and health, *International Journal of Therapy Rehabilitation,* 12(8), pp. 340-346.

Morrison, R.S. and Peoples, L. (1999) Using focus group methodology in nursing, *Journal of Continuing Education in Nursing,* 30, 2, pp. 6-67.

MS v Sweden (1999) 28 EHRR 313 at para 41.

Mulcahy v Ministry of Defence [1996] 2 All ER 758.

Murdock, D.B (2008) Trauma: where's there no time to count, *AORN Journal,* Feb, 87(2), pp. 322-32.

Murphy, S. (2009) *The Official British Army Fitness Guide,* Great Britain, Ministry of Defence, Army, Guardian Books.

Murray in his *Suggestions for Young Officers* In: Cramer S (1921) *Disciplining Americans,* North American Review, 214, July/Dec, p. 774.

National Health Service Act 1977. At: http://www.legislation.gov.uk/ukpga/1977/49/pdfs/ukpga_19770049_e n.pdf (last visited 20 November 2012).

National Health Service (Scotland) Act 1978. At: http://www.legislation.gov.uk/ukpga/1978/29/pdfs/ukpga_19780029_e n.pdf (last visited 20 November 2012).

National Service Act 2006. At: http://www.legislation.gov.uk/ukpga/2006/41/pdfs/ukpga_20060041_e n.pdf (last visited 20 November 2012).

National Service Frameworks At: http://www.nhs.uk/chq/Pages/1080.aspx?CategoryID=68&SubCategor yID=153 (last visited 20 November 2012).

National Health Service and Community Act 1990. At: http://www.legislation.gov.uk/ukpga/1990/19/contents (last visited 1 December 2011).

Naval Discipline Act 1957. At: http://www.legislation.gov.uk/ukpga/1957/53/pdfs/ukpga_19570053_e n.pdf (last visited 20 November 2012).

National Service Act 2006. At:

http://www.legislation.gov.uk/ukpga/2006/41/pdfs/ukpga_20060041_e n.pdf (last visited 20 November 2012).

NHS National Institute for Clinical Excellence (2005). *Post-Traumatic Stress Disorder, The management of PTSD in adults and children in primary and secondary care*, Clinical Guidelines 26, March 2005, London. Also at: http://www.nhs.uk/Conditions/Post-traumatic-stress-disorder/Pages/Introduction.aspx (last visited 20 November 2012).

Nettleship v Weston [1971] 2 Q.B. 691

Nichol J and Rennell T. (2009) *Medic, Saving Lives – from Dunkirk to Afghanistan, Viking Penguin Book,, ch.* 9, Battle Stations, p. 190.

Noble-Adams, R (1999) Ethics and nursing research 1: development, theories and principles, *British Journal of a Nursing*, 8(13), pp. 88-892.

North Atlantic Treaty Organisation. At: http://www.nato.int/cps/en/natolive/what_is_nato.htm (last visited 20 November 2012).

Nursing Midwifery Council, (2008) *The Code: Standard of Conduct, Performance and Ethics for Nurses and Midwives*, London.

—. (2008) *Consent, Advice Sheet*, London.

—. *Advice sheet: Providing care in an emergency situation outside the work environment, 2008*

—. (2009) *Confidentiality Guidance Sheet*, March 2009, London at 1. Also at: http://www.nmc-uk.org/Nurses-and-midwives/Advice-by-topic/A/Advice/Confidentiality/ (last visited 20 November 2012).

Obrusnikova, I. Block, M. and Dillon, S. (2010) Children's Beliefs Toward Cooperative Playing with Peers with Disabilities in Physical Education, *Adapted Physical Activity Quarterly*,27, pp. 127-142.

Official Secrets Act 1989. At: http://www.legislation.gov.uk/ukpga/1989/6/contents (last visited 20 November 2012).

Ohlsson, R. (1993) Who Can Accept Moral Dilemmas, *The Journal of Philosophy*, 90(8), pp. 405-415.

Orakhelashvili, A (2006) The Idea of European International Law, *The European Journal of International Law, 17* (2), pp. 315–347

Orend, B. (2004) Kant's Ethics of War and Peace, *Journal of Military Ethics,* 3(2), pp. 161-177.

Paddam, A. Barnes, D. and Langdon, D. (2010) Constructing vignettes to investigate anger in multiple sclerosis, *Nurse Research*, 17(2), pp. 60 - 73.

Paley, J. (2002) Virtues of autonomy: the Kantian ethics of care, *Nursing Philosophy*, 3(2), pp. 133-143.

Palmer RB and Iverson KV. (1997) Ethics of emergency medicine, *The Journal of Emergency Medicine*, 15(5), pp. 729-733.

Parks, W.H. (1990) Air war and the law of war, 32 *Air Force Law Review*.

Parahoo, K. (2006) *Nursing research, principles, process and issues,* 2nd edn., Macmillan.

Paris v Stepney [1951] 1 All ER 42.

Parker v The Commonwealth (1965) 112 C.L.R., at 302.

Paterick TJ. Carson, GV.   Allen MC. Paterick TE. (2008) Medical Informed Consent: General Consideration for Physicians, *Mayo Clinical Practice*, 83(3), pp. 313-319.

Pearce v United Bristol Healthcare NHS Trust (1999) BMLR 118.

Petition of Right Act 1860. The Stationery Office, London.

Pettrey, L. (2003) Who Let the Dogs Out?   Managing Conflict with Courage and Skill. *Critical Care Nurse/Supplement*, pp. 21-24.

Pieper, P. (2008) *Ethical Perspectives of Children's Ascent for Research Participation: Deontology and Utilitarianism*, Paediatric Nursing, 34(4), pp. 319-323.

Plambeck, C.M. (2002) Divided Loyalties, *The Journal of Legal Medicine*, pp. 23, pp. 1-35

Politt, D. and Beck, C. (2005) *Essentials of Nursing Research; Methods, Appraisal and Utilisation,* 6th edn, Lippincott Williams and Wilkins, Philadelphia

Powell, A (2005) Why Good Doctors Do Bad Things, *Harvard University Gazette*.   At: http://www.news.harvard.edu/gazette/2005/03.03/11-abu.html (last visited 1 December 2011)

Prescott, J.M (2008) Training in the Law of Armed Conflict-A NATO Perspective", *Journal of Military Ethics*, 7(1), pp. 66-75.

Price, A.W. (2009) *Intuitions of Fittingness, Common Knowledge*, (15)3, Fall 2009, pp 348 – 364.

Purtilo, R. (1999). *Ethical Dimensions in the Professions,* WB Saunders Company, London, ch 3, p. 47.

Price, A.W. (2009) *Intuitions of Fittingness, Common Knowledge,* (15)3, pp. 348 – 364.

Queen's Regulations for the Army 1975,   Unit Command, Control and Administration, Chapter 5, part 3, orders and duties,   5.121, a and b. The Stationery Office.

Queen's Regulations (1975), ch 3, Duties of Commanders, General Responsibilities, 3.001., a. The Stationery Office.

Queen's Regulations for the Army 1975, section 5.181.   London, The Stationery Office.

Queen's Regulations 1975, Part 4 - Naval, Military and Air Forces acting together command over Members of other Services, J2.041. London, The Stationery Office.

Queens Regulations, 1975, London, The Stationery Office.

Queen's Regulations for the Army 1975, PART 8 - MEDICAL, DENTAL AND HEALTH, PART 9 – DRESS, J5.362. The Stationery Office.

R v Bateman [1925] All ER Rep 45 at 49.

R (Burke) [2005] EWCA Civ 1003.

R (on the application of Smith) v Secretary of State for Defence [2010] UKSC 29.

R v Ponting [1985] Crim LR 318.

R (Smith) v Secretary of State for Defence [2009] EWCA Civ 441 at 31.

R v Shaylor [2003] 1 AC 247.

Re T (Adult: Refusal of Medical Treatment) [1992] 4 All ER 649 CA.

Rajecki, R. (2009) Rescuing Soldiers: MHCP embrace mission to serve in midst of battle, *Royal Navy*, Feb; 72(2), pp. 36-9.

Raiter, Y. Farfel, A. Lehavi, O. Goren, O.B. Shamiss, A. Priel, Z. Koren, I. Davidson, B. Schwartz, D. Goldberg A. and Bar-Dayan, Y (2008) Mass casualty incident management, triage, injury distribution of casualties and rate of arrival of casualties at the hospitals: lessons from a suicide bomber attack in downtown Tel Aviv, *Emerg. Med. J.* 25, pp. 225-229.

Rascona DA. (2007) A Moral Obligation for Military Medical Services in the United Kingdom, *Virtual Mentor,* 9(10), pp. 722-724.

Ratner, S, R (2011) Law Promotion Beyond Law Talk: The Red Cross, Persuasion, and the Laws of War, *The European Journal of International Law, 22* (2), pp. 459–506.

Re B (Adult, refusal of medical treatment) [2002] 2 All ER 449.

Redsell, S.A. Hastings, A.M. Cheater, F.M. Fraser, R.C. (2004) Devising and establishing the face and content validity of explicit criteria of consultation competence for UK secondary care nurses. *Nurse Education Today*, 24(3), pp. 180-187.

Reed, J (2005) Using action research in nursing practice with older people: democratizing knowledge, *Journal of Clinical Nursing*, 14, 5, pp. 594-600.

Reisman, W.M   and   Stevick, D, L (1998) The Applicability of International Law Standards to United Nations Economic Sanctions Programmes, *European Journal of International Law*, 9, pp. 86-141.

Re C (Adult, refusal or treatment) [1994] 1 All ER 81.

Re MB (an adult: medical treatment) [1997] 2 FCR 541 at 549.

Re F (A Mental Patient: Sterilisation) [1989] 2 All ER 545.

Re Post Traumatic Stress Disorder Group Litigation Multiple Claimants (Re PTSD) v Ministry of Defence [2003] at 2.C.8.

Re Post Traumatic Stress Disorder Group Litigation Multiple Claimants (Re PTSD) v Ministry of Defence [2003] at 2.C.12.

Re Post Traumatic Stress Disorder Group Litigation Multiple Claimants v Ministry of Defence [2003] EWHC 1134 at 2.C.13.

Re Post Traumatic Stress Disorder Group Litigation Multiple Claimants (Re PTSD) v Ministry of Defence [2003] at 2.C.17.

Re Post Traumatic Stress Disorder Group Litigation Multiple Claimants v Ministry of Defence [2003] EWHC 1134.

Re Post Traumatic Stress Disorder Group Litigation Multiple Claimants (Re PTSD) v Ministry of Defence [2003] at 2.C.8.

Re Post Traumatic Stress Disorder Group Litigation Multiple Claimants (Re PTSD) v Ministry of Defence [2003] at 2.C.12.

Re Post Traumatic Stress Disorder Group Litigation Multiple Claimants v Ministry of Defence [2003] EWHC 1134 at 2.C.13.

Re Post Traumatic Stress Disorder Group Litigation Multiple Claimants (Re PTSD) v Ministry of Defence [2003] at 2.C.17.

Re Post Traumatic Stress Disorder Group Litigation Multiple Claimants v Ministry of Defence [2003] EWHC 1134 at 2.c.12.

Re Post Traumatic Stress Disorder Group Litigation Multiple Claimants (Re PTSD) v Ministry of Defence [2003] at 2.C.8.

Re Post Traumatic Stress Disorder Group Litigation Multiple Claimants (Re PTSD) v Ministry of Defence [2003] at *2.C.12*

Re T (Adult: Refusal Of Treatment) [1992] 4 All ER 649 at 662.

Richards, D (1902) Martial Law, *18 L.Q.R.* 133 at pp. 140-141.

Richardson, R., Verweij, D. & Winslow, D. (2004) Moral fitness for peace operations, *Journal of Political and Military Sociology,* 32(1), pp. 99-113.

Robinson, P. (2007) Ethics Training and Development in the Military. *Parameters,* pp. 22-36.

Robertson, M, Morris, K and Walter, G (2007) Overview of psychiatric ethics v: utilitarianism and the ethics of duty, *Australasian Psychiatry*, 15(5), pp. 402-410.

Rochdale Healthcare (NHS) Trust v C [1997] 1 FCR 274.

Robinson P. (2007) Ethics Training and Development in the Military. Parameters, pp. 22-36.

Roche, M. Diers, D. Duffield, C. Catling-Paull, C (2010) Violence Towards Nurses, the Work Environment, and Patient Outcomes, *Journal of Nursing Scholarship,* 42(1), pp. 13-22.

Rogers, A.P.V. (2004) *Law on the Battlefield*, Manchester University Press Juris Publishing, 2nd edn.

Rossow-Kimball, B and Goodwin, D. (2009) Self-Determination and Leisure Experiences of Women Living in Two Group Homes, University of Alberta, *Adapted Physical Activity Quarterly*, 26, pp. 1-20.

Rowley, J. (2004) Combat Immunity and the Duty of Care, *Journal of Personal Injury Law*, pp. 280-290.

Royal College of Obstetricians and Gynaecologists (2010) Obtaining valid consent, *Clinical Governance Advice No. 6, paragraph 4.1.* At http://www.rcog.org.uk/files/rcog-corp/CGA6-15072010.pdf   (last visited 20 November 2012).

Royal College of Psychiatrists. At: http://www.rcpsych.ac.uk/mentalhealthinfo/problems/ptsd/posttraumati cstressdisorder.aspx (last visited 20 November 2012).

Richards, D (1902) Martial Law, *18 L.Q.R.* 133 at pp. 140-141.

Richman, J. and Mercer, D. (2002) The vignette revisited: evil and the forensic nurse, *Nurse Researcher*, 9(1), 70-82.

Rogers, W.A. (2006) Pressures on confidentiality, *The Lancet*, 367, pp. 553-4.

Rowley, J. (2004) Combat Immunity and the Duty of Care, *Journal of Personal Injury Law*, pp. 280-290.

Rubel, W.R. (2004) Leave No One Behind, *Journal of Military Ethics*, 3(3), pp.252-256.

Rubenstien, L.J.D. (2003) Dual Loyalty and Human Rights, *Journal of Ambulatory Care Manage* 2003, 26(3), pp. 270-272.

Rubenstein, L.S. (2004) *Medicine and War*, Hastings Center Report, Another Voice, November-December, p. 3.

Rubin, G.R.   (2002) United Kingdom Military Law: Autonomy, Civilisation, Juridification, *The Modern Law Review*, 64(1), pp. 36-57.

Sainsbury, M (2011), Context or Chaos: Statutory Interpretation and the Australian Copyright Act, Statute Law Review 32(1), pp. 54-75

Sandin, P. (2007) Collective Military Virtues, *Journal of Military Ethics*, (6)4, pp. 303-314.

Sandman, L and Nordmark A (2006) Ethical Conflicts in Pre-hospital Emergency Care, *Nursing Ethics*, 13(6), pp. 592-607.

Sassòli, S, Bouvier, A.A, and Quintin, A (2011) How Does Law Protect In War?   Outline of International Humanitarian Law, *International Committee of the Red Cross*. vol. 1. At http://www.icrc.org/eng/assets/files/publications/icrc-0739-part-i.pdf (last visited 21 April 2012).

Savitsky, L Illingworth, M. and DuLaney, M. (2009) Civilian Social Work: Serving the Military and Veteran Populations, *Social Work*, 54(4), pp. 329-339.

Sarikonda-Woitas, C. and Robinson, J (2002) Ethical Health Care Policy: Nurses Voice in Allocation, *Nurs Admin Q*, 26(4), pp. 72-80.

Sayer, N.A. Friedemann-Sanchez G, Spoont, M. Murdoch, M. Parker, L.E. Chiros, C. Rosenheck, R. (2009) A qualitative study of determinants of PTSD treatment initiation in veterans, *Psychiatry: Interpersonal & Biological Processes*, 72(3), pp. 238-55.

Scheltinga, Tjallie A.M.; Rietjens, Sebastiaan J.H.; De Boer, Sirp J.; Wilderom, Celeste P.M. (2005) Cultural Conflict within Civil-Military Cooperation: A Case Study in Bosnia, Low Intensity Conflict and Law Enforcement, 13(1), pp. 54-69.

Schoenberg, N.E. and Ravdal, H. (2004) Using vignettes in awareness and attitudinal research, *International Journal of Social Research*, 3(1), pp. 63-74.

Schloendorff v Society of New York Hospital (1914) 211 NY 125 at 126.

Schofield, J (2009) Review: Family Law Advocacy: How Barristers Help the Victims of Family Failure, [2009] Fam Law 1109

Scott v Shepherd (1558-1774) All ER Rep 295.

Secretary of the Navy, (2002); paragraph 2085, 3413. At: http://www.archive.org/stream/manualformedical00unitrich/manualfor medical00unitrich_djvu.txt (last visited 20 November 2012)

Seedhouse, D (2001) *Ethics: The Heart of Health Care*, 2nd edn., Wiley, London.

Shaw Savill and Albion Co Ltd v The Commonwealth of Australia (1940) 66 C.L.R. 344 at 356.

Shaw Savill and Albion Co Ltd v The Commonwealth of Australia (1940) 66 C.L.R. 344.

Shea MA. (2005) Treatment Refusals: The Process and the Proof, *Journal of Legal Nurse Consulting*, 16(9), pp. 21-22.

Sidaway v Board of Governors of the Bethlem Royal Hospital and the Maudsley [1985] 1 All ER 643.

Sidel, V.W. and Levy, B.S. (2003) Physician-Soldier: A Moral Dilemma, In T.E.Beam and L.R. Sparacino, eds., *Military Medical Ethics*, vol. 1, pp 293-312. Textbooks of Military Medicine, Washington, DC: Office of the Surgeon General, Borden Institute.

Simmons, A.T. and Rycraft, J.R. (2010) Ethical Challenges of Military Social Workers Serving in a Combat Zone, *Social Work*, 55(1), pp. 9-18.

Smith, J. and Arthur, M. (1992) Military Medicine: Not the Same as Practicing Medicine in the Military, *Armed Forces & Society (Transarion Publishers)*, Summer, 18, p 14. Saunders, M. Lewis, P. and Thornhill A. (2000) *Research methods for business students*, Financial Times/ Prentice Hall, 2nd edn.

Soldier Management (2004) *A Guide for Commanders*, p. 47-50. Earle & Ludlow Limited, Gloucestershire.

Soloman, M.Z. (2005) Healthcare Professionals and Dual Loyalty: Technical Proficiency Is Not Enough, *Medscape General Medicine*, 7(3), pp.1-4.

Southby J.R. (2003) Nursing ethics and the Military. In. Beam TE, Sparacino, LR (eds). *Military Medical Ethics*, ch. 20, vol. 2. Washington, DC: Bordon Institute, pp.661-686.

Soloman, J.A.Tandon, A. Murray, C.J.L. (2004) Comparability of self-rated health: cross sectional multi-country survey using anchoring vignettes, *British Medical Journal*, 328, 7434, 258.

Southby, J.R. (2003) Nursing and the Military, *Military Medical Ethics*, 2003; Falls Church, Va.: Office of the Surgeon General, 2(20), pp. 661-686 at p. 663.

Stanley v Powell [1891] 1 QB 86.

Standardization Agreement (STANAG). At: http://www.nato.int/cps/en/natolive/stanag.htm (last visited 1 December 2011).

STANAG, 2004 NATO Standardization Agency. *Standardization Agreement No. 2449 (Ediction1) –Training in the Law of Armed Conflict,* 29 March 2004. At: http://www.nato.int/cps/en/natolive/stanag.htm (last visited 20 November 2012).

Stein, M. S. (2002) Utilitarianism and the Disabled: Distribution of Resources, *Bioethics,* 16(1), pp. 1-19.

St Georges's Healthcare NHS Trust v S, R v Collins and others, ex parte S, [1998] 3 All ER 673.

St Petersburg Declaration of 1868. Declaration Renouncing the Use, in Time of War, of Explosive Projectiles Under 400 Grammes Weight. Saint Petersburg, 29 November / 11 December 1868. At http://www.icrc.org/ihl.nsf/INTRO/130?OpenDocument (last visited 20 November 2012).

The Lady Gwendolene [1965] 2 All ER 283 at 300.

Thorgen, A. and Crang-Svalenius, E. (2009) Birth Centres in the East Midlands: views and experiences of midwives, *British Journal of Midwifery*, 17(3), pp. 144-151.

Timmons, G. and Ridenour, N (1994) Legal approaches to the restraint of trade of nurse practitioners: Disparate reimbursement patterns, *Journal of the American Academy of Nurse Practitioners,* 6, pp. 55-59.

Tingle, J. (2002) The professional standard of care in clinical negligence, *British Journal of Nursing,* 11(21), pp. 1375-1377.

Tingle, J and Cribb A. (2002) Consent and the capable adult patient, *Nursing Law and Ethics,* p.101. Blackwell Publishing.

Tobin, J. (2005) The challenges and ethical dilemmas of a military medical officer serving with a peacekeeping operation in regard to the medical care of the local population, *Journal of Medical Ethics,* 31, pp.571-574.

Tschudin, V and Schmitz, C. (2003) The Impact of Conflict and War on International Nursing and Ethics, *Nurs Ethics,* 10(4), pp. 354 – 367.

Tarasoff v Regents of the University of California 17 Cal 3d 425, 551 P2d 334 [Cal 1976].

Tschudin, V. (1992) *Ethics in nursing; the caring relationship,* 2nd edn. Oxford: Butterworth Heinemann.

Tuckett, A.G. (1998) An ethic of the fitting: a conceptual framework for nursing practice, *Nursing Inquiry,* 5, pp 220-227.

The Golden Hour, at http://www.haworth21.karoo.net/The%20Golden%20Hour.htm   (last visited 20 November 2012).

The Joint Doctrine Concept Centre (2007) *Joint Warfare Publication, Joint Medical Doctrine,* paras 120 and 122, 2nd edn., Ministry of Defence, Swindon. At: http://ids.nic.in/UK%20Doctrine/UK%20(12).pdf   (last   visited   20 November 2012).

Toner, C. (2006) Military Service as a Practice: Integrating the Sword and the Shield Approaches to Military Ethics, *Journal of Military Ethics,* 2006, (3)3, pp.183-200.

Tripodi, P. (2006) Peacekeepers, Moral Autonomy and the Use of Force, *Journal of Military Ethics,* (5)3, pp. 214-232.

Tschudin, V. (1992) *Ethics in nursing; the caring relationship,* 2nd edn. Oxford: Butterworth Heinemann.

Tschudin, V and Schmitz, C (2003) The Impact of Conflict and War on International Nursing and Ethics, *Nurs Ethics,* 10(4), pp. 354 – 367.

Tasioulas, J. (1998) Consequences of Ethical Relativism, *European Journal of Philosophy,* 6(2), pp. 156-171.

The British Army. At:

http://www.armysearch.mod.uk/query.html?qt=history+of+the+army& charset=iso-8859-1&style=test2&col=armyweb (last visited 20 November 2012).

The British Psychological Society and The Royal College of Psychiatrists (2004) *Self-harm-The short-term physical and psychological management and secondary prevention of self-harm in primary and secondary care.* At: http://www.nice.org.uk/nicemedia/pdf/CG16FullGuideline.pdf (last visited 20 November 2012).

The Case of the King's Prerogative in Saltpetre (1607) 12 Co Rep. 12. 77 ER 1294, 17 *Digest* (Repl) 436, *87.*The Defence Medical Services. At: http://www.mod.uk/DefenceInternet/microsite/dms (last visited 20 November 2012).

The Golden Hour. At: http://www.haworth21.karoo.net/The%20Golden%20Hour.htm (last visited 20 November 2012).

The Royal Air Force. At: http://www.rafmuseum.org.uk/research/journals.cfm (last visited 20 November 2012).

The Royal Navy. At: http://www.seayourhistory.org.uk/index.php?option=com_rnm_homep age&Itemid=81&changeNav=3533&noRedirect=1 and http://www.royalnavy.mod.uk/history/ (last visited 20 November 2012).

Toner, C. (2006) Military Service as a Practice: Integrating the Sword and the Shield Approaches to Military Ethics, *Journal of Military Ethics,* 3(3), pp.183-200.

Tricarico, D.J. (1998) Readiness - Meeting the air force mission, *Today's Surgical Nurse,* 20, pp. 41-46.

The World Medical Association Declaration of Geneva (1948) Physician's Oath. Adopted by the General Assembly of World Medical Association at Geneva Switzerland, September 1948. At: http://www.cirp.org/library/ethics/geneva/ (last visited 20 November 2012).

Tjallie. A.M, Rietjens, S.J.H, Sirp, J. De Boer, and Wilderom, P.M (2005) Cultural Conflict within Civil-Military Cooperation: A Case Study in Bosnia, *Low Intensity & Law Enforcement,* 13 (1), pp. 54-69.

Tuckett, A. (2004) Truth-telling in clinical practice and the arguments for and against: a review of the literature. In *Nursing Ethics,* 11(5) pp. 501-509.

Tschudin, V (2002) Editorial, *Nursing Ethics,* 9(4).

Tschudin, V. and Schmitz, C. (2003) The Impact of Conflict and War on International Nursing and Ethics, *Nursing Ethics,* 10(4), pp. 354-367.

US Department of the Army (1997), *Combat Health Support in Stability Operations and Support Operations*, Washington DC; DA; 27 October, Field Manual 8-42.

US War Department (1899), The War of the Rebellion: A Compilation of the Official Records of the Union and Confederate Armies, Washington, D.C.: Government Printing Office, Series III, Volume 3, pp. 148-164. At: http://ebooks.library.cornell.edu/m/moawar/text/waro0124.txt (last visited 20 November 2012).

Van der Zalm, J.E. and Bergum, V. (2000) Hermeneutic-phenomenology: providing living knowledge for nursing practice, *Journal of Advanced Nursing*, 31(1), pp. 211-218.

Van Manen, M. (1990) Researching the Lived Experience: Human Science for An Action Sensitive Pedagogy. Ann Arbour, MI: Althouse Press.

Vellinga, A. Smit, J.H. Van Leeuwen, E. Van Tilburg, W. and Jonker, C. (2005) Decision-making capacity of elderly patients assessed through the vignette method: Imagination or reality? *Aging and mental Health,* January, 9(1), pp. 40-48.

Verpeet, E. DE Casterle, B.D. Van der Arend, A. and Gastmans C.A.E. (2005) Nurses' views on ethical codes: a focus group study, *Journal of Advanced Nursing*, 51(2), pp. 188-95.

Verweij, D. Hofhuis, K. and Soeters, J. (2007) Moral Judgement within the Armed Forces, *Journal of Military Ethics*, 6(1), pp. 19-40.

Vetter, S. (2007) Understanding Human Behavior in Time of War. *Mil Med* 172: S7-10.

Voyce, A. (2009) *Working Through an Ethical Dilemma*, Kai Tiaki Nursing New Zealand, 15(1), pp. 12-13.

Visser, S.L. (2003) The Soldier and Autonomy, Military Medical Ethics, In: Beam TE, Spracino LR, eds. *Military Medical Ethics*, 1(9), pp. 9, pp. 251-266 Falls Church, VA.; Office of the Surgeon General.

W v Egdell [1990] 1 All ER 835.

Walsh, E. (2010) Newsline Extra: Media Access and Children's Views, [2010] Fam Law 414 (2).

Wallenius, C. Larsson J. and Johansson, J (2004) Military Observers' Reactions and Performance When Facing Danger, *Military Psychology,* 16(4), pp. 211-219.

Walters, T.P. (2009) A balance between protection and liberty, *British Journal of Nursing,* 18(9), pp. 555-558.

Walzer, M. Just And Unjust Wars, p.143. In: May L. (2005), Killing Naked Soldiers: Distinguishing between Combatants and Non-combatants, Ethics & International Affairs, 19(3), pp. 39 -53.

Warburton, N. (2006) *Philosophy: The Classics,* 3ed, Routledge, London.

Walters, T.P. (2009) A balance between protection and liberty, *British Journal of Nursing,* 18(9), pp. 555-558.

Walzer M. *Just and Unjust Wars: A Moral Argument with Historical Illustrations,* London, Allen Lane, 1978.

Wasunna, A.A. (2003) Dual loyalty and Human Rights: Proposed Guidelines and Institutional Mechanisms, *Hastings Center Report,* p. 7.

Weigel, V.B. (2002) *Deep learning for a digital age: technologies untapped potential to enrich higher education* San Francisco Jossey-Bass.

Weld, K.K and Bib, S.C.G (2009) Concept Analysis: Malpractice and Modern-Day Nursing Practice, January-March, *Nursing Forum,* 44 (1).

Wells, S.H. Warelow, P.J. and Jackson, K.L. (2009) Problem based learning (PBL): A conundrum, *Contemporary Nurse,* 33(2), pp. 191-201.

Westhusing, T.S. (2006) Equality Within Military Organizations, *Journal of Military Ethics,* (5)1, pp. 5-11.

Weston, M.J. (2009) Defining Control over Nursing Practice and Autonomy, *Journal of Nursing Administration,* 38, pp. 404-408.

Weston, M.J. (2010) Strategies for Enhancing Autonomy and Control over Nursing Practice, *Online Journal of Nursing,* 15(1), pp. 1-10.

White, C. and Boucke, L (2010) *The Undutchables: An Observation of the Netherlands, Its Culture and Its Inhabitants, a Humorous and Irreverent Look at Dutch Customs,* 4th edn., Cultural Portrait.

Wheatley, S. (2001). *'Litigating bioethics: the role of autonomy and dignity',* Healthcare Law: the impact of the Human Rights Act 1998, Cavendish Publishing Limited, London.

Whitehouse v Jordan [1981] 1 All ER 267

Wicks, E. (2001). 'The right to refuse medical treatment under the European Convention of Human Rights', *Medical Law Review,* 9, Spring, pp. 17-40.

Wilks, T. (2004) The use of vignettes in qualitative research into social work values, *Qualitative Social Work,* 3(1), pp.78-87.

Williams, P.T (1996) To Kill of Not to Kill: a Question of Wartime Ethics, *Nurs Ethics,* 3(2), pp. 150-156

Williams, J.R. (2009) Dual Loyalties: How to Resolve Ethical Conflict, *South African Journal of Bioethics and Law,* 2(1), pp.8-12.

Williams, D. (2009) Forensic Nursing and Utilitarianism: The quest for being right, *Journal of Forensic Nursing*, 5, pp. 49-50.

Williams, G. (1982) Case law technique, Learning the Law, London Stevens and Sons, 11th edn., ch.6, p.67.

Williams, J. R. (2009). Physicians and Society. *Medical Ethics Manual* (2nd edn.) (pp.63-79). At: http://www.wma.net/en/30publications/30ethicsmanual/pdf/ethics_manual_en.pdf (last visited 20 November 2012).

—. (2009) Dual Loyalties: How to Resolve Ethical Conflict, *South African Journal of Bioethics and Law*, 2(1), pp.8-12.

Wilsher v Essex Area Health Authority [1986] 3 All ER 801 at 811.

Wilsher v Essex Area Health Authority [1986] 3 All ER 801 at 813.

Wilsher v Essex Area Health Authority [1986] 3 All ER 801 at 814

Wilsher v Essex Area Health Authority [1986] 3 All ER 801 at 832

Wilsher v Essex Area Health Authority [1986] 3 All ER 801

Witting, C. (2005) Duty of Care: An Analytical Approach, *Oxford Journal of Legal Studies*, 2005, 25(33)

Wolfendale J. (2009) Professional Integrity and Disobedience in the Military, *Journal of Military Ethics*, 8(2), pp. 127-140.

World Medical Association (2009) *Medical Ethics Manual*, Chapter 3, Physicians and Society, 2nd edn.

—. (2009) *Medical Ethics Manual*, Chapter 3, Physicians and Society, 2nd edn.

—. (1948) 2nd General Assembly of the World Medical Association, Geneva, Switzerland, September 1948. At: http://www.mma.org.my/Portals/0/Declaration%20of%20Geneva.pdf (last visited 1 December 2011). Also at: http://www.wma.net/en/30publications/10policies/c8/index.html   (last visited 20 November 2012).

World Medical Association International Code of Medical Ethics (1949) *Adopted by the 3rd General Assembly of the World Medical Association, London, England, October 1949.   At:* http://www.wma.net/en/30publications/10policies/c8/index.html   (last visited 20 November 2012).

Wynia, M, K. (2007).   Breaching Confidentiality to Protect the Public: Evolving Standards of Medical Confidentiality for Military Detainees. *The American Journal of Bioethics*, 7(8): 1-5.

World Medical Association (2004) Regulations in Times of Armed Conflict, Adopted by the 10th World Medical Assembly, Havana, Cuba, October 1956.   Edited by the 11th World Medical Assembly, Istanbul, Turkey, October 1957, and Amended by the 35th World

Medical Assembly, Venice, Italy, October 1983 and the WMA General Assembly, Tokyo 2004. At: http://www.wma.net/en/30publications/10policies/a20/index.html (last visited 20 November 2012).

Yeo, M. (1989) Integration of Nursing Theory and Nursing Ethics, *Advanced Nursing Science*, 11, pp. 33-42.

Yoshioka, T. Suganuma, T. Tang, A. Matsushita, S. Manno, S. and Kozu, T. (2005) Facilitation of Problem Finding Among First Year Medical School Students Undergoing Problem-Based Learning, *Teaching and Learning in Medicine*, 17(2), pp. 136-141.

Zander, R.M. (1994) *Experiences and moral life: a phenomenological approach to bioethics*. In: DuBose, E.R. Hamel, R.P. and O'Connell, L.J. eds. *A matter of principles? Ferment in US bioethics*, Valley Forge, PA: Trinity Press, 1994, pp 211-239.